The Politics of Metanoia

Europäische Hochschulschriften

European University Studies

Publications Universitaires Européennes

Reihe XXIII **Theologie**

Series XXIII Theology

Série XXIII Théologie

Band/Volume **947**

Theodros Assefa Teklu

The Politics of Metanoia

Towards a Post-Nationalistic Political Theology in Ethiopia

PL ACADEMIC RESEARCH

Bibliographic Information published by the Deutsche Nationalbibliothek
The Deutsche Nationalbibliothek lists this publication in the Deutsche Nationalbibliografie; detailed bibliographic data is available in the internet at http://dnb.d-nb.de.

Printed with financial support of the
Ethiopian Graduate School of Theology in Addis Ababa.

ISSN 0721-3409
ISBN 978-3-631-65850-5 (Print)
E-ISBN 978-3-653-05083-7 (E-Book)
DOI 10.3726/978-3-653-05083-7

PL Academic Research is an Imprint of Peter Lang GmbH.
Peter Lang – Frankfurt am Main · Bern · Bruxelles · New York · Oxford · Warszawa · Wien

This publication has been peer reviewed.

www.peterlang.com

To Stephania, Yahavel, Hila and Berith

My Family

Contents

Acknowledgements

I would like to thank my sponsoring institution – the Ethiopian Graduate School of Theology – and the School of Arts, Languages and Cultures at the University of Manchester whose offer of an Overseas Research Studentship award made it possible for me to buy some time – by being away from my work – in order to focus on my research. I would like to thank my family without whose dear support I could not complete this work. Special thanks are, of course, due to my PhD supervisor, Professor Graham Ward, for unreservedly dedicating his time and energy to my research, and, most of all showing confidence in me right from the start. I also would like to thank Professor Peter Scott for his academic support especially during the last stage of the study. I would like to thank the librarians of the Institute of Ethiopian Studies at the University of Addis Ababa for making accessible relevant material on Ethiopia. Likewise, I would also like to thank my former colleague Mary Evans at the Ethiopian Graduate School of Theology for proofreading the manuscript, and my colleague Dr Desta Heliso for his encouragement. Many thanks go to many people and friends, too numerous to mention their names, who supported and encouraged me during my research.

Introduction

Ethiopia in Academic Discourse

> Suppose that one day, after a nuclear war, an intergalactic historian lands on a now dead planet in order to enquire into the cause of the remote little catastrophe which the sensors of this galaxy have recorded. He or she – I refrain from speculating on the problem of extraterrestrial physiological reproduction – consults the terrestrial librarian and archives which have been preserved, because the technology of the mature nuclear weaponry has been designed to destroy people rather than property. Our observant, after source study, will conclude that the last two centuries of human history of planet Earth are incomprehensible without some understanding of the term 'nation' and the vocabulary derived from it.[1]

Taking a cue from this passage by Eric Hobsbawm, we recognize that this category called the 'nation', which remains significant to understand human action and suffering, is not a naturally given or a self-evident reality. Indeed, it is difficult to offer *a priori* definition of what a nation constitutes. In this regard, the aid of the dictionary is of no avail since the nation is not a semantic phenomenon but rather a modern political concept that is best understood in particular political and social formations. Owing to such a fact, then, the nation (being historically and locally rooted) can only be properly understood *a posteriori*.[2] Consequently, any inquiry relating to the nation – such as this one – must draw

1 Eric Hobsbawm, *Nations and Nationalism Since 1790: Programme, Myth, Reality* (Cambridge: Cambridge University Press, 1990), 1.

2 Scholars such as Hobsbawm have well argued that nations, as natural or God-given way of classifying people and determining their destiny, are historical constructs with an element of social engineering and are, of course, ideological processes. Thus, nationalism comes before nations (not vice versa). Following Ernest Gellner, the term 'nationalism' can be understood as 'primarily a principle which holds that the political and national unit should be congruent.' See Ernest Gellner, *Nations and Nationalism: New Perspectives on the Past* (Ithaca, New York: Cornell University Press, 1983), 1. For a different view, however, cf. John Armstrong, *Nations before Nationalism* (Chapel Hill: University of North Carolina Press, 1982).

attention to local, and modern, historical processes and their discourses. This study examines the case of Ethiopia.[3]

Although the name 'Ethiopia' evokes several images, Carlo Conti Rossini's illustrious cliché *èun museo di popoli* (a museum of people) best describes Ethiopia, which is home for diverse people groups, anthropologically.[4] When Conti Rossini coined this aphorism during the early years of the past century, Ethiopia was already a modern empire-state heading towards centralisation. At least two aspects are evident, here: Ethiopia as a bounded territorial state and Ethiopia as a population state composed of diverse groups.

Three historical conjunctures are important to understand the territorial construction of the modern empire-state. First, the centralisation of parcellised sovereignties within the fragmented Christian Abyssinian kingdom located in the central and northern highlands of Ethiopia including parts of present day Eritrea during the 19th century a period referred to as the *Zamana Masafent* (Era of the Princes) under emperor (*Atse*) Tewodros II; second, the conquests and expansions to the regions south of the Abyssinian kingdom – a process locally understood as *agar maqnat*, which implies cultivation and a Christianising or civilizing mission, under *Atse* Menelik of Shawa (present day central Ethiopia);[5]

3 Geographically, the country is located in the north-eastern part of Africa commonly known as the Horn of Africa and it borders Djibouti and Somalia in the east, Kenya in the south, Sudan and South Sudan in the west and south-west and Eritrea in the north. Covering an area of 1,112,000 square kilometers (472,000 sq. miles), which is almost the size of France and Spain combined, Ethiopia has varied topography and climate. Demographically, it has the second largest population in Africa: the population projection for 2014 (based on the 2007 census, 73,750,932) is 87,952,991. See Federal Democratic Republic of Ethiopia Central Statistical Agency, "Population Projection of Ethiopia for All Regions at Wereda Level from 2014-2017," n.p. Accessed 20 January 2014, http://www.csa.gov.et/

4 Cf. Carlo Conti Rossini, *Storia d'Etiopia* (Milan, 1928), chap.1 cited in Donald N. Levine, *Greater Ethiopia: The Evolution of a Multiethnic Society* (Chicago; London: University of Chicago Press, 1974), 19-20. Other common images in scholarly works include: Ethiopia as an ancient Christian polity; a state similar to European nations (somehow *in* Africa but not *of* Africa); a symbol of African pride; a colonial state imprisoning 'nations' within its territorial confines; and a country of famine and; cf. also John Sorenson, introduction to *Imagining Ethiopia: Struggles for History and Identity in the Horn of Africa* (New Jersey: Rutgers University Press, 1993).

5 Teshale Tibebu, *The Making of Modern Ethiopia 1896-1974* (Lawrenceville, NJ: The Red Sea Press, 1995), 40.

and third, the scrimmage of interests and treaties between European colonisers such as Britain, France and Italy and Ethiopian rulers.

Despite the divergent interpretations given to these historical conjunctures (which we will see later), the historical agency of these conjunctures have led to greater diversity of people groups subjected to a common law within a single polity: Ethiopia. Due to such processes, present day Ethiopia is composed of diverse ethnic, linguistic and religious groups: Oromo, Amhara, Tigre, Sidama, Gurage, Wolaytta, Hadiyya, Afar, Gamo, Gedeo, Somali, and others.[6] Over eighty languages are spoken: Amarigna (Amharic) is the official language; Oromiffa and Tigrigna are official regional languages; and other languages such as Somali, Sidama, Wolaytta, Gurage, Afar, Hadiyya, Gamo, and foreign languages such as English (official) and Arabic are also spoken, taught in schools and serve as working languages. Ethiopia is also home for various religions: Orthodox, Muslim, Protestant, traditional, Catholic, other.[7]

In view of such diversity, how do we understand Conti Rossini's aphorism – a museum of people – today? Does this imply that Ethiopia contained the diverse groups 'side by side' as closed self-contained and self-sufficient groups, or has Ethiopia been a 'melting pot' – a sphere of assimilation?[8] This is not only an academic question but one that also has strong practical or political implications. Under successive regimes, the management of the diverse population has taken different routes. The incumbent government (1991-present) claims to have taken a radical leap from the unitary centralist political culture of previous regimes that are considered to have misrecognised this diversity: the modernising autocracy of Haile-Selassie (1916/1930-74) and the military socialist regime (1974-1991).

The current government 'has adopted what some might see as a peculiarly anthropological approach to state-building, recalling Conti Rossini's famous aphorism' implying a re-imagining of Ethiopia as an 'assemblage of distinct ethnicities' – ethnic-federalism.[9] However, how this diversity should be

---

6 For population projection at region level, see Central Statistical Agency, "Population Projection of Ethiopia."

7 Based on Census 2007, Orthodox (43.5%), Muslim (33.9%), Protestant (18.6%), traditional (2.6%), Catholic (0.7%), other (0.7%); cf. Central Statistical Agency, "Population and Housing Census Report-Country – 2007," p. 109, Accessed 12 January 2012, http://www.csa.gov.et/

8 Cf. Teshale Tibebu, *The Making of Modern Ethiopia*, 66; Levine, *Greater Ethiopia*, 19-22.

9 Christopher Clapham, "Controlling Space in Ethiopia," in *Remapping Ethiopia: Socialism and After*, eds. Wendy James et al. (Oxford: James Currey, 2002), 15, 27.

understood and recognised is still unclear and an issue of contest in Ethiopia. People groups who once claimed to be Ethiopians are no longer identifying themselves as such, and even people groups who are 'being' or becoming Ethiopian do so in ways different from past times.[10] Indeed, embarking on such a study that relates to the 'nation' places one at the crossroads of various theoretical routes leading to different ways of understanding this abstract entity named 'the modern Janus'[11] by Tom Nairn. No less ambivalent is the subject of 'ethnicity' with a 'chameleon-like capacity'[12], as Katsuyoshi Fukui and John Markakis have rightly described it.

Underlying the political discourse on Ethiopian nationhood are contending intellectual trends. Over the past century, intellectual currents have emerged whose role in shaping the discourse of nationhood in Ethiopia has been significant. In their methodological presuppositions and their disciplinary location, these academic trends are diverse as well as divergent. If I may employ typological categorisation for heuristic purposes, they can be classified into two major trends: the functionalist paradigm or the integration model, and the instrumentalist paradigm or the conflict model.[13] The former paradigm, which is largely informed by structural functionalism and social evolutionary theories,

---

10 Here, we can think of events such as the radicalisation of the so-called the Ethiopian Student Movement, the rise of ethno-nationalist resurgent fronts struggling for their respective regions such as Eritrean, Tigrean, Oromo, Somali and Ogaden and the recent independence of Eritrea from Ethiopia and the restructuring of Ethiopia based on ethnic-federal principles and Constitution. See Donald Crummey, "Ethiopian Historiography in the Latter Half of the Twentieth Century: A North American Perspective," *Journal of Ethiopian Studies* Xxxiv (2001): 7.

11 SeeTom Nairn, *Faces of Nationalism: Janus Revisited* (London: Verso, 1997), 71.

12 Cf. Katsuyoshi Fukui, and John Markakis, eds., *Ethnicity and Conflict in the Horn of Africa* (Athens: Ohio University Press, 1994), 3.

13 I developed these typologies based on a familiar sociological distinction of society into 'integration model' and 'conflict model'; Cf. P. Cohen, *Modern Social Theory* (London, 1968) cited in Anthony D. Smith, *Theories of Nationalism* (London: Duckworth, 1971), 41. Since the disposition of the former is largely shaped by the functionalist view, I simply designate it as the functionalist paradigm. And because the latter is informed by Marxist conflict theories, I prefer to call it the instrumentalist paradigm. Nevertheless, I am not claiming that there cannot be an element of functionalism in the instrumentalist mode of thought. Nor can I say that the functionalist mode of thought does not include an account of conflict. For other ways of classification; see Merera Gudina, *Ethiopia: Competing Ethnic Nationalisms and the Quest for Democracy, 1960-2000* (Maastricht: Shaker Publishing, 2002) and Crummey, "Ethiopian Historiography," 7-18.

emphasises the survival or persistence of Ethiopia and the integration of its people while the latter, which draws upon Marxist and neo-Marxist theories, centres on conflict and the need for change – i.e., of asserting the right to national self-determination. These are contending ways of understanding Ethiopia – a museum of people.

Such trends have sought to explain the historical conditions under which Ethiopians have developed as a people. However, while the concern of these currents of thought is somehow related to or inseparable from the problematic or philosophy of the human subject, they have not yet given rise to philosophical -theological consideration that takes human action and suffering earnestly. Recently, of course, a philosophical discourse has emerged, which seems to have set a new trend, albeit, arguably, highly coloured by the functionalist mode of thought and liberal political pragmatism.[14] In reaction to the instrumentalist mode of thought, this philosophical discourse claims to give due attention to the native condition of Ethiopia, which it considers as being marginalised by Eurocentric views adopted to understand, analyse, and redirect Ethiopian socio-political realities. While this mode of thought has its own inadequacies, it strongly asserts the significance of drawing attention to metaphysical and religious dimensions that should not be relegated to a marginal position in understanding the country's past and present.

This later discourse paves the way for a new possibility of approaching the Ethiopian situation from the theological angle. I will briefly demonstrate how this current of thought relates to my own approach below. And the present study seeks to explore this possibility. It endeavours to offer a theological contribution to the academic discourse of Ethiopia, which to date has been a lacuna. Whilst there is a proliferation of academic works that investigate the political context, few interdisciplinary approaches have attempted to provide a theological outlook. It is precisely the connection between the two discourses – the political and the theological – that I intend to make in this study.

In order to elaborate the nature of this theological contribution, I must further expand this introductory outline. The question I want to confront in this introduction – 'why is a theological turn appropriate and desirable for the Ethiopian case?' – is what justifies my contribution in this study. Since one way of approaching this question is to demonstrate how the theological figures in the two paradigms, I wish to review briefly these modes of thought below.

14 Cf. Messay Kebede, *Survival and Modernization: Ethiopia's Enigmatic Present: A Philosophical Discourse* (Lawrenceville, NJ: The Red Sea Press, 1999).

The Functionalist Paradigm

The work of Donald Levine, the Chicago sociologist, especially his book *Greater Ethiopia: the Evolution of a Multiethnic Society* best represents and imbues this paradigm.[15] Akin and complementary to this current of thought are the 'western *éthiopisant* school' who studied the 'Christian Orient' or Semitic Ethiopia.[16] Central to this mode of thought is the Durkheimian understanding of integration, or social cohesion. Nationalism or patriotism, according to this paradigm, is considered as one of the stabilising collective ideologies. Drawing upon Talcott Parsons (who synthesises the works of Émile Durkheim and Max Weber), Levine brilliantly combines structural functionalism with social evolutionism in his work.

Of course, Levine is aware of the weaknesses of the social evolutionary theory.[17] Despite its weaknesses, Levine deems social evolutionary theory useful to understand or interpret Ethiopia. Levine considers three major concepts of this theory: first, the idea of *emergent novelty* – that is, 'over time human groups have created social and cultural forms which previously did not exist'; second, *functional specialisation* implying that 'new forms have been retained because they better satisfied certain needs'; and third, the reality of *social integration* – that is, 'the new forms have increased the scope of human association, relating larger numbers of persons within societal systems'.[18]

---

15 As Anthony D. Smith observes, some political scientists have drawn from Durkheim (and also Rousseau), to analyse the political development of the new states of Asia and Africa. This is true of the Chicago School propounded by Edward Shils and Clifford Geertz, for example, who wrote 'The Political development of the New States' and 'The Integrative Revolution' respectively. Levine also further develops a similar way of thinking. See for example, Edward Shils, *Political Developments in the New States* (Netherlands: Mouton, 1962), 7-9; Clifford Geertz, *Old Societies and New States: The Quest for Modernity in Asia and Africa* (New York: London: Free Press; Collier-Macmillan, 1963), 108-113; Clifford Geertz, *The Interpretation of Cultures* (London: Hutchinson, 1975), 240-249.

16 Scholars such as Edward Ullendorff, Harold Marcus, Sergew Hable Sellassie, and Tekletsadiq Mekuria, to mention but a few. This school eulogises the Orthodox Christian Abyssinia, and draws upon the works of 'the Ethiopian highland *literati*' (ecclesiastical chroniclers), which, as historical sources are said to be ecclesiastically and politically biased; see Bahru Zewde, *Society, State and History* (Addis Ababa: Addis Ababa University Press, 2008), 20.

17 Social evolutionary theory is criticised for its view that social development follows a fixed (irreversible) set of stages and that highly evolved ones are morally superior to less evolved ones.

18 Levine, *Greater Ethiopia*, 165-166. Note here, we see a different appropriation of Durkheimian differentiation. Such an appropriation should not give the impression

Applied to the Ethiopian situation, such concepts construct an understanding of Ethiopia (a) in terms of survival that looks backwards into the past (an historical explanation) and (b) how such mechanism of survival moves forward into the future (a *telic* explanation). Accordingly, this paradigm emphasises historical continuity and hence, follows a *longue durée* approach with the idea that Ethiopia extends back to millennia. The interest of this paradigm is not, however, limited to describing the historical events *per se* but rather seeks to explain this survival sociologically. In consequence, the diverse people of Ethiopia, which are classified as the 'Ethio-Semitic', the 'Cushitic', the 'Omotic' and the 'East Sudanic' (or rather Nilo-Saharan), who occupy diverse ecological niches, are said to have undergone processes of social evolution, which culminates in the formation of the modern state of Ethiopia.

What is important to note for our purpose here is not only the undertaking of this paradigm to offer a functional explanation of the 'nation' (Ethiopia) in 'objective' sociological terms as a whole (vis-à-vis parts and counter-parts), but also its historic determinism. The latter becomes significant and often problematic particularly in its legitimation of nation-building during the 19th century by the dominant *ethnie* (i.e., the Amhara) and the manner in which all other people groups including the Tigreans and the Oromo had to follow the Amhara. Beside the strength of Amhara socio-cultural system including military prowess accentuated by access to modern weaponry, the revival of the myth embodied in a book called *Kebrä Nägäst*, 'Glory of Kings', which makes Ethiopia's rulers descendants of successors of Israel and the Jews through a legendary union of King Solomon with the Queen of Sheba, is regarded by this mode of thought as significant in understanding Ethiopia's modern nation-building. As a 'national epic' or 'societal script', this ideology of chosen-*ness* (covenant) is regarded as fulfilling both legitimising and integrative functions.

The Instrumentalist Paradigm

Drawing upon Marxist and neo-Marxist concepts, socialist movements, particularly the Ethiopian Student Movement, began to shape the discourse on the so-called 'nationalities question' in Ethiopia from the late 1960s.[19] The radical writer

---

that it is because of Levine's faulty appropriation that functionalism failed. It will not affect my argument as we see in what follows. Durkheim's differentiation refers to individuals whereas Levine appropriates it to ethnic groups. Each ethnic group develops its own specialisation.

19 Randi Rønning Balsvik, preface to *Haile Sellassie's Students: The Intellectual and Social Background to Revolution, 1952-1977* (East Lansing: Michigan State University, African Studies Centre, 1985), xiii.

Addis Hiwot[20], who typifies a profound left-critique of Ethiopian society, seems to be the first to establish an academic landmark, as early as 1974, in the deconstruction of the assumptions of the functionalist paradigm. In his analysis, Addis Hiwot deploys the analytical concepts of feudalism, capitalism, and imperialism. This kind of analysis had implications for subsequent works that focused on the idea of class and the question of nationalities.

Literatures, after Addis Hiwot, on Ethiopia, mainly since the 1980s, sought to demystify the myth of Greater Ethiopia. Unlike the functionalist paradigm, this mode of thought emphasises the recent 'invention' of Ethiopia – only a hundred years and so – and it also focuses on the domination and exploitation of people groups of Ethiopia. For example, Gebru Tareke's published thesis de-centers the story of the Ethiopian modernising state through exposing various regional revolts or 'protests'.[21] In their book *The Invention of Ethiopia*, Bonnie K. Holcomb and Sisai Ibssa employ the concepts of 'colonialism' and 'imperialism' to explain how modern Ethiopia was invented and how it colonised people groups such as the Oromo.[22] Published in 1993, Asafa Jalata's *Oromia and Ethiopia* presented Ethiopia, or Abyssinia, and Oromia as though the two were contending nations that co-existed in pre-modern times until Abyssinia gained the favour of European imperialists whose ally and support enabled Abyssinia to colonise Oromia with the ideology or the politics of empire building (1850-1935).[23] Several other works also attempt to expound the relation between the dominant social class and the subordinate groups in light of centre-periphery dialectics.[24]

---

20 Addis Hiwot, *Ethiopia: From Autocracy to Revolution*, Occasional Publication No.1 (London: Review of African Political Economy, 1975).

21 Gebru Tareke, *Ethiopia: Power and Protest* (Cambridge: Cambridge University Press, 1991).

22 Bonnie K. Holcomb and Sisai Ibssa, *The Invention of Ethiopia* (Trenton, NJ: Red Sea Press, c1990).

23 Asafa Jalata, *Oromia and Ethiopia: State Formation and Ethnonational Conflict, 1868-1992* (London: L. Rienner, 1993); and *Oromo Nationalism and the Ethiopian Discourse: The Search for Freedom and Democracy* (Lawrenceville, NJ: Red Sea Press, c1998).

24 See Donald L. Donham, *Marxist Modern: An Ethnographic History of the Ethiopian Revolution* (Berkeley, Oxford: University of California Press, 1999); those works not least the once elaborated in the book edited by Baxter et al, cf. P.T.W. Baxter, Jan Hultin, & Alessandro Triulzi, eds., *Being and Becoming Oromo: Historical and Anthropological Enquiries* (Uppsala: Nordiska Afrikainstitutet, 1996); John Markakis, *National and Class Conflict in the Horn of Africa* (Cambridge: Cambridge University

The debate on national self-determination, whether among the Ethiopian Student Movement of the 1960s and 70s, or the works mentioned-above, from the 1980s and 90s, inappropriately resonate around the question of 'what is a colony?' rather than 'what is a nation?' Where they ought to have inquired into what constitutes the nation, proponents of this current of thought moved into issues of colonisation because the reality of the nation and the belief that every nation should have its own state were simply taken for granted. Accordingly, this paradigm construes Ethiopia as the 'prison of nations' – an expression borrowed from Ernest Gellner – and the political will, which resists the freedom of the 'nations' (that is, Greater Ethiopian nationalism), is regarded as 'great-nation chauvinism' (echoing Lenin).[25] As a result, this mode of thought elevates the category of the 'nation' or the 'ethnic', leading to identity politics as ethnic politics.

In a similar manner, the metaphor of prison also applies to religion: the state takes on a new significance in ensuring that religious groups, as interest groups, exercise their freedom and assert their rights.[26] Nonetheless, what reverberates in the literature within this paradigm is the charge that religion (that is, Ethiopia's Orthodox Christianity), in the past, was in the service of the ruling ideology in order to manipulate the 'masses'.

Why A Theological Turn? Why Political Theology?

Having cursorily reviewed these two paradigms, it is now possible to address the question posed earlier in this introduction concerning the theological turn. To this end, I now want to draw attention to how the theological figures in the two paradigms. And later I also want to add the point that there is already a cultural exigency in Ethiopia that welcomes the theological turn. Although the functionalist mode of thought considers religion as a key aspect of Ethiopian society, religion is narrowly understood in terms of its function as a cohesive force promoting social bond between the whole, the parts and

---

Press, 1987); Seyoum Hameso, "Myths and Realities of the Ethiopian State," in *Arrested Development in Ethiopia: Essays on Underdevelopment, Democracy and Self-determination*, eds., Seyoum Hameso and Mohammed Hassen (Trenton, NJ: The Red Sea Press, 2006), 97-111.

25 See Walleligne Mekonen, "On the Question of Nationalities in Ethiopia," *Struggle* 5, 2 (November 1969): 4-7.

26 See Girma Bekele, *The In-Between People: A Reading of David Bosch through the Lens of Mission History and Contemporary Challenges in Ethiopia* (Eugene, Oregon: Pickwick Publications, 2011), 357-367.

counter-parts. Such an understanding of religion in terms of what it does in society – as either legitimising authority (power system), or sacralising consensus (social conventions) – is reductive because it downgrades, if not totally denies, the transcendent dimension of religion or the theological that is often scandalous (i.e., it has a critical capacity). Moreover, it justifies the nationalistic absorption of religion (I will explain this later in Chapters 1 and 4). The functionalist discourse on the differentiation of spheres, as we noted above, leads to the affirmation of secularism. But the story does not end there as this differentiation then leads to the subordination of the theological by the political.

The instrumentalist paradigm charges Christianity and its practices as ideologically distortive. Religion is relegated to the private sphere and the freedom of religion is not as such about its public contribution but its qualification for being treated as one of the interest groups in society. What we observe, here, is the inappropriate positioning of the theological by these secular discourses. And, hence, it is my contention that the repositioning of the theological vis-à-vis these dominant worldviews requires the emergence of a particular Christian theological standpoint.[27] Such a theological turn will allow the repositioning of the theological within the Ethiopian society.

These secular sociologies are flawed not only because of the nature of the religious or the theological, but also because of their views on the human subject and especially the nature of collective social existence. Both paradigms affirm 'original violence'[28] as constitutive of the social. Despite its emphasis on integration, the functionalist paradigm embraces the necessity of foundational violence. Even more evidently, the instrumentalist paradigm presupposes imagined 'ethnic conflict' underlying social realities because of which society needs a social pact. As I shall argue, these views are not compatible with the views held

27 Such a theological standpoint is a socially 'situated' epistemic project that challenges the 'epistemic dominance of secular, material and immanent worldviews'; cf. Graham Ward, *Cultural Transformation and Religious Practice* (Cambridge: Cambridge University Press, 2005), 75 and for an extended discussion of the theological standpoint, see Ward, *Cultural Transformation and Religious Practice*, 72-84.

28 This notion implies 'a reading of the world which assumes the priority of force and tells how this force is best managed and confined by counter-force'; see John Milbank, *Theology and Social Theory: Beyond Secular Reason*, second edition (Oxford, Blackwell, 2006), 5; See also John Milbank, *The Future of Love: Essays in Political Theology* (London: SCM Press, 2009), 243-244.

by 'Christian sociology'[29]. I will make the case that Christianity recognises no 'original violence' but rather, in John Milbank's expression, 'harmonious peaceful order'[30] and towards this end, I will outline a political theology (in Part III). Here, my embrace of Milbank is limited to his social ontology in Part IV of *Theology and Social Theory* rather than his critique of secular social theories in the foregoing parts.

With regard to the cultural exigency in Ethiopia, I wish to turn to Messay Kebede's work. His philosophical work, as I mentioned above, give attention to metaphysical and religious notions whose significance he recognises brilliantly. In this regard, we share similar concerns. However, in his attempt to accentuate the Ethiopian native condition – vis-à-vis Eurocentric worldviews that he supposes to have eroded Ethiopian values – and to establish Ethiopian autochthony, he does two things: first, he attempts to whitewash the past and associates religion, and myth, only with consensus. Second, he argues that since the spheres of the religious and the political should be differentiated, the interplay between the Church and the political must be understood at and restricted to the national level. He strongly suggests that the Orthodox Church should be the custodian of Ethiopian nationalism.[31] I disagree with this affirmation of nationalist ideology and the nationalistic absorption of Christianity.

Nonetheless, what I am suggesting is not separating the theological from the political but rather the subordination of one by the other. To be sure, there is no impassable gulf between the two discourses and here, the distinction between the two discourses – the political and the theological – is simply heuristic. The political theology, which I will develop, will blur the boundaries between these two discourses – both of which are imaginative practices.

A Hermeneutical Approach

In this study, I will adopt a hermeneutical approach, a cultural hermeneutics.[32] Epistemologically, this approach differs from the previous paradigms

---

29 This is Sergie Bulgakov's term to express a theological standpoint; see Rowan Williams, *Sergii Bulgakov: Towards a Russian Political Theology* (Edinburgh: T & T Clark, 1999), 275.

30 Milbank, *Theology and Social Theory*, 5-6.

31 Messay Kebede, *Survival and Modernization*, 379-396.

32 My approach (i.e., hermeneutical) stands to evoke an association with Paul Ricoeur's philosophy of imagination; see Introductory Lecture to *Lectures on Ideology and Utopia* (New York: Columbia University Press, 1986); and Graham Ward's 'cultural

which manifest 'objectifying' tendencies. Of course, I am not claiming that this hermeneutics is completely original since a few others – to some extent – have employed this approach to study the Ethiopian case.[33] However, the degree of interdisciplinary sophistication, which will be evident in this study are lacking in those other works.

The benefits of a cultural hermeneutic approach for my study are two-fold. First, there is a method-content symbiosis: an appropriateness of the methodological tools for addressing the content of the research case. The content is constituted by key terms such as myth, ideology, historical narratives, and identity and of course, these are complex terms/concepts that need to be defined well (in Part I) before they are employed. Second, it allows me to work with a constructive logic of inquiry that draws together differing disciplines such as critical theory and theology – the latter without losing its disciplinary identity. Allow me, here, to briefly explain the nature of this interdisciplinary approach.

Theology and Social Theories

Theology and social theories are not necessarily at odds. For any academic inquiry that aims at a meaningful engagement between theology and the contemporary cultures that contextualise theology, theological discernment and theological critique or construction are two important aspects that require sufficient attention. Without proper discernment, theology can simply accommodate cultural productions without a critical contribution. Since the theological task of discernment precedes the theological task of construction, a theologian who seeks a hermeneutical engagement, must start by posing the question: 'what is the time?' or where are we culturally? Theology's own resources – sacred or classic texts, sacraments, liturgies, doctrinal formulations – cannot serve as analytical tools; although these can facilitate, to some extent, 'theology's own self-reflection', they 'are not fashioned for theology's engagement with its contextualising cultures'.[34] This implies that theology has to borrow analytical tools developed in the social and human sciences for its understanding of the contextualisation of cultures. Thus, there can be a constructive relation between theology and social theories.

With such a remark, we can move to determining the analytical tools appropriate for this inquiry. As we have already seen in the two paradigms, which

hermeneutics', or Christian *Kulturkritik* (Christian apologetics); cf. *Cultural Transformation and Religious Practice*, 62-72, 94.

33 For example, Sorenson, *Imagining Ethiopia*, 38-76.

34 Ward, *Cultural Transformations and Religious Practice*, 2.

we cursorily reviewed, the category of the nation is central. Nevertheless, the 'nation' has under-determined meaning in the Ethiopian context as we shall see in Part II. The reason such a category, the 'nation', has become important in Ethiopia has its own intellectual and political history. Applying certain theories of nationhood, the mode of thought I designated as the 'Instrumentalist Paradigm' ultimately constructed an image of Ethiopia as the 'prison of nations'. Such construction has not been without its political repercussions. It eventually led to a social engineering, which involved the reconstitution of Ethiopian as an assemblage of *beher, behereseboch, hezboch* (nations, nationalities and peoples); however, the meanings of these terms are not yet clear (more of this in Part II). Obviously, the use of such terms exhibit divergence from the use of the term 'nation' in Europe and North America. What must be highlighted about such developments in Ethiopia with regard to nationhood is intellectual and social reification. A brief discussion on the relation of theories of nationhood to intellectual and social reification can clarify my point, here.

Usually, theories of nationhood are discussions about nations. And, as Rogers Brubaker remarks, nations have been understood 'as real entities, as communities, as substantial, enduring collectivities. *That* they exist is taken for granted, although *how* they exist – and how they *came* to exist – is much disputed'.[35] Even though such a 'realist ontology of nations' has been problematized by the emergence of 'constructivist' theories that conceive 'groupness as constructed, contingent, and fluctuating' lately, the substantial view of nations still lingers.[36] For example, the usual questions that preoccupy the studies are 'what is the nation?' and 'when is the nation?' and such questions simply presuppose the existence of nations.

Such substantialist illusion characterises not only the so-called primordialists 'who emphasize the deep roots, ancient origins, and emotive power of national attachments' but also 'modernists' and 'constructivists' who understand nations as formed by such forces as 'industrialization' (e.g., Ernest Gellner), 'uneven development' (e.g., Tom Nairn), and 'the growth of communication and transportation networks' (e.g., Benedict Anderson).[37] The substantial view is not confined only to those who treat nations 'objectively' in terms of 'language,

---

35 Rogers Brubaker, "Rethinking Nationhood: Nation as Institutionalized Form, Practical Category, Contingent Event," *Contention* 4, 1 (Fall 1994): 3.

36 Brubaker, "Rethinking Nationhood," 3.

37 The examples given in parentheses are mine. See Gellner, *Nations and Nationalism*; Nairn, *Faces of Nationalism*; Benedict Anderson, *Imagined Communities: Reflections on the Origin and the Spread of Nationalism*, Revised edition (London: Verso, 1991).

religion, and so forth' but also characterises those who see nations 'subjectively' in terms of 'myth, memories, and self-understanding'.[38] The major problem of this view is that it 'adopts *categories of practice* as *categories of analysis*', which contributes to the problem of reification in practice as well as in theory.[39]

Theoretically, a better promising way of conceiving nations is to understand them 'not as substantial but as institutionalized form; not as collectivity but as practical category; not as entity but as contingent event'.[40] In light of such a conclusion, we note that the Ethiopian case fails at this point. In this study, I do not prefer to use the 'nation' as a category of analysis lest I contribute to the reification. Rather, I intend to problematise it. However, this does not imply that nations can simply be ignored. The set of analytical tools, which I will deploy, will treat the nation as an institutionalised form – as a social formation or reproduction – intimately linked to the operation of ideology, which constitutes subjects.

Therefore, the question of national-formation cannot be divorced from ideology and subject formation and this is a topic less discussed in the academic discourse of Ethiopia (see what I have said about such lacuna above). Academic trends and political discourses in Ethiopia put remarkable emphasis on the assertion of national and ethno-national identities, but the mechanisms by which such identities are constructed have not been subjected to critical analysis. Since the question of identity or subject formation cannot be exhaustively answered by a single theoretical approach, I wish to generate some conceptual tools, which will offer insights for the task. To this end, I will draw upon three critical thinkers: Louis Althusser, Michel Foucault, and Paul Ricoeur. Of course, the choice is eclectic (I will elaborate on this below).[41] Herein, we have to accept the risk of employing theories honed elsewhere (in the West) because local theoretical frameworks are still undeveloped. The cultural hermeneutics, which will be employed here, will also have a three-fold theological task of self-criticism, critique and construction.

---

38 Brubaker, "Rethinking Nationhood," 4. Cf. Anthony D. Smith, *Myths and Memories of the Nation* (Oxford; New York: Oxford University Press, 1999); Adrian Hastings, *The Construction of Nationhood: Ethnicity, Religion, and Nationalism* (Cambridge: Cambridge University Press, 1997).

39 Brubaker, "Rethinking Nationhood," 5.

40 Brubaker, "Rethinking Nationhood," 5-6.

41 Althusser is a structuralist thinker while Foucault and Ricoeur are post-structuralists. Ideologically, the first two are clearly Marxist and post-Marxist respectively while Ricoeur is a Christian philosopher.

Theoretical Frameworks

Drawing upon the above-named theoreticians whose theories are founded on different, often divergent, philosophical premises can rightly be judged as eclectic in approach. Of course, theoretical eclecticism is not without any precedents in various academic studies.[42] Often times, theoretical eclecticism is a response to a theoretical failure. When a single theoretical paradigm fails to be satisfactorily efficient to analyse a given research case, eclecticism presents itself as an alternative. What justifies the eclecticism of this study is the theoretical problem in Africa in general. This is not to say, however, that eclecticism is the only alternative in such moments of theoretical failure. For example, theoretical synthesis can be another viable alternative. In his essay entitled 'Toward a Sociology of Africa', Pierre van der Berghe, for example, proposes that synthesising certain elements of functionalism with Hegelian-Marxist dialectic is important for analysing pluralistic and rapidly changing societies of Africa.[43] Even though Berghe proposes a theoretical synthesis, he does not offer explicit criteria as to which elements to synthesise and thus far, developments in this direction seem to be lacking in Africa.

Recently, Achille Mbembe has lamented on the incommensurability between the theories deployed and the social dynamics analysed in Africa. Mbembe links such theoretical poverty to the lack of openness in the social sciences or the humanities such as philosophical inquiry; the enlightenment legacy of the division of intellectual labour, which is still behind the 'compartmentalization of knowledge'; and generally, the relative lack of the postmodern 'crisis of representation' that has affected various disciplines elsewhere; and critiques the lack of interdisciplinarity in the academia that allows the development of 'cultural studies,

42 The work of the feminist philosopher Judith Butler can be an example, here; cf. Terrell Carverand and Samuel Chambers, *Judith Butler's Precarious Politics: Critical Encounters* (London: Routledge, 2008), 1-8. See also Aijaz Ahmad, a post-colonial scholar, who raises the issue of uncontrolled theoretical eclecticism in Edward Said's image of 'travelling theory'. Of course, the charge is not against the use of eclecticism as such but its control. Ahmad notes, in the work under critique, 'poststructuralist denunciations of Marxism [...] delivered in the name of Gramsci, using the terminology drawn from Althusser, and listing the names of communist poets like Aimé Césaire, Pablo Neruda and Mahmoud Darwish'; see Aijaz Ahmad, "Orientalism and After," in *Colonial Discourse and Post-colonial Theory: A Reader*, eds. Patrick Williams and Laura Chrisman (New York: Columbia University Press, 1994), 169.

43 Pierre van der Berghe, *Race and Ethnicity: Essays in Comparative Sociology* (London: Basic Books, 1970), 79-80.

postcolonial, or postmodern criticism.'[44] Cognizant of such theoretical crisis and because local theoretical frameworks are still undeveloped, I prefer to follow an eclectic approach. However, the theoretical eclecticism, here, is not simply arbitrary but a thematically controlled one: it is narrowly focused on gathering theoretical responses to the fundamental question of subject formation. As we shall see in Part I, there is no singular approach that can adequately address this question: how do we become subjects?

While drawing upon these thinkers, I do not presume that they have compatible philosophical foundations. The intention, here, is not to furnish a synthesised theoretical framework out of the structuralism of Althusser and the post-structuralism of Foucault and Ricoeur, but to elaborate an eclectic set of analytical tools to analyse the Ethiopian case. Such an eclectic set of analytical tools, which will help us address the question of subject formation, is related to (a) the concept of ideology including key conceptual terms such as 'interpellation', 'apparatuses', 'mastery', '*dispositif*', and 'nation-form'; (b) 'technologies of the self' including terms such as 'subjectivity', 'self-writing', 'practices of freedom' and 'subjectivization'; and (c) human agency including terms such as 'action', 'narratives' and 'utopian imagination'. In what follows, I shall briefly discuss how such diverse conceptual tools are interwoven together in a generative way.

Outline of the Argument

In what follows, I shall outline the summary of the argument. Underlying contemporary socio-political practices, or political anthropologies, in Ethiopia are contending secular modes of thought. Such modes of thought, and the political practices they endanger, put considerable emphasis on the enactment of identity – national or ethnic – leading to an equivocal situation wherein the ethos that binds people together has been greatly eroded. Such secular modes of thought are flawed not only on the notion of the human subject but also inappropriately position the religious or the theological. However, a theological turn, as this study argues, will generate theological resources for a social horizon of hope – for the apotheosis of the bond of togetherness – which risks thinking politics in an altogether different way beyond the ethno-national logic. This, as I shall argue, paves the way for the possibility of a new political subject, and the reinvention of politics.

---

44 See Achille Mbembe and Sarah Nuttall, "Writing the World from an African Metropolis," *Public Culture* 16, 3 (2004): 350. Of course the studies Mbembe mentions here are studies that do not define themselves in disciplinary terms and are actually eclectic in their approach drawing concepts across a varied range of disciplines.

The outline of the argument will proceed in three stages. Since the problem of national or social formation is generally associated with social imagination, we need to frame the Ethiopian case with concepts related to ideology and ideology critique. To this end, the first Part, Imaginative Practices, will clarify key conceptual issues pertaining to the role of imagination in politics.[45] 'Social imagination', according to Ricoeur, 'is constitutive of social reality'.[46] Any bifurcation between imagination and reality, interpretation and practice is defied in such understanding. Social imagination is intimately interlinked with the notion of the human subject – human action or agency.[47] Thus, the basic philosophical question that brings together these diverse voices mentioned above (Althusser, Foucault and Ricoeur) is 'how do we become subjects?'

In Chapter 1, I will start with Althusser's theory of ideology. Here, the works of other thinkers such as those of Judith Butler and Étienne Balibar will also figure insofar as they support the analysis by Althusser. The concept of ideology will be employed in connection to national formation. This will provide a considerable light for understanding practices that shape or construct identities, whether national or ethno-national, which are now contestable issues in Ethiopia. However, even though Althusser offers an account of how the subject is formed as an outcome or construct of ideological conditioning, he fails to offer an adequate account of how individuals or subjects participate in their own ideological formation.

Foucault's 'technologies of the self' complements and develops Althusser's concept of 'ideological state apparatuses' in Chapter 2. Foucault's work helps to understand the construction of subjectivity – how the subject is actively constituted by her own actions. This notion of subjectivity has great relevance for understanding the Ethiopian situation in which individuals are encouraged to reflect upon and assert their ethnic identity or belongingness. Foucault's work in the social construction of subjectivity helps to understand the intersection, and offers a theoretical bridge, between coercive ideology, as conceived by Althusser, and moral agency, as conceived by Ricoeur. Here, the work of Jacques Ranciére will also figure insofar as he supports Foucault's analysis particularly with respect to 'subjectivization'.

---

45 Tentatively, I employ the term ideology as an imagination that helps to preserve a social order and utopia as an imagination that helps us to rethink an alternative society (another order).

46 Ricoeur, preface to *Ideology and Utopia*, xxxv.

47 Ricoeur, preface to *Ideology and Utopia*, xxiii.

I shall begin the third chapter by discussing Ricoeur's account of the narrative self because it further deepens Foucault's conception of the self or agency. Since this account of the self has a critical capacity, it will prepare the ground for the understanding that subjects are not simply conditioned by ideology and its practices but also that they can distance themselves to make a critique of ideology.[48] The conceptual discussion will be concluded with the discussion of ideology critique: the necessity of utopia as a social horizon of hope to formulate a critique of ideology. The principal relevance of the conceptualization in this chapter for the Ethiopian case is to highlight the fact that subjects are not only formed *in* and *through* ideological institutions and their practices, but also they can act to change and reproduce these institutions.

The conceptual discussion – developed in Part I – provides the hermeneutical tools to analyse the case of Ethiopia in the next stage (Part II). This part, Ethno-political Imagination, will focus on the ideological practices of nationalism and ethno-nationalism. Here, I will examine two contending ideologies in two consecutive chapters (Chapter 4 and 5) in light of the conceptual tools elaborated in Part I. The main focus of Chapter 4 will be on how Ethiopians – diverse people as they are – come to imagine themselves as a 'unified' people or how they come to represent their unity. Since the history of a nation is always presented to us in the form of a narrative, I will begin the analysis with the so-called narrative of Greater Ethiopia. Then, I will further develop the analysis under the following two thematics: the imaginary singularity of Ethiopians and the nationalistic absorption of religion (Orthodox Christianity). Then, I will conclude the chapter by offering a brief historical context for the rise of ethno-political imagination as an alternative imaginative practice to nationalistic ideology.

The discussion in this chapter sets the stage for the following chapter (Chapter 5), which charts the narratives that contend the narrative of Greater Ethiopia and the contemporary practices that institute ethnic and national identity. Of particular interest, here, are the 'identity formation mechanisms'[49] by which Ethiopians are encouraged to reflect upon their ethnic identity and to express or assert it for political ends and how the management of ethnic difference emerges as an aspect and preoccupation of the government. This chapter will discuss

48 Ricoeur clearly outlines the ethical implications of the 'narrative self'. For him, narratives are between description and prescription where the ethical aim (the 'good') cannot be ignored; cf. Paul Ricoeur, *Oneself as Another*, trans. Kathleen Blamey (Chicago: Chicago University Press, 1992).

49 Aprád Szakolczai, *Identity Formation Mechanisms: A Conceptual and Genealogical Analysis* (San Dominico, Italy: European University Institute, 1998), 1.

the pitfalls of this political culture and why a critique of this ideology of ethno-nationalism is needed. Instead of directly proceeding to the final part, however, I shall attend to an emergent perspective: the discourse of nativism. This discourse is a projection based on philosophical reflection on Ethiopia's native condition. The scope of the discussion will be limited to the reason why this approach appears to be a viable alternative but becomes inadequate for offering a vision of an alternative society. Having examined the historical processes and discourses on ethno-nationalism, the study turns to the theological resources that enable us to engage with the issues precipitated in Part II.

Part III –Theo-political Imagination – is intended to offer a projection of *another* (alternative) society. It is a post-nationalistic political theology that demonstrates the possibility of a new political subject: a theo-political subject. Here, my use of the term 'post-nationalistic' should not be understood in terms of rigid etymology, which may refer to a temporal or chronological concept. Nor do I conceive it as a total rejection of anything 'national' or local (for example, in favour of abstract cosmopolitanism). Rather, I intend to define a political theology that engages or contests ethno-national or national discourses, which place considerable emphasis on the assertion of ethnic and national identity, and legitimise particular forms of social order and practices that endanger common life.

Although I will make use of various theologians (only tangentially), I seek to develop my own political theology specifically through the work of the Russian philosophical-theologian, Sergie Bulgakov.[50] Such a choice is not simply arbitrary. Bulgakov's theological system can address the issues raised by ethno-nationalistic ideology efficiently. His intellectual critique of Marxism and liberalism, the Russian radical intelligentsia, the church's conservatism are all meaningful aspects of Bulgakov that I consider as important when thinking of his relevance to the Ethiopian case. Here, I have in mind some parallels shared between Ethiopia and Russia.[51] I also have in mind Bulgakov's ecumenical interest often reflected in his theology. But still a possible objection can be raised concerning the drawing of external sources for the theological construction, especially from those involved in and influenced by the discourse of nativisim that gives greater attention to the local construction of knowledge from local sources and I will defend myself from this objection in the Theological Introduction (Chapter 6).

---

50 A similar objection (as in the case of the critical theorists) could be asked on such choice and I will justify the reasons later (see Theological Introduction).

51 For example, the shifts from monarchic rule to socialism, Orthodox Christianity, the rise of radical intelligentsia, etc. Bahru Zewde, *Society, State and History*, 433.

In Chapter 7, I shall provide a theological account of Christian agency based on divine-humanity. This will serve as a protocol against Christian tendencies that cannot offer resistance against ideology. Following this chapter, which is more or less a theological self-criticism, I shall proceed to the chapter (Chapter 8) that offers a Christian ontology and ecclesiology as a theological critique against the ontology and anthropology engendered by ethno-national ideology as well as being a resource for the following constructive chapter. In a nutshell, this articulation of ontology aims at a Christian ordering of society: a peaceful harmonious order.

Finally, having articulated both a counter-anthropology and counter-ontology, I shall move on to the more constructive chapter (Chapter 9) that develops the outlook articulated in the previous expository chapters by giving expression to a political perspective consistent with the theology developed in the previous chapters: the Politics of Metanoia.[52] Such politics announces a form of Christian humanism that inspires us to risk thinking politics in an altogether different way beyond ethno-national logic. At the centre of this humanism is the possibility for a new culture of the self and the reinvention of politics. This will be a constructive theological contribution that offers an account of an alternative social order and a new way of looking at the interplay between the theological and the political in Ethiopia. Finally, I want to conclude this introduction with the clarification that the book is narrowly focused on the problem of nationalism in Ethiopia and that it excludes any discussion either on the problem of high theory in France or the problem of nationalist theology in Russia. What I said of the eclectic approach in relation to theory also applies here.

---

52 *Metanoia* is a Greek word for conversion or transformation. The translation of this term as 'repentance' is an unfortunate one; cf. Treadwell Walden, *The Great Meaning of Metánoia: An Undeveloped Chapter in the Life and Teaching of Christ* (New York: Thomas Whittaker, 1896), Ch. 2. Here, the politics of metanoia implies recognition of transformative potential of Christianity. It draws subjects to a new comprehension of Christianity and its dogmas insofar as this leads to action that co-ordinates Christianity with contemporary life.

Part I

Imaginative Practices

Having cursorily reviewed the two paradigms and methodological approaches; namely, the functionalist paradigm and the instrumentalist paradigm, in the Introduction, I would like to elaborate my own approach here. As I have already indicated earlier, I opt to call the mode in which I situate my own methodological approach a hermeneutical approach. Such a methodology will draw upon mainly three thinkers: Louis Althusser, Michel Foucault and Paul Ricoeur. The key philosophical question I shall raise will be: how do we become subjects?

I shall start with Althusser who will lay the foundation for our inquiry with his materialist and functionalist account of ideology (Chapter 1). Our particular interest will be on his doctrine of interpellation and ideological apparatuses and their practices in relation to the question of the subject. Secondly, we will see how Foucault's notion of subjectivity complements and develops Althusser's account of subjectivation (Chapter 2). Specifically, we will focus on Foucault's technologies of the self. The discussion on Foucault will be the theoretical bridge between coercive ideology (Althusser) and agency (Ricoeur). Finally, we will turn to Ricoeur whose work can rescue the loss of agency in both Althusser's and Foucault's accounts of subject formation (Chapter 3).

1 Ideology and Identity

1.1 Introduction

The discussion of this chapter will focus on the theory of ideology, as conceptualised by Althusser. To some extent, the works of Étienne Balibar and Judith Butler will also figure insofar as they support the analysis on Althusser. The main purpose of my engagement with Althusser's work is to analyse how ideology constitutes the subject. First, I will open the discussion with a cursory remark on Althusser's anti-positivist approach to ideology (1.2). The purpose of doing this is to set the theoretical frame, that is, a materialist and a functionalist account of ideology. Within such a framework, first, I will look at how the subject comes into being as a result of interpellation (1.3). I will also demonstrate how and why we need to relate identity to the polyvalent notion of the subject; and how this discussion will be relevant to identitarian – ethnic or national – ideology. Then, I will describe how the subject – whether ethnic or national – relates to ideological apparatuses or institutions and their practices in 1.4. Finally, I will conclude the discussion on Althusser by forwarding some critical remarks (1.5).

1.2 A Materialist Account of Ideology

Does ideology have a reality of its own? If it does, what is the nature of its existence? Answering these questions will have significant implications for our subsequent discussion. Generally speaking, the inquiry will place us in a position to understand clearly the function of ideology and the nature of its critique. Let us, then, seek the answers to these questions in the thoughts of Althusser.

First, Althusser contrasts his conception of ideology with that of his predecessors', which are positivist theories of ideology that conceive ideology as pure dream or illusion – i.e., as nothingness. He associates such conceptions with pre-Freudean notions of dream, as purely imaginary – i.e., as null.[1] He makes allusion to Marx, who, in *The German Ideology*, employs the proposition in relation to metaphysics: 'ideology has no history'. Althusser argues that this proposition,

1 Louis Althusser, *On Ideology* (London: Verso, 2008), 34.

for Marx, implies a negative sense because he (Marx) conceives ideology as a 'false-consciousness'.[2]

By rejecting the positivist and historicist thesis of *The German Ideology*, Althusser gives this proposition, that is, 'ideology has no history', a completely new meaning and a positive sense.[3] The Freudean notion of the unconscious is the basis for Althusser's radical shift in his conception of ideology. Following Freud's proposition that 'the unconscious is eternal', Althusser asserts: 'ideology is eternal' – that is, ideology has a 'non-historical reality' or an '*omni*-historical reality'.[4] The implications of this proposition are basically twofold: first, ideology has a history and a reality of its own and second, ideology has a concrete material existence.

Allow me to elaborate briefly what these implications actually mean. First, what does Althusser mean when he claims that ideology has a reality of its own? This reality, according to Althusser, is the reality of the imaginary or the illusory. The imaginary is something that does not 'correspond to reality', nevertheless, despite this fact, people always hold different sorts of 'world outlooks' or ideologies: religious, ethical, political, legal, etc. Ideology constitutes an illusion because it does not correspond to reality, but at the same time, it makes allusion to reality – hence, ideology is equated to or associated with illusion and/or allusion.[5]

Then, Althusser suggests that the question we need to ask should not be about the cause of the imaginary distortion but rather 'why is the representation given to individuals of their (individual) relation to the social relations which govern their conditions of existence and their collective and individual life necessarily an imaginary relation?'[6]

---

2 According to Engels: 'Ideology is a process accomplished by the so-called thinker consciously, it is true, but with a false consciousness. The real motive forces impelling him remain unknown to him; otherwise it simply would not be an ideological process.' While admitting that Marx and Engels have differences, Martin Seliger argues that similar elements are inherent in Marx's conception of ideology even if Marx did not use the term 'false-consciousness' but this makes no difference as far as Marx used 'incorrect', 'twisted', 'untrue' and 'abstract' besides nouns like 'illusion', 'block'... etc. instead of 'false'. We may thus take 'false consciousness' to denote Marx's view as well.' See Martin Seliger, *The Marxist Conception of Ideology: A Critical Essay* (New York: Cambridge University Press, 1977), 30-31.

3 Althusser, *On Ideology*, 34-35.

4 Althusser, *On Ideology*, 33-35. Althusser's particular interest, here, is proposing a theory of ideology 'in general' (on which particular ideologies depend) by following Freud's theory of the unconscious in general.

5 Althusser, *On Ideology*, 36.

6 Althusser, *On Ideology*, 39.

Althusser accepts neither the pre-Marxist view, which holds that certain individuals (such as Priests and Despots) as sources of ideological 'mystification', nor the Marxian-Feuerbachian conception, which attribute ideological distortion to the 'the alienated character of the real world'.[7] What is distorted in ideology, according to Althusser, is not reality as such or the conditions of existence but rather the imaginary relation. This is so because what humans 'represent to themselves' in ideology is not 'their real conditions of existence' but 'their relation to those conditions'.[8]

Althusser conceives the existence of an imaginary relation between real individuals and real relation. He calls this relation a 'lived' relation, which 'is a kind of 'a second degree relation' – it looks 'simple' but is 'complex' and it appears 'conscious' but is 'unconscious'.[9] As Ricoeur suggests, such a mixture of the 'real' and the imaginary, as a concept, is closer to Freud's (than to Marx's) concept of a 'compromise formation'.[10] In this particular definition, Althusser holds that ideology is active in principle through the 'overdetermination' of the 'real' and the imaginary and vice versa.[11]

Althusser's second conclusion is that '[I]deology has a material existence'.[12] Ideology has not only a reality of its own, which is an 'imaginary reality', but also this reality is endowed with a material existence. Put differently, this imaginary reality is not an ideal but a material reality. Althusser affirms this, saying: '... the 'idea' or 'representations', etc., which seem to make up ideology do not

7 Althusser, *On Ideology*, 37-39. Althusser does this at the expense of rejecting Marx's highly valued concept of alienation and the possibilities of de-alienation. The 'real' and the imaginary, which are in opposition in the young Marx, are herein conjoined by Althusser.

8 Althusser, *On Ideology*, 38.

9 Louis Althusser, *For Marx* (London: Allen Lane, 1969), 233.

10 Ricoeur, *Ideology and Utopia*, 136. Ricoeur observes that the 'real' and the imaginary, which are in opposition in the young Marx, are herein conjoined by Althusser.

11 Here 'overdetermination' is not applied to the relation between instances (infrastructure and superstructure) but rather to the relation between the 'real' and the imaginary; Ricoeur, *Ideology and Utopia*, 136. Althusser defines overdetermination as 'the representation of dream-thoughts in images privileged by their condensation of a number of thoughts in a single image (condensation)', or by the transference of psychic energy from a particularly potent thought to apparently trivial things [...]' For Althusser, 'overdetermination of a contradiction is the reflection in it of its conditions of existence within the complex whole'; Louis Althusser and Étienne Balibar, eds., *Reading Capital*, trans. Ben Brewster (London: Verso, 1979), 315.

12 Althusser, *On Ideology*, 39.

have an ideal (*idéale* or *idéelle*) or spiritual existence, but a material existence.'[13] Althusser, then, relates the actions of individuals to practices since 'practice', rather than 'action', expresses better the material reality. Also Althusser replaces the use of notions such as 'ideas' and 'consciousness' by concepts such as 'practices' and 'rituals' with the aim of emphasising the materiality of ideology.

To explain this, he employs the concepts of ideological apparatuses and *dispositif* that shape the behaviour of individuals or subjects (we will discuss these later).[14] *Dispositif* is a conceptual device that blurs the dichotomy between ideas (ideas of belief or consciousness) and material practices or attitudes of subjects. Apparatuses and *dispositif* are quite intricate concepts. Althusser talks about 'actions inserted into practices' that are 'inscribed within the material existence of an ideological apparatus'.[15] It is in and through the ideological apparatuses that individuals involve in practices or rituals. Althusser finds in the Pascalian formula a good illustration and confirmation of this case: 'Pascal says [...]: 'Kneel down, move your lips in prayer, and you will believe. According to Althusser, this exemplifies a scandalous inversion of the order of things.[16] Then, based on Pascal's inversion, Althusser concludes,

> I shall therefore say that, where only a single subject (such and such an individual) is concerned, the existence of the ideas of his belief is material in that his ideas are his material actions inserted into material practices governed by material rituals which are themselves defined by the material ideological apparatus from which derive the ideas of that subject.[17]

Althusser uses the word 'material' in four different ways. If we read this text against the background of Christian practice, for example: kneeling is a *material action*; kneeling as a religious practice is a *material practice*; kneeling as part of a service of worship is a *material ritual*; and finally, the church as an institution is a *material ideological apparatus*.[18] In fact, Althusser's use of the Pascalian formula

---

13 Althusser, *On Ideology*, 39.
14 Althusser, *On Ideology*, 41.
15 Althusser, *On Ideology*, 42.
16 Althusser, *On Ideology*, 42.
Althusser is careful in his use of the notion of 'inversion' lest it gives the impression that he shares Marx's method of conversion that aims at inverting Hegel's dialectic; see Althusser, On Ideology, *43-44.*
17 Althusser, *On Ideology*, 43.
18 See Ricoeur, *Ideology and Utopia*, 147.

is not far from Marx's method of conversion.[19] Marx argues that material circumstances determine ideas[20] and, likewise, Althusser holds the notion that the ideas of the subject derive from the *dispositif* or practice: the existence of ideas is 'inscribed in the actions of practices governed by rituals defined in the last instance by an ideological apparatus'[21].

Thus far, we have followed through Althusser's argument that ideology has a reality of its own – the reality of the imaginary (with a material existence). This is akin to his definition of ideology in *For Marx*, which is a positive construal. He defines ideology as '... a system (with its own logic and rigour) of *representations* (images, myths, ideas or concepts, depending on the case) endowed with a historical existence and role within a given society'.[22] By calling ideology 'a system', Althusser highlights its objectivity. He also emphasises its historical existence throughout social formations. The positive attribution and the indispensability of ideology are clearer in his claim that every human society secretes ideology, which is essential for its 'historical respiration and life'.[23]

Althusser acknowledges the positive role of ideology and its inevitable historical existence. He is also critical of any 'end-of-ideology' thesis. With Althusser, it is impossible to think of a non-ideological or a post-ideological society – there is no

---

19 Marx is indebted to Feuerbach for the method of conversion. Feuerbach, by criticising religion as 'a dream of the human brain', reverses the formula (of German philosophy) that makes God (Idea) the 'Subject' and 'man' the 'predicate'. Following Ludwig Feuerbach, Marx claimed that 'man makes religion; religion does not make man'. See Karl Marx, preface to *Critique of Hegel's Philosophy of Right*, ed. Joseph O'Malley (Cambridge: Cambridge University Press, 1970), xxx-xxxi; and Ludwig Feuerbach, *The Essence of Christianity*, trans. George Eliot (New York: Harper & Brothers, [1841] (1957), 13-14.

20 Cf. Karl Marx, "The German Ideology," in *Early Writings*, trans. Rodney Livingstone and Gregor Benton (Penguin Books in association with New Left Review, 1975), 47. Marx's dialectical method takes the objective material world as its departure and thought or consciousness cannot be independent of material reality. Marx writes, '[T]he production of ideas, of conceptions, of consciousness, is at first directly interwoven with the material intercourse of men, the language of real life.' Consciousness is always a consciousness of something – it is object-oriented and socially-determined or conditioned. Consciousness, for Marx, is not passive or arbitrary but it is an 'efflux', 'echo', or 'reflex' of the material relations of humans.

21 Althusser, *On Ideology*, 43-44.

22 Louis Althusser, *For Marx* (London: Allen Lane, 1969), 231.

23 Althusser, *For Marx*, 232.

ideology-free zone or no individual could be non-ideological. Althusser himself acknowledges that he (the writer) and the reader are both ideological; there is no exteriority to ideology.[24] Althusser does not discard the possibility of utopia (or any discursive break in history) but what he stresses here is the fact that there is no end to ideology. With Althusser only a shift of one's allegiance from one ideological state to another is possible. Of course, this is not a voluntary choice in Althusser.

Generally, ideology is of organic importance for the wellbeing of any society. Althusser claims that ideology exists even in a classless society: 'It is in ideology that the classless society lives the inadequacy/adequacy of the relation between it and the world', and he continues that 'it is in it and by it that it transforms men's "consciousness," that is, their attitudes and behaviour so as to raise them to the levels of their tasks and the conditions of their existence'.[25] The role ideology plays in a classless society is to empower individuals in their life. Here, ideology seems to fulfill ethical and existential functions because ideology has an existential dimension that helps people make sense of catastrophe and suffering. As Ricoeur points out, contradictory happenstances of life are considered as a 'lived' contradiction between 'our capacity to adjust' and the 'demands of reality' rather than 'abstract', 'logical' or 'structural' ones.[26] Here, Althusser's view manifests slight resemblance to the conception of ideology by 'strain theory' that conceives ideology as 'therapeutic'.[27]

Thus, if ideology is to be understood in anti- or post-positivistic sense, then, what can be said of ideology critique? Althusser distinguishes ideology from science to emphasise the (social) functionality of ideology. Ideology 'as a system of representations, is distinguished from *science* in that (in it) the *practico-social* function is more important than the *theoretical* function (function as knowledge)'.[28] This implies that, for Althusser, ideology is more sociological, focusing on the social functions of ideology than epistemological, which is concerned about the truth-value of ideas. What Althusser highlights is the subject's orientation to practical task in society.[29]

---

24 Judith Butler, *Psychic Life of Power: Theories in Subjection* (Stanford: Stanford University Press, 1997), 110. According to Butler, Althusser "enacts what he thematizes" Cf. Louis Althusser, "Ideology and Ideological State Apparatuses (Notes Towards an Investigation)," in *Lenin and Philosophy and Other Essays*, trans. Ben Brewster (New York: Monthly Review Press, 1971), 171, 110.

25 Althusser, *For Marx*, 235.

26 Ricoeur, *Ideology and Utopia*, 139.

27 Geertz, *Interpretation of Cultures*, 204-205.

28 Althusser, *For Marx*, 231. Italics added.

29 Terry Eagleton, *Ideology: An Introduction* (London: Verso, 2007), 3, 21-22.

Here, ideology is not understood in purely pejorative sense and its critique is not based on the criteria of truism and falsity. Rather critique is based on the function of ideology – whether an ideology is 'good' (profits all) or 'bad' (profits some only). In this regard, Althusser's concept of ideology does not only provide us the model for the critique of ideology but also it is a critique of ideology-critique. Even though Althusser's discussion of ideological interpellation and ideological apparatuses are limited to class society, he offers us a model of critique of ideology. With these introductory remarks, then, I would like to proceed to Althusser's notion of interpellation.

1.3 Interpellation and Identity

(From Identity to the Place of the Subject in Institutions)

How does ideology function? Or how does ideology relate to the subject? It is to this fundamental question on subject formation that Althusser's doctrine of interpellation addresses itself. According to Althusser, the subject comes into being as a result of interpellation. He postulates: '*ideology interpellates individuals as subjects*'.[30] Interpellation is an 'act' or 'function' of ideology by which individuals are transformed to subjects.[31] It is a way of recruiting subjects among individuals (in fact it recruits them all).[32] To illustrate this concept, Althusser assumes a theoretical scene:

> There are individuals walking along. Somewhere (usually behind them) the hail rings out: 'Hey, you there!' One individual (nine times out of ten it is the right one) turns around, believing/suspecting/knowing that it is for him, i.e. recognizing that 'it really is he' who is meant by the hailing.[33]

Using this hypothetical scene, Althusser highlights the compulsiveness as well as the 'obviousness' of ideology. As soon as the 'hailing' rings out, the right individual turns recognising and accepting the terms of the hail. There is always such obviousness about ideology; we recognise it without necessarily understanding the whole mechanism.[34] The distinction between the hailing and the recognising is simply hypothetical and it is meant for demonstrating an initial submission

30 Althusser, *On Ideology*, 44. Italics in original.
31 Althusser, *On Ideology*, 48.
32 Althusser, *On Ideology*, 48.
33 Althusser, *On Ideology*, 48.
34 Althusser, *On Ideology*, 45-47.

to ideology by which the subject comes into being.[35] Althusser explains that in concrete situations there is not any 'succession' between the hailing and the recognising because, he claims, that the 'existence of ideology and the hailing or interpellation of individuals as subjects are one and the same thing'.[36] What happens in the street – as in the theoretical scene – also happens in ideology. The fact that the voice comes out of an authoritative figure makes it difficult to refuse and it compels the individual to turn towards the voice. This turning towards the authority is a turning against oneself – thus, subjection.

But (echoing Judith Butler): why does the subject turn? In anticipation of what does the subject turn? As a matter of fact, Althusser himself draws attention to this dilemma calling it (the turning) a 'strange phenomenon'.[37] As for Butler, the subject turns because of guilt[38], in anticipation of the 'conferral of identity'.[39] She indicates that the turn is not simply imposed by the hailing but rather it becomes 'compelling' for the reason that 'it promises identity'.[40] Then, in anticipation of identity, the subject turns towards the 'law' or 'institution'. Herein, three things need proper attention: the subject, identity and institution. Althusser's doctrine of interpellation makes it possible for us to address the relationship between these in the context of identitarian ideology.

Althusser further elaborates the notion of interpellation by way of offering an example of what he refers to as the 'Christian religious ideology'. His assumption is that all social ideology (ethical, legal, political, etc.) works in an analogous way to this 'ideology' or 'divine performative act' (to use Butler's words) and that the 'formal structure of all ideology is always the same'.[41] He employs a rhetorical figure (God) that addresses (through Scripture, Tradition, etc.) a human individual by calling him, by his name, 'Peter'. The address is made possible only because of the existence of the one addressed – i.e., the name 'Peter' (both the address and the addressee [the name] are the same in this case). As Butler remarks, 'a name creates what it names' and 'there appears to be no 'Peter' without

35 See Butler, *Psychic Life of Power*, 119.

36 Althusser, *On Ideology*, 48-49.

37 Althusser, *On Ideology*, 48.

38 Althusser, *On Ideology*, 4-5, 107.

39 Althusser, *On Ideology*, 107.

40 Althusser, *On Ideology*, 108-109.

41 Althusser, *On Ideology*, 51. Butler makes reference to Althusser's account of the divine performative act but only with reluctance. She critiques Althusser's use of the religious metaphor for its lack of "power to diffuse the force of ideology." Cf. Althusser, *Lenin and Philosophy*, 171. Butler, *Psychic Life of Power*, 110.

the name 'Peter'.[42] She continues, 'the name supplies the linguistic guarantee' for the existence of 'Peter'.[43] In this manner, Christian 'individuals' are transformed, by interpellation, into subjects. The address, 'this is who you are: you are Peter', should receive an affirmative response, 'Yes, it is really me!' if interpellation has been successful.[44] With such recognition, interpellants, as subjects, occupy their pre-allocated places designated for them – their identity, placement, vocation and responsibility.

Let us now relate this to ethnic/national ideology. As the individual is transformed into a subject by a linguistic guarantee, ethnic/national ideology interpellates individuals by a collective name, which is the name of a given ethnic group or nation. Such a name makes it possible for identitarian ideology to aggregate dissimilar individuals as a 'homogenous' group of ethnic/national subjects (for political ends). In the words of Balibar, this is 'a singularizing strategy' or 'a false and provisional totalization' (as Butler would call it).[45] Insofar as 'identity' is bestowed upon them, subjects are able to make symbolic identification with their respective collectivities. This implies that the success of interpellation is in having subjects assume their pre-allocated positions, as ethnic/national selves, and accept their given 'identity' as 'truly' theirs.

For Althusser, such an 'inevitable and natural reaction' of ideological recognition is *mis*cognition[46]. Based on the example of a divine performative act, we can see the necessity for relating ethnic or national identity to a broader variable, which is the polyvalent notion of the subject: 'there is identity only by and for subjects; there is culture only by and for institutions'[47] (Balibar). This will become clearer in what follows.

However, a possible objection could be raised, here, on my usage of 'symbolic identification' for ethnic identity (mentioned above), which seems to be more proper only to national groups. This relates to the question of the nature of the collection: since members of ethnic groups are said to share one or more visible resemblances – such as physical, psychological/behavioural, and moral – is it appropriate to use the term 'symbolic' to ethnic groups?

---

42 Butler, *Psychic Life of Power*, 111.
43 Butler, *Psychic Life of Power*, 111.
44 Althusser, *On Ideology*, 51-52.
45 Étienne Balibar, "Culture and Identity (Working Notes)," in *The identity in Question*, ed. John Rajchman (New York: Routledge, 1995), 187; cf. Butler, *Psychic Life of Power*, 112.
46 Althusser, *On Ideology*, 46.
47 Balibar, "Culture and Identity," 183.

To answer this question, I shall turn to Balibar who adopts Jean-Claude Milner's typologies of 'classes' or 'collections'. Milner delineates between classes of the symbolic and classes of the imaginary. Classes of the imaginary are 'founded upon the *attribution* of one or several "properties" common to individuals, supposed to be distinct and to exist independently of the act of attribution'[48] (the resemblances could be visible [as in the case of race] or generally representable such as moral, psychological makeup, etc [as in the case of ethnic groups]). But classes of the symbolic are 'founded upon the irremediably nonrepresentable fact that subjects *respond* to the same name' – a name that interpellates them (e.g., Frenchman, Christian, Communist).[49]

What is illuminating in Milner's typologies, however, is that he places 'typical behaviours' under the imaginary but 'rites', or cultural performances, under the symbolic. This poses the question as to whether the two can function independently of each other. Although Milner speaks of the '*imaginarization* of symbolic classes', he does not pose the inverse question of 'the symbolization of imaginary classes'.[50] Here, Balibar highlights the significance of the symbolization of imaginary classes. For example, we note the symbolization of imaginary classes when social groups such as 'race' are defined 'institutionally' or 'juridically'.[51] Thus, my usage of symbolic identification is on this ground that the institutional definition of a given ethnic group, based on an understanding that both the imaginary and the symbolic, do not exist independently of each other.[52]

Therefore, notions of the ethnic and identity should be related not only to a broader variable – the subject – but also to that of 'institution'. In fact, here lies the difference between ethnicity as a cultural phenomenon and ethnicity as a political identity. We will discuss 'institutions' later under the next thematic.

Althusser employs the '*speculary*'-stage, or the mirror-structure, in his notion of recognition: self recognition and a mutual recognition between subjects and the Subject, and the subjects between themselves. In the divine performative act, Moses and the multitude subjects of God's people become 'the Subject's interlocutors-interpellates: his *mirrors*, his *reflections*'.[53] The people of God reflect God's image – as

48 Balibar, "Culture and Identity," 188.

49 Balibar, "Culture and Identity," 188.

50 Balibar, "Culture and Identity," 188.

51 Balibar, "Culture and Identity," 189.

52 Recent scholarship has already established the symbolic nature of community including the ethnic community; cf. Anthony Smith, *Ethno-symbolism and Nationalism: A Cultural Approach* (London: Routledge, 2009).

53 Althusser, *On Ideology*, 53.

all humans are bearers of this image.[54] The Subject needs its subjects and vice versa. The subjects also need each other. Analogously, ethnic/national subjects always 'contemplate' their own 'image (present and future)' in this 'double mirror-connexion'.[55] Their self-knowledge is continually reflected in and determined by their relation to ideology within this mirror-structure. Because of their symbolic identification, ethnic/national subjects (totalised or singularised by interpellation) recognise each other as members in solidarity – the solidarity of the *ethnos* or the nation.[56]

The mirror-structure, which Althusser employs for illustrating mutual recognition, also displays the relationship of subsumption. For example, Althusser narrates the redemptive work of God: humans fall in 'sin' – the cause for the separation of subjects from the Subject – and God, through his Son, 'duplicates himself' and the Son, 'forsaken' in the crucifixion, becomes subject while he himself is the Subject, for the purpose of preparing the way for final redemption and resurrection. Now, if individuals subject themselves to the Subject, 'they will re-enter the Lord's Bosom, like Christ, i.e. re-enter the Subject'.[57] To be a subject means to be subordinated/submitted to: 'there is no ideology except by the subject and for subjects'. Individuals who could have multiple identifications: for example, a single individual could be an Ethiopian, an Oromo (by ethnicity), a Christian, and a socialist. Logically, all categories are irreducible to one another and in fact, making one category subsume the other(s) is not only a singularising strategy but also reductionistic.[58] What ethnic essentialisation or nationalism does is reduce or conflate one or more categories. In ethnic/national ideology, the subsumption is followed not by a confirmation but by a conflation of one category by the other. The subject is totally subjected by and to ideology, that is, the 'I' will be lost in or floats between 'we' or/and 'they'.

As God's nominative call could illustrate, the Subject (God) who takes the central place demands the submission of his subjects. God calls Moses who responds

54 Althusser, *On Ideology*, 53.
55 Althusser, *On Ideology*, 54.
56 It does not mean that this solidarity is a perfect solidarity that really includes what it includes but there could be internal exclusion and hierarchisation within the inclusion; Balibar, "Culture and Identity," 188. Solidarity of the *ethnos* implies 'a community bound together by the power of shared fate, memories, solidaity and belonging' and can contradict the positive and ethical principles of the demos; see Seyla Benhabib, *Another Cosmopolitanism*, ed. Robert Post (Oxford: Oxford University Press, 2008), 8, 65.
57 Althusser, *On Ideology*, 54.
58 Balibar, "Culture and Identity," 188.

to the call and surrenders his will to God. As a proof of his submission, he makes his people obey God's Commandments. As the result, not only Moses but also the multitudenous subjects of God's people become 'the Subject's interlocutors-interpellates' – his subjects subjected to him.[59] Ethnic/national ideology, as a Subject, takes a central position subjecting all possible subjects around it.

At the end of his exposition of interpellation, Althusser assures us that there is an 'absolute guarantee' that 'everything will be alright' for subjects who 'behave accordingly'; except for some 'bad subjects', Althusser concludes that, all good 'subjects 'work by themselves'.[60] The implication is that unless and otherwise they obey, they will not escape from the coerciveness of the repressive State apparatus. Thus, those subjects who work by themselves are those who become committed to self-mastery; however, this mastery is nothing other than self-indoctrination and reproduction of ideology. This takes us to the discussion of ideological apparatuses and their practices.

1.4 Ideological Apparatuses and Practices

(From Practices in Institutions to the Discourse of Identity)

The notion of mastery is related to the operation of ideology in and through State, or social, institutions. Althusser refers to the school, the family, religious institutions (e.g. the Church), the legal firm, political parties, the trade-union, the media (press, radio and television, etcetera), and culture (literature, the arts, sports, etcetera) as ideological State apparatuses.[61] The functions of such ideological apparatuses are synchronised by the ruling ideology. In their symphony, they secure the subjection of 'citizens' to the State. Althusser affirms that the ruling ideology ensures the unity between the diversified and contradictory nature of the ideological

---

59 Althusser, *On Ideology*, 53.

60 Althusser, *On Ideology*, 55. His use of 'bad subjects' is an oxymoronic expression. Such expression tends towards the oxymoronic because 'to be "bad" is not yet to be a subject' whereas to be "good" is to be a subject. Althusser does not elaborate his reference to 'bad subjects' but he gives the impression that that he actually praises them; see Althusser, *On Ideology*, 64. Such an expression suggests that interpellation leaves room for the resistance of ideology. Of course, this raises a theoretical question that if 'conscience of guilt' is in operation in the constitution of good subjects, can it be said that 'good conscience' is indispensable for the constitution of bad subjects? Neither Butler nor Althusser answers this question; Butler, *Psychic Life of Power*, 119.

61 Althusser, *On Ideology*, 17.

apparatuses.[62] He observes that the communications apparatus, for example, crams citizens with 'daily doses of nationalism'.[63] And the School ensures subjection to the ruling ideology or mastery of its 'practice'. Similarly, all the other apparatuses work towards this goal of subjecting subjects to the ruling ideology.

Ethnic or national subjects placed in or under institutions undergo ideological practices that effect, consolidate or concretise symbolic identification. The identification of ethnic/national subject could be either with 'the institution itself' or with 'other subjects by the intermediary of the institution'.[64] A symbolic identification is not a matter of singular accomplishment (limited to a single event) but rather a daily process (always unfinished). Balibar refers to this process as '*a processing of the imaginary*: a behavior, a history or a singular strategy of the subject in his relation to the imaginary ("his," that of "others")'[65]. A processing of the imaginary is not something imaginary or merely a mental process. Rather it is something that emanates from what Althusser terms *dispositif*. Such a processing of the imaginary is about material practices that define the subject and out of which the ideas of the subject derive. In this context, we could also see Benedict Anderson's 'imagined communities'[66] as the function of *dispositifs* – monuments, maps, the press, the census – that create and consolidate symbolic identification with a given national group.

We can further link the notion of mastery to the practice of language, which has implications for our understanding of national formation. Althusser relates the efficacy of interpellation to the attainment of 'mastery'; especially, to learning how to 'speak properly'.[67] Mastery is figured by Althusser as submission, and both mastery and submission take place simultaneously. The aim of mastery is to enable or capacitate oneself to manage or to be managed by others. Mastery concerns the distribution of statuses, obligations, and responsibilities in a given society in such a way that it functions for the social reproduction or the maintenance of the *status quo* of the division of labour. The link between mastery and language as such (in general) has broader implications for social reproduction. Giorgio Agamben regards language as the most ancient *dispositif* or apparatus by which

62 Althusser, *On Ideology*, 23.
63 Althusser, *On Ideology*, 28.
64 Balibar, "Culture and Identity," 187.
65 Balibar, "Culture and Identity," 187.
66 *Cf. Anderson,* Imagined Communities; *and for that matter, the imaginarisation could also involve biometrics (e.g. Identification Card on which the holder's ethnic group and nationality appear [a case in former USSR and present Ethiopia]).*
67 Althusser, *On Ideology*, 29-31. See also Butler, *Psychic Life of Power*, 115.

humans are captured.[68] Similarly, Balibar calls it the 'institution of institutions' – that which determines an individual as belonging to this or that culture.[69]

Balibar develops the Althusserian notion of interpellation (and its efficacy; i.e., mastery) vis-à-vis the practice of language with respect to national formation or the nationalisation of society.[70] For Balibar, '[*E*]*very social community reproduced by the functioning of institutions is imaginary*, that is to say, it is based on the projection of individual existence into the weft of a collective narrative, on the recognition of a common name and on traditions lived as the trace of an immemorial past (even when they are fabricated and inculcated in the recent past)'.[71] Modern national formations or the 'imaginary singularity of national formation', Balibar argues, involves the producing of the people (the national community) through the practice of a common language in which individuals are instituted as *homo nationalis* and of course, simultaneously formed as *homo economicus, homo religious,* etc.[72]

To the community formed by language, Balibar gives the name 'fictive ethnicity'. Fictive ethnicity 'makes it possible for the expression of a pre-existing unity to be seen in the state, and continually to measure the state against its "historic mission" in the service of the nation and, as a consequence, to idealize politics'.[73] The institution of the community by the nation-state has become the dominant political form in our globe:

---

68 Giorgio Agamben, *What Is an Apparatus? And Other Essays*, ed. Werner Hamacher, trans. David Kishik and Stefan Pedatella (Stanford, CA: Stanford University Press, 2009), 14. Agamben defines the Foucauldian apparatuses (*dispositifs*) as 'literally anything that has in some way the capacity to capture, orient, determine, intercept model, control, or secure the gestures, behaviors, opinions, or discourses of living beings'; see Agamben, *What Is an Apparatus?*, 14.

69 Balibar, "Culture and Identity," 183-184. Balibar defines institution as 'generally a name signifying that any human practice involves a certain distribution of statuses (or obligations) and functions (utility, efficiency, communication), susceptible of being expressed and legitimated in discourses – whether they be codes, stories or programs.' The individual is 'chosen' by language more than he or she 'chooses' it and this implies that the subject occupies a position in a given language; see Balibar, "Culture and Identity," 184.

70 See Étienne Balibar, "The Nation Form: History and Ideology," in *Race, Nation, Class: Ambiguous Identities* (eds. Étienne Balibar and Immanuel Wallerstein. London: Verso, 1991), 86.

71 Balibar, "The Nation Form," 93.

72 Balibar, "The Nation Form," 93.

73 Balibar, "The Nation Form," 96.

> By constituting the people as a fictive ethnic unity against the background of a universalistic representation which attributes to each individual one – and only one – ethnic identity and thus divides up the whole humanity between different ethnic groups corresponding potentially to so many nations, national ideology does much more than justify the strategies employed by the state to control populations.[74]

It is not only language but also race (heredity; fictive kinship/genealogy), which constructs ethnicity. Both are competing, but often complementary, forms of collectivity whose aim is aggregating individuals/subjects (trans-individual phenomena). In fact, the latter is not more 'natural' than the former, however, both (linguistic and hereditary ethnicities) are 'ideal representations'.[75] Both combine in them the element of 'anthropological universality': hereditary ethnicity (race symbolism) is based on the notion of generational succession/continuity while fictive or linguistic ethnicity exhibits an 'ideal openness' to integrate diverse groups.[76]

The nation form is a result of the two competing but complementing operations. While on the one hand, linguistic ethnicity is an open process that has 'a strange plasticity' naturalising 'new acquisitions', on the other hand, hereditary ethnicity serves as 'a principle of closure' (demonstrating the fact that the language community 'assimilates anyone, but holds no one').[77] For this reason, Balibar refers to this closure as a 'second-degree fiction'.[78] This has the following implications:

> Whereas the language community can only create equality between individuals by simultaneously 'naturalizing the social inequality of linguistic practices, the race community dissolves social inequalities in an even ambivalent 'similarity'; it ethnicizes the social difference which is an expression of irreconcilable antagonisms by lending it the form of a division between the 'genuinely' and the 'falsely' national.[79]

Balibar concludes by highlighting the need for every society, which has evolved as an outcome of a process of ethnicisation, to transcend identitarian ideology.[80]

1.5 Conclusion

Althusser furnishes us with valuable critical insights on how subjects are formed, by interpellation, through the mediation of ideological apparatuses and *dispositifs*.

---

74 Balibar, "The Nation Form," 96.
75 Balibar, "The Nation Form," 103.
76 Balibar, "The Nation Form," 103.
77 Balibar, "The Nation Form," 98-99.
78 Balibar, "The Nation Form," 99.
79 *Balibar, "The Nation Form," 99-100.*
80 Balibar, "The Nation Form," 105.

Based on Althusser's account of the function of ideology, we have related identity (whether national or ethnic) to broader notions of the subject and institution. However, such account raises some questions, for example: are we conditioned exclusively by ideology? If yes, how can we then resist 'bad' ideology? How can ethnic/national subjects resist national/ethnic-interpellations? Can we not have a utopian moment of recognition beyond any ideological distortion – *mis*cognition? How can ethnic/national subjects, captured by contradictory *dispositifs* or polarised by divisive ethno-political devices, change their circumstances? Or how can solidarity beyond the *ethnos* made possible? These questions relate to the issue of agency. The major criticism against Althusser's work is this lack of agency.

Althusser's critics such as Mladen Dolar argue that there is an element of the subject that is 'pre-ideological' or 'pre-subjective' (*materia prima*) that does not pass into subjection – this *materia prima* is an 'immaterial interiority' (subjectivity) that can never be reduced to materiality.[81] The Pascalian machine, Dolar argues, is a 'senseless ritual' unless the 'remainder' or the 'kernel of interiority' is reclaimed.[82] Butler, however, makes a counter-argument rejecting Dolar's criticism as Cartesian and praises Althusser for undermining the ontological dualism that was presupposed in conventional Marxist distinction between the material base and the ideal/ideological superstructure.[83]

Like Dolar, Ricoeur criticizes the behaviourist framework of Althusser's *dispositif*. His contention is that such a framework does not make reference to motivation or action because it is not directly related to human action but rather actions inserted in practices.[84] Althusser's reason for rejecting the idea of 'action' is that it is too anthropological and hence, ideological. Both Dolar and Ricoeur agree that there must be a pre- or non-distorted imaginary; otherwise, if everything is distorted it is as if nothing is distorted.[85] Ricoeur suggests that Althusser's work needs to be complemented with a symbolic structure of action as a precondition of any ideological distortion.[86]

The other objection by Ricoeur is that Althusser reduces all recognition to *mis*cognition and hence, breaks the whole possibility of recognition.[87] He is against Althusser's correlation of the 'mirror-relation' with the 'relation of

81 Butler, *Psychic Life of Power*, 120.
82 Butler, *Psychic Life of Power*, 122.
83 Butler, *Psychic Life of Power*, 121.
84 Ricoeur, *Ideology and Utopia*, 168.
85 Ricoeur, *Ideology and Utopia*, 116.
86 Ricoeur, *Ideology and Utopia*, 157.
87 Ricoeur, *Ideology and Utopia*, 150.

subsumption' – how can subjectts resist apparatuses when ideologically tied to the mirror-stage of imagination?[88] The frame that Althusser offers us is 'subjection', not subjectivity. For him, the term 'subject' does not imply 'a free subjectivity', the subject as 'a centre of initiatives, author of and responsible for its actions', but rather, the subject is devoid of 'all freedom except that of freely accepting his submission'.[89] Such ambiguity about freedom of the subject needs further discussion.

In our discussion on Ricoeur, we will address this crucial question of agency. Prior to that however, as I have already stated in the Introduction, I will proceed to the discussion on Foucault. Even though Foucault follows a similar materialist approach as Althusser, his later thought on 'Technologies of the Self' clearly distinguish the notion of subjectivity from subjection. For this reason, I would like to place the discussion on Foucault as a theoretical bridge between ideology (Althusser) and agency (Ricoeur).

---

88 Ricoeur, *Ideology and Utopia*, 150.
89 Ricoeur, *Ideology and Utopia*, 157.

2 Technologies of the Self

2.1 Introduction

Foucault describes the focus of his later work as directed towards the analysis of those forms of understanding that the subject generates about herself.[1] Such conceptual development addresses the following question: 'How are we constituted as moral subjects of our own actions?'[2] According to Foucault's thought, the subject participates in her own subjection as well as 'freedom'. His thought can be approached as a bi-polar constellation of 'constraints' – the experience of our limits – and 'freedom' (going beyond our limits). The first pole deals with the 'limits' of *what we are* while the second pole deals with the development of new forms of subjectivity that enable us to refuse *what we are* because of imposed identities.

In view of this, and in view of its relevance for the politics of identity, I will draw upon Foucault's practices of the self such as 'confessional' and 'self-writing' techniques insofar as they address issues pertaining to the construction of modern subjectivities (identities) (2.2). Subsequently (2.3), I will focus on Foucault's strategic thought on the politics of our selves, which aims to counter normalising aspect of ethics. Finally, I will draw upon Jacques Rancière's insights on emancipation – the relation between the subject, politics and subjectivization – insofar as it complements Foucault's idea on the practices of freedom (2.4). This will clarify how Foucault's practices of freedom become relevant for the politics of identity before I offer a brief conclusion of the whole discussion (2.5).

2.2 Self-techniques and Modern Identities

The art of governing, according to Foucault, embraces not only constraint-techniques but also self-techniques. He understands government not simply

1 Despite the claims of some, I consider Foucault's conception of the constitution of the subject in his later work exhibits continuity with his early work. See Michel Foucault, "About the Beginning of the Hermeneutics of the Self," in *The Essential Works of Foucault 1954-1984*, volume 1, ed. Paul Rabinow (Penguin Books, 1994), 203.

2 Michel Foucault, "What is Enlightenment?" in *The Essential Works of Foucault 1954-1984*, volume 1, ed. Paul Rabinow (Penguin Books, 1994), 318.

as being governed by others, but rather as the nexus for the control by others and relationship with oneself. This means that one has to govern her conduct and government ensures (by regulating or guiding) that conduct. In brief, government, for Foucault, implies the 'conduct of conduct'[3]. Disciplinary power is simply one aspect of the art of governing but there is also another aspect of governing society. Governing in its broad meaning conveys not only mere obedience to the rules of the governing body but it 'is always a versatile equilibrium, with complementarity and conflicts between techniques which assure coercion and process through which the self is constructed or modified by himself'.[4] Thus, government, or rather, more appropriately, 'governmentality'[5] effectively combines such coercion-techniques and self-techniques.[6]

In his genealogical[7] work on modern practices of self-formation, Foucault draws attention to 'the way in which the subject constitutes himself in an active fashion'[8]. As we shall see later, the practices of the self are characterised in terms of juridical and discursive forms of subjectivation. In modern societies, the subjectivation of truth has become an important aspect that defines morality and the meaning of the good life. For this reason, attention to the practices of the self seems important to understand a given society. In what follows, I wish to start with a brief account of Christian confessional technologies and the practice of

3 Michel Foucault, "Preface to *The History of Sexuality*, Vol. 2," *The Foucault Reader*, ed. Paul Rabinow (New York, 1984), 337-338.

4 Kim Atkins, *Self and Subjectivity* (Oxford: Blackwell, 2005), 214.

5 Cf. Luther H. Martin, Huck Gutman, and Patrick H. Hutton, eds., *Technologies of the Self: A Seminar with Michel Foucault* (London: Tavistock, 1988), 19.

6 All Power relations can not be reduced to domination: As we will see later there is 'the dual possibility of being both *constituted* by the law and *an effect of resistance* to the law'; see Butler, *Psychic Life of Power*, 98; see Michel Foucault, "Security, Territory, and Population," in *The Essential Works of Foucault 1954-1984* volume 1, ed. Paul Rabinow (Penguin Books, 1994), 68-9.

7 Genealogy is 'an analysis which can account for the constitution of the subject within a historical framework'; Michel Foucault, *Power/Knowledge: Selected Interviews and Other Writings*, 1972-1977, ed. Colin Gordon (Brighton: Harvester, 1980), 117. The advantage of the genealogical approach over the archaeological is the former 'provides historical rather than epistemological answers to the questions of what constitutes knowledge and truth'; see also Jon Simons, *Foucault & the Political* (London: Routledge, 1995), 27. Foucault's aim is that 'the historical ontology of ourselves' should avert from those projects (metaphysical and ahistorical) that claim to be 'global or radical' because limits, according to Foucault, are not universal but contingent; cf. Foucault, "What is Enlightenment?" 316.

8 Foucault, "What is Enlightenment?" 11.

'Self Writing' insofar as they explain the historical development of techniques of ethical self-formation, self-representation and self-relation.

Confessional Technologies

If we follow Foucault through his genealogical work, we come across how practices of the self – self-relation and self-representation – developed on the model of Christian confession as an 'act of truth'.[9] Foucault recognises two concepts that correspond to practices of confession: *exomologĕsis* and *exagoreusis*. His study of *exomologĕsis* shows that this term is broad and has different types of usages. One kind of *exomologĕsis* designates making an 'act of affirmation' an 'object of affirmation'; one has to affirm not only that one believes, but one needs to affirm 'the fact of that belief'.[10] The aim of this affirmation is authentication of the belief either to oneself or another. The effect is that the subject ties herself to 'that affirmation and accepts the consequences': the subject has to live in accordance with what has been professed or affirmed, and moreover, *exomologĕsis* as an 'act of faith' is not simply a matter of personal beliefs but is vital and obligatory for the Christian so that she can 'accept the authority that authenticates' the beliefs.[11]

Foucault refers to another kind of *exomologĕsis* related to the sacrament of penance, which is more dramatic and without verbal confession. Although the prescription in *Didascalia* was that confession of sins to be verbalised to a congregation, this type of confession became related to a public ritual that involved the sinner's physical (bodily) expression such as wearing garments, abstaining from marriage and ministry. The focus became on 'mortifications' or 'ascetic macerations' that reveal or disclose the sinner.[12] This kind of confession survived from the 2nd to the 5th century. But later from the 12th and 13th centuries onward, the sacrament of penance became more organised and became verbalised. This is the kind of confession called *exagoreusis*. In *exagoreusis*, Foucault analyses three key aspects: 'the mode of dependence with respect to the elder or teacher, the way of conducting the examination of one's own conscience, and the obligation to describe one's mental impulses in a formulation that aims to be

9 Father T. De Vio, *De Confessione questions*, in *Opuscula* (Paris: Regnault, 1530) cited in Foucault, "On the Government of the Living," in *The Essential Works of Foucault 1954-1984*, volume 1, ed. Paul Rabinow (Penguin Books, 1994), 81. Foucault discusses ethical self-representation and self-relation (though he does not distinguish between these two explicitly).

10 Foucault, "Government of the Living," 81-82.

11 Foucault, "Government of the Living," 82.

12 Foucault, "Government of the Living," 82.

exhaustive'[13]. The model of *exagoreusis* is continued verbal confession as an act of renunciation of self or self-will.

Finally, Foucault conjoins both *exomologĕsis* and *exagoreusis*. He observes that there is a common element to both because one cannot disclose without renouncing. In both models, either through disclosure or verbalisation of one's self to authorities, there is a renunciation of one's own self or will. Foucault's hypothesis is that these techniques, which were operative until the 17th century, were later reinserted in the modern human sciences (ascetic social practices – which 'contribute to the strategies of power'[14]) that used them without the element of renunciation.[15]

Foucault remarks that this positive (self-affirmative) constitution of the self is a crucial hiatus from practises of the self with an element of renunciation. For Foucault, such regulative or normalising ethical subjectivations, which make one to externalise himself or herself, are characteristic features of Western 'truth-regimes' that are codified: law/rule-oriented. According to Foucault, truth is 'produced only by virtue of multiple forms of constraint. And it induces regular effects of power. Each society has its own regime of truth, its "general politics" of truth: that is, the type of discourse which it accepts and makes function as true'.[16] The modern government of people – 'truth regimes' – requires not only submission or obedience but also 'acts of truth' in order 'to reveal what one is by stating it'.[17] Therefore, the subjectivation of truth is an important element for self-conduct and the guiding of that conduct by authorities (government): the conduct of conduct (ultimately inscribing the subject into disciplinary apparatuses).

The conjunction of self-relation and self-representation in the verbalisation of asceticism is significantly important to understand contemporary politics of identity. Here, verbalisation of asceticism can be defined as 'an attempt at a conscious, willed formation of the self through the use of techniques of introspection and self-knowledge, the public declaration of the identities thus found, and a deep

13 Foucault, "Government of the Living," 83.

14 See Hubert L. Dreyfus and Paul Rabinow, *Michel Foucault: Beyond Structuralism and Hermeneutics* (London: Harvester Wheatsheaf, 1982), 180-181.

15 Martin et al., *Technologies of the Self*, 48-49.

16 Michel Foucault, *Power/Knowledge*, 131 cited in Charles Taylor, "Foucault on Freedom and Truth," *Political Theory* 12, 2 (May): 153. The modes of ethical subjectivation might vary in every society depending on the process of secularisation but codifications are global phenomena. Some societies could be more drawn to divine law (religious) while others to 'rational' or secular law.

17 Foucault, "Government of the Living," 81.

emotional involvement with the identity thus created'.[18] In pluralistic societies, the development of multiple subjectivities and practices of the self often tend to enclose subjects in 'different kinds of straitjacket labels', which can obliterate 'human bonds' and hypostasise 'human beings into antagonistic abstract categories'.[19]

Ethno-national politics (as a truth regime) disciplines its subjects insofar as they reflect upon their identity and disclose it; and ethnic/national subjects are supposed to align their behaviour to the requirements of that identity (participating in what Balibar calls the processing of the imaginary).[20] As noted above, the subjectivation of truth cannot be separated from governmental subjectivation and this is significant to understand truth regimes that emphasise cultural (national) identity. Here, drawing upon Balibar, cultural identity can be understood as the ensemble of these two poles: objective structures (truth concerning collectivities, the social and the historical) and processes of subjectivation ('dimensions of "lived experience," of "conscious" or "unconscious" individuality').[21] For that matter, Balibar accounts not only for the reciprocity between truth and individual subjectivity but also the disjunction in discourses of identity: moments of crisis.[22] Prior to discussing how the subject resists truth regimes, we need to see the importance of writing as an aspect of self-formation.

Self-Writing

Foucault notes that Christian texts of the Greco-Roman world of the first two centuries concerning 'the practices of the self placed a good deal of stress on writing'.[23] He starts his analysis from early Christian texts such as that of Athanasius's *Vita Antonii* in which the self-formation (transformation) of the Christian subject is highly emphasised. 'Writing about oneself' (particularly 'the notation of actions and thoughts'), which became 'indispensable element of the ascetic life', was an important art of governing oneself as well as others.[24]

Then, Foucault makes a retrospective analysis of the technologies of the self prior to Christianity in Greco-Roman philosophical tradition to enable him to see the differences between the two. Commenting on Epictetus's text, Foucault

---

18 Szakolczai, *Identity Formation Mechanisms*, 27.

19 Szakolczai, *Identity Formation Mechanisms*, 30.

20 Balibar, "Culture and Identity," 187.

21 See Balibar, "Culture and Identity," 174.

22 Balibar, "Culture and Identity," 174.

23 Michel Foucault, "Self Writing," in *The Essential Works of Foucault 1954-1984* volume 1, ed. Paul Rabinow (Penguin Books, 1994), 208.

24 Foucault, "Self Writing," 207-208.

observes that writing 'constitutes an essential stage in the process to which the whole *askēsis* leads: namely, the fashioning of accepted discourses, recognized as true, into rational principles of action'.[25] As part of self-writing, writing (alluding to Plutarch), has 'an ethopoietic function', which implies that it is 'an agent of the transformation of truth into ēthos'.[26] Thus, writing, as a form of governing oneself and the other, constitutes a way of being and behaviour, which cannot be dissociated from the field of action.

Foucault briefly elaborates ethopoietic writing appearing in two forms: the *hupomnēmata* and the 'correspondence'. The former contains fragmentary texts such as a collection of sayings and passages from respected books, which may help one to write 'more systematic treatises in which one presented arguments and means for struggling against some weaknesses (such as anger, envy, gossip, flattery) or overcoming some difficult circumstance (a grief, an exile, ruin, disgrace)'.[27] Foucault remarks (echoing Seneca), the 'writing of *hupomnēmata* is an important relay in the subjectivation of discourses' because 'the soul must make them [the discourses] not merely its own but itself'.[28] Foucault identifies the cultural context, in which *hupomnēmata* emerged, as one that can be characterised by an ethic 'oriented by concern for the self toward objectives defined as: withdrawing into oneself, getting in touch with oneself, living with oneself, relying on oneself, benefitting from and enjoying oneself'.[29] The *hupomnēmata* are caught by the principle of repetition – that is, the detaching of the self from 'concern for the future' and redirecting it 'toward contemplation of the past' (enchantment with tradition).[30] In general, the function of *hupomnēmata* has to do with constructing a unified self via disparate discourses.

The latter form of writing called 'correspondence' functions as ethopoeitic writing, which shapes the self by working 'toward the subjectivation of true discourse'.[31] The 'assimilation' and 'transformation' of correspondence is regarded as a 'personal asset', and according to Foucault, correspondence is 'something more than a training of oneself' but 'it also constitutes a certain way of manifesting oneself to oneself and to others'.[32]

---

25 Foucault, "Self Writing," 209.
26 Foucault, "Self Writing," 209.
27 Foucault, "Self Writing," 210.
28 Foucault, "Self Writing," 210.
29 Foucault, "Self Writing," 211.
30 Foucault, "Self Writing," 213.
31 Foucault, "Self Writing," 216.
32 Foucault, "Self Writing," 216.

Therefore, the act of written correspondence involves the 'objectification of the soul' in which the self enters 'the exchange of soul service': put differently, both the correspondents are impacted in the exercise of correspondence.[33] In correspondence, one finds the narrative of the self, which is 'the account of one's relation to oneself'.[34]

Generally, the two forms of self-writing precipitate the following important aspects in understanding the constitution of the subject. Writing informs and connects the subject to the field of action. It is the condition for the subjectivation of truth, which becomes an internal motivating force for the subject. Furthermore, self-writing is not only about the self but also about the *other*. More precisely, it is a two-way interchange that aims at bringing the 'gaze' of the self into congruence with the 'gaze' of the *other*.[35] This has implications for understanding the relation of the subject to truth-regimes and institutions (governmentality) in general, and ethno-nationalist pedagogy and the culture of the self, in particular.[36]

At this juncture, we can already note how Foucault's discussion of self-writing, as a practice of the self, can deepen the notions of mastery and the processing of the imaginary, which we discussed in the previous chapter. Understood at the level of the collective, ethopoeitic writing can have a significant role in understanding what defines the self-understanding of a community and its collective action. This implies that certain modes of self-writing and the mastery of their practices can be absorbed into the collective social *imaginaire*.[37] Furthermore, the characteristic features of self-writing – the enchantment with tradition (the past) and the subjectivation of truth as intimately linked to action – can help us to examine contemporary contending discourses of identity in a pluralist social context.

2.3 Ethics as Practices of Freedom

Foucault's genealogy unfolds a discourse of critique that counters the logic of governmental subjectivation. Foucault writes:

> If governmentalization is really this movement concerned with subjugating individuals in the very reality of a social practice by mechanisms of power that appeal to a truth,

---

33 Foucault, "Self Writing," 217.
34 Foucault, "Self Writing," 217.
35 Foucault, "Self Writing," 221.
36 Cf. John Ambrosio, "Writing the Self: Ethical Self-formation and the Undefined Work of Freedom," *Educational Theory* 58, 3 (2008): 263-265.
37 Cf. Achille Mbembe, "African Modes of Self-Writing," *Public Culture* 14, 1 (Winter 2002): 239.

> I will say that critique is the movement through which the subject gives itself the right to question truth concerning its power effects and to question power about its discourses of truth. Critique will be the art of voluntary inservitude, or reflective indocility. The essential function of critique would be that of desubjectification in the game of what one could call, in a word, the politics of truth.[38]

Here Foucault's politics is both oppositional and constructive. He expresses the need to counter subjectification through the questioning of political rationality itself, which is the mechanism of domination. He also indicates that such questioning or critique should be embodied in a new form of practice – the art of bodily resistance, which implies *refusing what we are*.[39] Thus, Foucault's two poles are always in tension and they reciprocate: subjectification abuts desubjectification.

In search of a non-normalising ethics, Foucault turns to Greek and Greco-Roman ethics. His aim is not a retrieval of an old 'alternative' for he explicitly acknowledges the fact that we 'can't find the solution of a problem in the solution of another problem raised at another moment by other people'; rather, what fascinates Foucault about Greek ethics is 'the idea of the *bios* as a material for an aesthetic piece of art'.[40] Foucault's conception of the 'aesthetics' of life does not imply an ethics divorced from politics, however. Rather it is a political strategy ('ethico-political choice') albeit a 'hyper – and pessimistic activism' aimed at countering the normalisation of ascetic social practices.[41]

Foucault outlines four major aspects of ethical subjectivation or relationship to oneself – techniques of the self – to show the contrast between normalising and non-normalising ethics. First, he speaks about the ethical substance that requires ethical attention: that is, identifying the problem or 'the part of us, or of our behaviour, which is relevant for ethical judgment'[42]. In Greek ethics it was *aphrodisia* denoting 'acts linked to pleasure and desire in their unity', but in Christianity,

---

38 Foucault, "What is Critique?" in *What is Enlightenment? Eighteenth-Century Answers and Twentieth-Century Questions*, ed. James Schmidt (Berkeley: University of California Press, 1996), 386.

39 Agamben also attests that a 'desubjectifying moment is certainly implicit in every process of subjectification' – both processes of subjectification and processes of desubjectification reciprocate; see Agamben, *What Is an Apparatus*? 20-21.

40 Foucault, "On the Genealogy of Ethics: An Overview of Work in Progress," in *The Essential Works of Foucault 1954-1984*, ed. Paul Rabinow (Penguin Books, 1994), 256, 260. Foucault, "the Genealogy of Ethics," 260.

41 Foucault, "the Genealogy of Ethics," 256.

42 Foucault, "the Genealogy of Ethics," 263.

the ethical substance is desire.[43] Thus, the ethical substances or objects on which subjects work on vary in different perspectives, eras, and societies.

The second mode of ethical subjectivation concerns the question – how or what ethical rule of conduct can address the ethical problem identified. This is the mode of subjectivation: 'the way in which people are invited or incited to recognize their moral obligations'.[44] This also varies: for the Greeks, for instance, the mode of subjectivation was both aesthetic and political – 'power, glory, immortality, and beauty are all linked'; later, for the Stoics, it became rationality; and in the Christian era, it became divine law.[45] Thirdly, Foucault raises the issue of how the self transforms itself: the 'self-formative activity' – that is, the means by which we change ourselves to become ethical subjects can be generalised in one broad term 'asceticism'.[46]

The final mode of ethical subjectivation is the goal to be achieved or the *telos* of ethics: the kind of beings ethical subjects strive to become whether achieving purity, or immortality, or freedom, or self-mastery.[47] Based on this genealogy of ethics, what Foucault attempts to explicate is that the significant changes that occurred between the different societies whether Greek or Christian are not in the 'code', which remain almost constant, but in what he calls the 'ethics', which is 'the relation to oneself'.[48] He argues that our self-relation can follow a non-normalising course if we make the aesthetic mode of the Greeks our choice, 'the aesthetic choice' or the 'political choice'.[49]

The crux of this argument is that for the subject to desubjectify herself, she needs to replace ascetic practice by aesthetics of life or practices of freedom.[50] This implies that 'ethics can be very strong structure of existence, without any relation with the juridical *per se*, with an authoritarian system, with a disciplinary structure'.[51] From Foucault's standpoint, we must have a new form of ethical relation to the self, which is not based ascetic values or moral austerities but rather on new 'aesthetic values' or 'stylistic criteria', the self must transform its relation to itself and in transforming itself as the work of art, the self will practice freedom

43 Foucault, "the Genealogy of Ethics," 263.
44 Foucault, "the Genealogy of Ethics," 264.
45 Foucault, "the Genealogy of Ethics," 264-265.
46 Foucault, "the Genealogy of Ethics," 265.
47 Foucault, "the Genealogy of Ethics," 265.
48 Foucault, "the Genealogy of Ethics," 266.
49 Foucault, "the Genealogy of Ethics," 266.
50 Foucault, "the Genealogy of Ethics," 282.
51 Foucault, "the Genealogy of Ethics," 348.

through refashioning itself as an ethical subject. In this regard, the practice of freedom is a counter movement in relation to forms of ethical subjectivisation: it is a problematisation of the taken-for-granted values.

Foucault establishes a new relation between ethics and freedom – he makes the latter an 'ontological condition' for the former.[52] Ethics, for Foucault, is the 'reflective part of freedom', which implies that he treats freedom as an ethical problem. He explains that the Greeks understood freedom as *ēthos*, which is 'a way of being and behavior'.[53] For Greeks, freedom implies 'non-slavery' (because 'a slave has no ethics') freedom is ethical as well as political. The mode for individual freedom or civil liberty, for Greeks, revolved on the imperative 'Take care of yourself'.[54] Foucault argues that care of self is ontologically prior to care for others but he warns that this imperative should not be misunderstood as emotivism or egoism. Rather, care of self embraces care for others – the 'art of governing' and even that of managing the 'space of power' (power relations).[55] This leads us to the issue of power relations with respect to ethics.

Foucault conceives the care of self as a 'conversion of power': '[F]or it is true that slavery is the great risk that Greek freedom resists, there is also another danger that initially appears to be the opposite of slavery: the abuse of power'.[56] What Foucault calls 'power' is power relations, which is everywhere: between/among individuals, within families, schools, political institutions, etc.[57] According to Foucault, power relations are fluid and reversible and participants can modify them; power is neither 'subjective' – a thing to be possessed – nor is it static, but rather it something to be exercised and is diffuse throughout the social body.[58] Rather practices of freedom coexist with relation of power and of course, the former control the latter.

For this reason, Foucault's notion of practices of freedom differs from processes of liberation. Foucault distinguishes between power relations and 'states

52 Foucault, "the Genealogy of Ethics," 284.
53 Foucault, "the Genealogy of Ethics," 286.
54 Foucault, "the Genealogy of Ethics," 284.
55 Foucault, "the Genealogy of Ethics," 287. Foucault's position on the relation between self care and care for others; see A. B. Hofmeyr, "The *meta*-physics of Foucault's ethics: Succeeding where Levinas fails," *South African Journal of Philosophy* 25, 2 (2006): 119.
56 Foucault, "the Genealogy of Ethics," 288.
57 Foucault, "the Genealogy of Ethics," 283, 291.
58 Cf. Foucault, "Society Must Be Defended," in *The Essential Works of Foucault 1954-1984*, ed. Paul Rabinow (Penguin Books, 1994), 59.

of domination'.[59] In the case of the latter, liberation might be appropriate but still Foucault insists that 'liberation is not in itself sufficient to define practices of freedom that will still be needed if this people, this society, and these individuals are to be able to define admissible and acceptable forms of existence or political society'.[60] This is the reason why Foucault emphasises practices of freedom over processes of liberation. Foucault argues that processes of liberation cannot define practices of freedom because for him the 'ethical problem of the definition of practices of freedom' is far more significant than a mere affirmation that an identity has to be liberated.[61]

From Foucault's aesthetics of life, we can draw some conclusions relevant to the analysis of ethno-national politics. Since the construction of identity, as we noted earlier, is a process never free of power relations implying that subjects can question a 'truth' about identity or particularly, the political rationality of ethno-national politics. It is such critique that gives way to a mode of resistance against nation/ethnic-interpellations and normalising ascetic social practices; for example, a nationalist-pedagogy. A critique of political rationality entails being critical of political liberation 'granted' by the state: the litmus test for such liberation being practices of freedom. At the centre of the cultivation of the self should be the ethos of the care of self and others in order to foster practices of freedom.

Briefly summarised, our discussion, thus far, has been on Foucault's conception of the constitution of the subject by her own actions or moral practices. In this account, we have seen a strong relationship of the subject, truth-games and power relations. The practices of freedom as envisioned by Foucault serve as the means by which the strong bond between the subject, games of truth and power are loosened; thereby, ensuring that power is exercised with a minimum domination.

2.4 The Logic of Subjectivisation

While the significance of Foucault's bipolar constellation of constraints (limits) and freedom (going beyond limits) for understanding or analysing the politics of identity is clear, it is not self-evidently clear how practices of freedom could lead to post-identitarian politics or identitarian ideology. To be more precise, the notion of freedom raises the question that whether or not the self or the subject of identity politics should assert or enact her identity in order to oppose

59 Foucault, "the Genealogy of Ethics," 283.
60 Foucault, "the Genealogy of Ethics," 282-283.
61 Foucault, "the Genealogy of Ethics," 283.

imposed identities. Foucault's genealogical interest in the construction of identity as a historically contingent reality strongly suggests and he is also explicit on the fact that his project problematises or destabilises naturalised categories such as madness, illness and sexuality that assign identities to subjects.

Therefore, Foucault's emancipatory trajectory is far from the assertion of identities, which his project seeks to question and destabilise. It is here that Rancière's notion of emancipation offers a clarification of Foucault's practices of freedom.[62] What Rancière calls the logic of subjectivisation, which implies a process of 'disidentification' rather than an identification of politics with identity, can be of great value here.[63]

Prior to elaborating this process with respect to self-formation, I wish to start by drawing attention to Rancière's definitions of three interrelated concepts: policy, politics, and the political. He argues that politics is not simply the process of governing, which involves 'the distribution of shares and the hierarchy of places and functions'.[64] To this process, he gives the name policy. He draws attention to another process that he refers to as 'equality', which 'consists of a set of practices guided by the attempt to verify this supposition': these sets of practices are named emancipation or synonymously politics.[65] The political, according to Rancière, is the encounter between these two processes of governing (policy) and of emancipation (politics).

Politics or the politics of emancipation, Rancière claims, is the 'politics of the self as another' implying the logic of a 'heterology' – such politics has to do with the 'verification of the equality of the self with any other and is always enacted in the name of a category denied either the principle or the consequence of that equality'.[66] Such enactment, however, is never the enactment of identity

---

62 The relation between Foucault and Rancière is best understood by considering the latter's work as a development of and complementary to the former. The latter begins where the former ends. In fact,Rancière himself explicitly states that his work is inspirited by Foucault's methodology that rejects metaphysics; see Jacques Rancière, *The Politics of Literature*, trans. J. Rose (Cambridge: Polity, 2011b), 30. Both Foucault and Rancière articulate a notion of emancipation that accounts for the action of subject: that is, something that is done by subjects than something that is done to them; cf. Gert Biesta, "Toward a New 'Logic' of Emancipation: Foucault and Rancière," *Philosophy of Education* (2008), 175-176.

63 Jacques Rancière, "Politics, Identification, and Subjectivization," in *The identity in Question*, ed. John Rajchman (New York: Routledge, 1995), 61.

64 Rancière, "Politics, Identification, and Subjectivization," 58.

65 Rancière, "Politics, Identification, and Subjectivization," 58.

66 Rancière, "Politics, Identification, and Subjectivization," 59-62.

or the self of the community in question. Rather than being an act of identity, the enactment of equality entails a process of subjectivisation in which case the 'place of truth is not a ground or ideal' but a *topos* for an 'argumentative plot'.[67] For example, the logic of protest in the form of syllogism unfolds such process: 'Do French workers belong to the category of Frenchmen? If not, the Declaration of Rights has to be changed. If so, they must be treated as equals, and they act to demonstrate it'.[68] This implies that the utilisation (evoking) of the category, which is wronged, is meant to serve as a *topos* for rhetoric but not as an act of identity. Rancière argues that the identification of politics with the self/identity of the community – national or local/ethnic – only leads to a political dead-end.[69]

As noted above, the process of subjectivisation, for Rancière, implies not identification but disidentification or 'declassification': 'the enactment of equality – or the handling of a wrong – by people who are together to the extent that they are between. It is a crossing of identities, relying on a crossing of names: names that link the name of a group or class to the name of no group or no class, a being to nonbeing or a not-yet-being'.[70] In other words, political subjectivisation entails 'impossible identification' with others to 'act as political subjects in the interval or the gap between two [or more] identities, neither [none] of which we could assume'.[71] In point of fact, Rancière's account of the other not only develops but also complements Foucault's ethics as the practice of freedom, which focuses on the self rather than on the other. As mentioned above, Foucault's account of care of self, as he argues, does not completely neglect the other. Nevertheless, Foucault's reference to the other is not adequately convincing.

However, the aim, here, is not to argue this point but simply to highlight the operation of the logic of subjectivisation. Thus, the logic of subjectivisation is radically opposed to the logic of identification. The crisis of identity politics lies precisely in the degeneration of the politics of the self as another: solidarity beyond identity. The problem at stake now is not as such a matter of engaging a political problem but rather that of reinventing the self and re-inventing politics itself.[72]

---

67 Rancière, "Politics, Identification, and Subjectivization," 60.
68 Rancière, "Politics, Identification, and Subjectivization," 60.
69 Rancière, "Politics, Identification, and Subjectivization," 58-61.
70 Rancière, "Politics, Identification, and Subjectivization," 61.
71 Rancière, "Politics, Identification, and Subjectivization," 62.
72 Rancière, "Politics, Identification, and Subjectivization," 64.

2.5 Conclusion

In what Foucault calls the practises of the self, Foucault furnishes us with a conceptual framework that allows us to develop a reading of politics as ethics – the development of subjectivity is the individual's will to truth, and truth regimes and power relations hold on the subject's own moral will. Self-techniques, intertwined with coercive-techniques, inscribe the subject in disciplinary apparatuses. The technologies of the self, we concisely discussed, emphasised the significance of confessional techniques and self-writing as these have strong theoretical relevance to identity politics we are analysing. What is more insightful in Foucault is not the notion of the limits that can be placed on the self but rather the conception that illustrates the possibility of going beyond the limits of the self. Particularly, the understanding of the self as the work of art has great relevance to conceive ethical self-formation on new aesthetic values and stylistic criteria that offer new possibilities of thinking our ethical relation to the self.

From the discussion on Foucault's hermeneutics of the self, we are now able to draw two important protocols relevant to identitarian politics: first, the self not only involves in practices, whether confessional or written, which bind the subject to her imposed identity but also has the capacity/potentiality to go beyond the limits imposed. Second, practices of freedom do not imply an assertion of essential identity that needs to be dis/re-covered. Practices of freedom discourage the identification of politics with the self/identity of the community. Only this dis-identification process can curb processes of governmental/political subjectivisation.

3 Agency and the Self

3.1 Introduction

In the previous chapter, we considered Foucault as a theoretical transition to fill the gap between coercive ideology (Althusser) and agency (Ricoeur). The present chapter will demonstrate how the subject can be conceived as an agentful being insofar as it complements the materialist and behaviourist framework of *dispositifs* by Althusser and Foucault. The discussion will proceed in the following way: first, I shall begin by showing how human action and material circumstances are interlinked in Ricoeur's configuration of the hermeneutics of the self (3.2). This is but a preliminary discussion that anticipates the second discussion, in continuation of the analysis of agency, on the narrative identity (3.3), via the notion of temporality.

The brief exposition of Ricoeur's narrative identity will precipitate certain key aspects relating to the problem of temporality and the relation between the selective function of narratives to collective memory that raises the question of ideology. Third, I shall then discuss how utopian mentality opens up the possibility of creating a critical distance to resist ideology (3.4). Finally, in 3.5, I shall conclude the chapter with a concise note on how the discussion on Ricoeur fills the gap in Althusser and Foucault as well as its application to ethno-politics.

3.2 Preliminary Remarks on Ricoeur's Action Theory

How can we overcome the dichotomy between material circumstances or frameworks and human action? Another way of phrasing this question might be: how can we arrive at a conception of the self, which can reclaim the sense of agency lost in Althusser (and to some extent in Foucault), yet, free of a Cartesian resonance? Ricoeur's hermeneutical approach to philosophical anthropology precisely addresses this issue. He holds a conception of the self that is neither Cartesian nor radical anti-Cartesian.[1] Ricoeur's hermeneutics of the self is equidistant to both cogito philosophies, which assert the independence of the ego

1 See Ricoeur, *Oneself as Another*, 4-16.

from the body, and anti-Cartesian conceptions of the self that conceive the self as a product of material circumstances or impersonal systems.[2]

The self, for Ricoeur, is not only embodied, or, mediated by material and cultural situations, but also capable of action or initiating something new. As Ricoeur elaborates, initiating something new involves desire, which conjoins two 'irreducible orders of causality', namely, the physical and the intentional orders.[3] Desire is two-sided in that it is 'a *force* that compels and moves' and it is also 'a *reason* for acting'.[4] This double allegiance of desire is the source of the opposition between cause ('what can be explained') and motive ('what can be understood').[5] The two-sidedness of desire helps us to conceive a given initiative as 'motive to force and to sense, to nature and to culture, to *bios* and to *logos*'.[6] Thus, the self, as an agent, belongs to the domain of 'explanation' or 'causation', which refers to impersonal material (physical or natural situations), and to that of 'understanding' or 'motivation'.[7]

Ricoeur claims that desire makes an action intelligible or meaningful but it cannot help us to understand what action or initiative is. An action, Ricoeur explains, is that which 'intervenes in the world': an action introduces change in the world.[8] Based on such an understanding of action, Ricoeur poses two questions: one on the nature of the world and the other on the nature of action itself: '[W]hat must be the nature of the world… if human beings are to be able to introduce changes into it?' and '[W]hat must be the nature of action… if it is to be read in terms of change in the world?'[9]

By drawing upon G. H. von Wright's work entitled *Explanation and Understanding*, Ricoeur sets out to answer the first of these questions. The analysis by von Wright conjoins the 'conditions of explanation' with the 'conditions of understanding' in the notion of what he calls an 'intentional intervention' in the world.[10] Von Wright's analysis is important for Ricoeur's theory of action for it helps him (Ricoeur) to overcome the dualism between causation and motivation, or, between what Ricoeur calls 'explanation' and 'understanding'.

---

2 Ricoeur, *Oneself as Another*, 23.
3 Ricoeur, *Oneself as Another*, 111.
4 Paul Ricoeur, *From Text to Action: Essays in Hermeneutics, II,* trans. Kathleen Blamey and John B. Thompson (London: Continuum, 2008), 130.
5 Ricoeur, *From Text to Action*, 130.
6 Ricoeur, *From Text to Action*, 130.
7 Ricoeur, *From Text to Action*, 130-31.
8 Ricoeur, *From Text to Action*, 131.
9 Ricoeur, *From Text to Action*, 131.
10 Ricoeur, *From Text to Action*, 131.

Von Wright's argument lies upon system theory. He takes the notion of a 'closed system' that can permit us to think of an 'initial state' and a 'terminal state', and, in between, 'various stages' or 'internal alternatives'.[11] It is in relation to such a system that von Wright conceives the interference of human action in the world because to set the system in motion, an initial state must be produced by 'exercising a power, by intervening in the course of affairs'.[12] The initial state, intervention and the exercise of power are all related like a chain-reaction and one cannot happen without the other.[13] As Ricoeur argues, '[A]cting is always doing something so that something else happens in the world. On the other hand, there is no action without the relation between knowing how to do something (being able to do something) and that which the latter brings about'.[14] Thus, this implies that there is an intersection between explanation that belongs to the domain of system theory and understanding, which can belong to the domain of 'intentional' or 'motivated human action'.[15]

As Ricoeur would argue, 'the course of things' and 'human action' can be conjoined in the notion of 'intentional intervention' or interference in the world.[16] Such a notion of intervention requires a causation that is different from that of Hume's: Ricoeur substitutes Hume's causal connection, which holds the 'logical independence' between 'antecedents' and 'consequences', with the logical connection between intention and action, between motive and project.[17] This kind of understanding does not set out motive in opposition to action or initiative, but rather the former is included in the latter.

In response to the second question on the nature of action, Ricoeur, based on Kantian reflection on antinomies related to the causality of freedom, claims that action is related to initiative.[18] Initiative, as Ricoeur defines it, 'is an *intervention* of the agent of action in the cause of the world, an intervention which effectively causes changes in the world'.[19] Finally, there is no intervention without purpose and it is here that we recognise the centrality of the notion of temporality to Ricoeur's action theory.

---

11 Ricoeur, *From Text to Action*, 131.
12 Ricoeur, *From Text to Action*, 131.
13 Ricoeur, *From Text to Action*, 133.
14 Ricoeur, *From Text to Action*, 133.
15 Ricoeur, *From Text to Action*, 132.
16 Ricoeur, *From Text to Action*, 131-132.
17 Ricoeur, *From Text to Action*, 129-132.
18 Ricoeur, *From Text to Action*, 102.
19 Ricoeur, *Oneself as Another*, 109.

According to Ricoeur, every action is meaningful and it takes place in historical time in relation to past action and anticipating a future response. At the intersection of what Reinhart Koselleck calls the 'space of experience' and the 'horizon of expectation' is what Rocoeur refers to as the historical present.[20] Ricoeur raises the question of the historical present from the perspective of initiative on the collective and social and community level. Rather than the 'persistence of the past in the present', Koselleck opts to use a space of experience, because, first, the term 'experience' has a broader meaning that is inclusive of the legacy of the experience of past generations as well as the experiences of existing institutions, which is similar to the notion of a *habitus*.[21] It is a past remembered in the present.

Second, the term 'space' relates to the idea of various alternative routes and it indicates a 'layered structure, composed of clusters and stratifications'.[22] A space of experience allows the past to reside in the present insofar as it informs actions or initiatives in the present. The term 'expectation' in the expression 'horizon of expectation', refers to manifestations relating to the future: whether 'fear' or 'hope', 'wishing' or 'willing', 'care', 'rational calculation', 'curiosity' and so on.[23] It is a 'future-become-present', which is the expectation of the future inscribed in the present and the use of 'horizon', rather than 'space', is meant to 'emphasize the power of unfolding'.[24]

Both there is always a conditioning of the space of experience and the horizon of expectation with each other; and historical action keeps the dialectic between the two. To situate the discussion of the historical time in relation to the context of human action or agency, we need a sort of discourse that can frame these two notions. Precisely, narrative is the discourse that addresses both concepts. The dialectical relation between the space of experiences and the horizon of expectation can be related to 'the selection of narrated events' with 'existential projects'.[25]

At this juncture, before we proceed with our discussion of narrative identity, we can note how the overcoming of the dichotomy between material circumstances or events and human action can help us to revisit Althusser and Foucault's materialist frameworks. Consequently, we are able to think of its implication for our analysis of ethno-politics. It is this: the ethno-political subject is not merely an outcome of action formed *in* and *by* institutions and their practices but also one who can act to intervene so that he or she (re-)produces or changes them.

---

20 Ricoeur, *From Text to Action,* 214.
21 Ricoeur, *From Text to Action,* 214.
22 Ricoeur, *From Text to Action,* 214.
23 Ricoeur, *From Text to Action,* 214.
24 Ricoeur, *From Text to Action,* 214.
25 Ricoeur, *Oneself as Another*, 160.

3.3 Narrative Identity and Ideology

To ask about identity is to tell a story or a narrative. Ricoeur says that 'identity can be called [...] the identity of the character'.[26] This identity of the character or 'identity on the level of emplotment' is a paradoxical composition of concordance and discordance.[27] Ricoeur calls such a unity or 'the synthesis of the heterogeneous', which composes competing elements of 'concordance' and 'discordance', a 'discordant concordance'.[28] In the narrative configuration, there are manifold of dialectics or diversity of mediations in the plot. Ricoeur relates this to the notion of 'dynamic identity' that reconciles Locke's contraries 'identity' and 'diversity'.[29]

The self, which is constructed by narratives, is structured as a unity. Alasdair MacIntyre calls this the 'narrative unity of the self'.[30] Narratives display 'temporal unity' since they configure multiplicity of events of the past, the present and the future in a 'narrative unity'.[31] In the emplotment of action, both concordance and discordance are synthesised to form this temporal unity. The character in the story recounted is understood as an outcome of this synthesis. The dialectics between concordance and discordance can be placed in the discussion on the dialectics of 'Sameness' and selfhood.[32]

Narrative identity poses a key question: is a subject identical with itself in the diversity of its different states? Or, following Hume and Nietzsche, must we hold that this identical subject is nothing more than a substantialist illusion? Ricoeur's notion of narrative identity differs from a substantialist (formal) identity of the 'Same' for it is 'constitutive of self-constancy' and it is inclusive of 'change, mutability, within the cohesion of one lifetime'.[33] Self-constancy of individuals and communities, for Ricoeur, refers to 'a self instructed by the works of a culture

26 Ricoeur, *Oneself as Another*, 141. 'A character is the one who performs the action in the narrative.' Ricoeur, *Oneself as Another*, 143.

27 Ricoeur, *Oneself as Another*, 141.

28 Concordance is 'the principle of order that presides over what Aristotle calls "the arrangement of facts"' and discordance refers to 'the reversals of fortune that make the plot an ordered transformation from an initial situation to a terminal situation'; cf. Ricoeur, *Oneself as Another*, 141.

29 Ricoeur, *Oneself as Another*, 143.

30 Alasdair MacIntyre, *After Virtue* (Notre Dame: Notre Dame University Press, 1981), 219, 217-221.

31 Ricoeur, *Oneself as Another*, 141.

32 Ricoeur, *Oneself as Another*, 147.

33 Paul Ricoeur, *Time and Narrative,* vol.3, trans. Kathleen Blamey and David Pellauer (Chicago: The University of Chicago, 1988), 246.

that it has applied to itself', and in this sense, narratives become the 'actual history' of communities.[34] In what Freud called 'working-through', the analysand recognises her self-constancy; and, a series of rectifications and corrections are applied to life stories or previous narratives. And Ricoeur, regarding psychoanalysis as a laboratory for a philosophical inquiry into the notion of narrative identity, compares this with new historians bringing about certain changes to previous historiographical works on people or institutions ('history always proceeds from history').[35]

The correlation of action and narrative is emphasised by Ricoeur, as in MacIntyre: except in the case of fictions, stories are always lived before they are told.[36] Lived experience is always related to narrative configuration. For Ricoeur, '[T]he person, understood as a character in a story is not an entity distinct from his or her "experience"'.[37] For Ricoeur, human action or activities are enacted narratives. Narrative theory correlates action and character. When we make the passage from action to the character, however, the question about the correlation between the story recounted and the character arises: 'the character preserves throughout the story an identity correlative to that of the story itself', and Ricoeur claims that 'characters [...] are themselves plots'.[38] In the process of emplotment, the conjunction between action and character is the answer to the *aporia* of ascription.[39] To ask the question 'who of action' ('who did this?' or 'who is the agent?') is (following Hannah Arendt) 'to tell the story of a life', and '[T]he story told tells about the action of the "who" therefore itself must be a narrative identity'.[40] Put differently, '[T]elling a story is saying who did what and how, by spreading out in time the connection between these various viewpoints'.[41] Thus, 'stories are about agents and sufferers' since humans always act and suffer.[42]

Narrative identity entails a reference to others, which is a social dimension. Narratives influence social behaviour. And as Proust would have it: the 'subject

34 Ricoeur, *Time and Narrative,* vol.3, 247.
35 Ricoeur, *Time and Narrative,* vol.3, 247.
36 MacIntyre, *After Virtue,* 212.
37 Ricoeur, *Oneself as Another*, 147.
38 Ricoeur, *Oneself as Another*, 143.
39 Ricoeur, *Oneself as Another*, 146.
40 Ricoeur, *Time and Narrative,* vol.3, 246.
41 Ricoeur, *Oneself as Another*, 146.
42 The dissymmetry between those who act in violence and those who suffer (victims of disesteem) concerns the connection between action theory and ethical theory. See Ricoeur, *Oneself as Another*, 146.

then appears both as a reader and the writer of its own life'.[43] This implies that humans are not only agents in the course of their life but also they are sufferers – who are never free of their circumstances. Individuals or communities are not simply sole-authors of their own narratives but rather they are co-authors with others. Here, MacIntyre's statements support Ricoeur's view:

> We are never more (and sometimes less) than the co-authors of our own narratives. Only in fantasy do we live what story we please. In life, as both Aristotle and Engels noted, we are always under certain constraints. We enter upon a stage which we did not design and we find ourselves part of an action that was not of our making.[44]

This leads us to consider some limitations or problems associated with narratives three of which demand attention. Ricoeur discusses the following fragilities, which, in the first place, relates to time: self-constancy – the notion of being identical: how can a community become self-same through long periods of time, for example? Ricoeur discusses the fragilities of both identity and memory: the fragility of the former consists in responses (lack of a singular answer) given to the question 'what/who I am/we are'.[45] Second, the confrontation with others – as we have already discussed both in the previous and the current sub-chapters, identity is understood as the function of the 'Other'. Here, Ricoeur relates (pathological) collective memory to the *others* who are basically considered 'threats'.[46] Third, founding violence – many nation-states, historically, have groups (ethnic or religious) on whom violence had been enacted during their state/nation-building projects; hence, such historical events can be stored, as 'wounds', 'in the archives of collective memory'.[47] All these fragilities are pertinent for discourses of ethno-nationalism because whether the question of self-sameness of communities through time or the issue of boundary making mechanisms or even foundational national myths, in one way or the other, are intertwined with notions of collective memory and narratives.

Ricoeur connects such fragilities of collective memory to the selective function of narratives: a history, a nationalist narrative or story-telling are central in

43 Cf. Ricoeur, *Time and Narrative*, vol.3, 246.

44 MacIntyre, *After Virtue*, 213.

45 Paul Ricoeur, *Memory, History, Forgetting*, trans. Kathleen Blamey and David Pellauer (Chicago: Chicago University Press, 2004), 81.

46 Ricoeur, *Memory, History, Forgetting*, 85.

47 What we consider as pathological is not only the narratives of founding events but also the dangers of the claim for assuming the status of the victim (for the victim's questions remain endless and tends to place 'everyone else in the position of owing a debt'). Ricoeur, *Memory, History, Forgetting*, 85-86.

understanding nationalism. Here, we can also connect Ricoeur's statement to what Balibar calls a processing of the imaginary – 'a behaviour', 'a history' or 'any singularising strategy', which we already related to Althusser's notion of *dispositifs*. The issue of ideologised memory should be considered when theoretically engaging with ethno-nationalism in both its hegemonic and counter-hegemonic (subaltern) forms. As Ricoeur indicates, 'it is through the narrative function that memory is incorporated into the formation of identity'[48].

Memory, Ricoeur argues, 'can be ideologized through the resources of the variations offered by the work of narrative configuration', and he continues, '[A]nd, as the characters of the narrative are emplotted at the same time the story is told, the narrative configuration contributes to modeling the identity of the protagonists of action as it molds the contours of the action itself'.[49] The 'selective function' of the narrative, as Ricoeur argues, opens up the possibility of the manipulation of collective memory.[50] Ricoeur argues that history is quasi-fictive as fiction is quasi-historical and that the two are intricately interwoven.[51] For him, narrative identity of an individual or a community is 'the union of history and fiction'.[52] The past is often interpreted in the light of the present. Such an interpretation is seldom possible without fictive imagination. The fragility of memory rests on its proximity to imagination.[53] Representations of the past, through reference to collective memory, are often imaginative ideological projects of taking the past forward. As we have already observed so far, narrative identity helps us to reclaim an account of agency – the capability of humans to act and suffer – and thereby, link capabilities of action and narration. Finally, we have also seen that narratives or narration cannot be ideologically-free. Thus, this would logically lead us to the question of ideology-critique or the question of transcending the circularity of ideology.

3.4 Utopian Imagination

In his books entitled *The Course of Recognition* and *Oneself as Another*, Ricoeur concludes his discussion of identity with a discourse on ethics.[54] In fact there are

48 Ricoeur, *Memory, History, Forgetting*, 85-86.
49 Ricoeur, *Memory, History, Forgetting*, 85.
50 Ricoeur, *Memory, History, Forgetting*, 85.
51 Ricoeur, *Time and Narrative*, vol.3, 245.
52 Ricoeur, *Time and Narrative*, vol.3, 246.
53 Ricoeur, *Memory, History, Forgetting*, 81.
54 In the former, the author attempts to reconcile Kantian and Hegelian notions. He constructs a theory of mutual recognition drawing upon Axel Honneth's 'systematic

good reasons for relating to ethical theory, via narrative identity, following the Ricoeurian formula: description (action theory)-narration-prescription (ethical theory). Although this could be a possibility or an alternative in the architecture of my argument, I shall not follow Ricoeur into his excursion of ethics. Rather, I opt to extend my discussion into trajectories by which Ricoeur understands the social imaginary – that is, the two 'imaginative practices' called ideology and utopia.[55] It is from the viewpoint of, or the juxtaposition of, these two poles that Ricoeur addresses the question of ideology-critique.

How critique of ideology is made possible? Is it possible by assuming a non-ideological position to critique ideology? We have already discussed the impossibility of a non- or a post-ideological position when we first opened our discussion on Althusser. Althusser, in *Essays in Self-Criticism*[56], accuses himself of being 'too theoretical' (by opposing science to ideology). In fact, even in *On Ideology*, as we have already noted, he acknowledges the fact that he (the author) and the reader are both ideological. On the other hand, others such as Karl Mannheim suggest that we can strive to transcend the circularity of ideology by having a 'total view', or 'total reflection' as opposed to 'particular views', which are distortive ideologies.[57] But the question is whether a total view is a possibility for humans. Even the Habermasian mode of ideology-critique, as Ricoeur remarks, 'presupposes a reflective act', which is itself not part of the ideological process.[58] Nonetheless, adhering to the previous arguments made on Althusser, I claim that an exclusively non-ideological position for the critique of ideology is never available.

I agree with Ricoeur that 'judgment on ideology is always the judgment from a utopia'[59]. Ricoeur writes: [I]s it not always the utopian possibilities of individuals and groups which nourish our capacity to distanciate ourselves from

---

renewal' of Hegel's notion of recognition. Finally, he replaces the notion of the struggle for recognition with what he calls the states of peace. In the latter, he utilises the Aristotlian notion of the 'good', as an ethical aim, and he draws upon from contemporary thinkers on justice such as that of John Rawls. Especially, in his work Paul Ricoeur, *The Just*, trans. by David Pellauer (Chicago; London: University of Chicago Press, 2000).

55 Ricoeur, *From Text to Action*, 177.

56 Louis Althusser, *Essays in Self-Criticism* (London: NLB, 1976).

57 Karl Mannheim, *Ideology and Utopia: An Introduction to the Sociology of Knowledge* (London: Routledge and Kegan Paul, 1936, 1968), 102-107 cited in Ricoeur, *Ideology and Utopia*, 172.

58 Ricoeur, *Ideology and Utopia*, 171.

59 Ricoeur, *Ideology and Utopia*, 172.

ideologies?'[60] And the only way out of the circularity of ideology is through utopia. Utopia implies the notion of 'nowhere' to look at ourselves – our government, society, power – radically.[61] Utopias are subversive. Ricoeur remarks that the nowhere of utopia may be 'a pretext for escapism' and that the escapism of utopia belongs to 'a logic of all or nothing'; however, Ricoeur insists on questioning: 'is not this eccentricity of the utopian imagination at the same time the cure of the pathology of ideological thinking, which has its blindness and narrowness precisely in its inability to conceive of a nowhere?'[62] Imagination, as Ricoeur explains, 'through its utopian function – has a *constitutive* role in helping us *rethink* the nature of our social life' – offers imaginative variation on the issue of society, power and government (a vision of 'an alternative society').[63]

Now we should ask: what is/are the criterion/criteria for utopia? And what is utopia? Mannheim sets two criteria for utopia: first, noncongruence with reality: utopia is transcendent of the 'operating order of life', which is both 'infrastructural and superstructural'[64]; and second, a utopia tends 'to shatter, either partially or wholly, the order of things prevailing at the time'.[65] Obviously, the first criterion also applies to ideology. Ricoeur opts for the second criterion because it is differential (to utopia) so that he can oppose ideology to utopia. Both ideology and utopia are 'situationally transcendent' but the latter cannot be realised without shattering the existing order.[66]

Ricoeur remarks, '[W]e cannot get out of the polarity between utopia and ideology. It is always a utopia which defines what is ideological, and so characterisation is always relative to the assumptions of conflicting groups'.[67] As long as ideology and utopia are concerned there is 'a mutual labelling process': from the perspective of those in power/authority and emergent group is utopian. Mannheim says, '[W]henever an idea is labelled utopian it is usually by a representative of an epoch'.[68] The reason that a dominant group labels an ascendant group's idea as utopian is to undermine its realisability. This leads us to raise the question: 'which group is advocating the concept?' As we have seen above, there can

60 Ricoeur, *Ideology and Utopia*, 178.
61 Ricoeur, *Ideology and Utopia*, 15-17.
62 Ricoeur, *Ideology and Utopia*, 17.
63 Ricoeur, *Ideology and Utopia*, 16.
64 Ricoeur, *Ideology and Utopia*, 174.
65 Ricoeur, *Ideology and Utopia*, 192-193.
66 Ricoeur, *Ideology and Utopia*, 175.
67 Ricoeur, *Ideology and Utopia*, 178.
68 Mannheim, *Ideology and Utopia*, 203 cited in Ricoeur, *Ideology and Utopia*, 177.

be competing ideologies – dominant and emergent – that may make use of this criterion and as a result, it is difficult to distinguish between ideology and utopia on the ground of realisability.[69] Ricoeur's conclusion is that realisability cannot be a good criterion because 'utopias themselves are never realized to the extent that they create the *distance* between what is and what ought to be', otherwise, society must be dead if 'there would be no distance, no ideas, no projects at all'.[70]

As Ricoeur holds, the subversiveness of utopia is likened to the issue of power. Ideology is a functional concept connected with the issue of legitimation of power (authority), and so is utopia connected with the issue of power. The question should not only be who is in power but how that power is legitimised. Although implicit to Althusser's discussion of the unity of ideological state apparatuses is the issue of legitimating power or authority, we need to elaborate the link between power and its ideological legitimation based on Ricoeur's examination of Max Weber's analysis of power in *Economy and Society*.

Ricoeur deals with the ideological structure of legitimacy. He first unfolds the categories of political order in Weber starting right from his concept of action. Weber's understanding of action makes sense not only to the subject but also in relation to other subjects: it is constitutive of the dimension of meaning and interpretation.[71] Weber defines social action as that: '[...] which includes both failure to act and passive acquiescence, may be oriented to the past, present, or expected future behavior of others. Thus it may be motivated by revenge for a past attack, defence against present, or measures of defence against future aggression'.[72]

Weber, then, introduces four typologies of orientations of social action, which later become crucial for his typologies of legitimacy. These orientations are what he calls 'instrumental rational', 'value-rational', 'affectual' and 'traditional'.[73] According to Weber, the first orientation, with its emphasis on rules, goes with a bureaucratic form of authority; the second and the third orientations are relied upon by charismatic leadership; and finally the fourth type correlates with a system of legitimacy where followership becomes a matter of the leaders' traditional status.

Once having delineated what constitutes action ('what makes action human'), and the notion of meaningful social relations (in orientation/motivation),

69 Ricoeur, *Ideology and Utopia*, 178.
70 Ricoeur, *Ideology and Utopia*, 179-180.
71 Ricoeur, *Ideology and Utopia*, 184-185.
72 Max Weber, *Economy and Society*, 22 cited in Ricoeur, *Ideology and Utopia*, 184-185.
73 Ricoeur, *Ideology and Utopia*, 186.

Ricoeur moves on to outlining Weber's intermediary notion of order – which links the notions of action and meaning to power. Ricoeur points to a distinction in Weber between 'order' and 'imperatives' and forwards an important remark: '[W]e cannot speak of an order which is merely enforced and which does not at all claim legitimacy. The claim of legitimacy is constitutive of order'.[74] The notions of order, legitimacy and motives are quite interlinked. Ricoeur follows Weber further into the sociology of authority and domination because the legitimacy of order is a problem of authority.[75] Summarised, the notions of claim by Weber are (a) the 'claim of an order in general'; (b) the 'claim of the ruling group in an organization'; and (c) 'the claim of those in power to have the capacity to implement order by the use of force'.[76] This last type of claim is relevant to the notion of belief to legitimise power.

In Weber's description of the typology of claim, belief does not receive equal status as that of claim. The classification of the types of domination is according to claim but belief is that which is merely supplementary: when Weber states the several 'motives for obedience', he states '[C]ustom, personal advantage, purely affectual or ideal motives of solidarity, do not form a sufficiently reliable basis for a given domination. *In addition* there is normally a further element, the belief in legitimacy'.[77] *In addition* here denotes the belief in legitimacy and it is here that Ricoeur inserts his hypothesis: first, there is always a discrepancy between the *belief* of the ruled and the (rationally warranted) *claim* of the governing authority. Second, ideology fills the gap between the belief of the ruled and the claim of the authority. This leads, finally, to the need for a conception of *surplus value* related to power (not work as in Marx) – ideology supplements the necessary belief (always more than rationally warranted) to fill the gap or discrepancy.

Even though Weber's classification of his types of domination is explicitly according to claims only, Ricoeur argues that they are also presented based on belief.[78] Within the nexus, which binds the demand for legitimacy of authority claim and the response of the governed in terms of belief, arises ideology.[79] Ricoeur traces the surplus-value of belief to claim in all the three types of domination. In the last two, the phenomenon of belief seems more obvious (we do not

74 Ricoeur, *Ideology and Utopia*, 188.
75 Ricoeur, *Ideology and Utopia*, 189.
76 Ricoeur, *Ideology and Utopia*, 198-199.
77 Ricoeur, *Ideology and Utopia*, 200. Emphasis added.
78 Cf. Max Weber, *Economy and Society*, 215 cited in Ricoeur, *Ideology and Utopia*, 202-203. Emphasis added.
79 Ricoeur, *Ideology and Utopia*, 183ff.

need elaboration here) than in the first. However, Ricoeur argues that even the bureaucratic type (legality) depends on belief. Weber writes '[L]egal authority rests on the *acceptance* of the validity of the following mutually interdependent ideas'.[80] Legality rests on acceptance in the form of recognition: in a majority rule the minority should accept that the 'rule of the majority is the rule of the whole' and the majority likewise should accept that it is the rule of the majority.[81] Indeed, there exists an element of acceptance (consensus, agreement), which is the belief of subjects.

Utopia, is precisely that which unmasks the ideology that insinuates itself between the claim for legitimacy of power and the belief of those who are ruled. Utopia challenges legitimacy of power. This function of utopia is akin to Foucault's idea of challenging the legitimacy of political rationality in order to dismantle the logic of subjection. To confirm his hypothesis on utopia, Ricoeur draws upon Saint-Simon's work (on utopia), that 'both ideologies and utopias deal with power; ideology is always an attempt to legitimate power, while utopia is always an attempt to replace power by something else', and such a replacement of power (or shattering of reality) is 'merely asserted' but 'no practical means for implementation of the dream is set forth'.[82] Imagination, as Ricoeur holds, 'has a function of a social dream' and utopia is that which 'attempts to fill [the] gap between the dream and the present state of things'.[83] Utopia is an imagination or a mentality 'a [*G*]*eist*, a configuration of factors which permeates the whole range of ideas and feelings' (in Geertz's terminology 'the dominant wish').[84]

Finally, Ricoeur's discussion, on Charles Fourier's work (whose account of utopia goes beyond politics and economics into the domain of passions) is worth-mentioning since it is pertinent for the conceptual analysis of nationalism, which is often associated with sentiments and passions. According to Ricoeur, Fourier's contribution is basically the emancipation of passions.[85] Two key concepts are relevant for our purposes here: the first is the metaphor of inversion and the second is the 'cosmology of attraction'.[86] First, Ricoeur pays attention to what Fourier refers to as 'inverting' what we see in life by saying the contrary in utopia:

---

80 Ricoeur, *Ideology and Utopia*, 204. Emphasis added.

81 Ricoeur, *Ideology and Utopia*, 204.

82 Ricoeur, *Ideology and Utopia*, 288.

83 Ricoeur, *Ideology and Utopia*, 288.

84 'Geertz', 209 cited in Ricoeur, *Ideology and Utopia*, 275.

85 Ricoeur, *Ideology and Utopia*, 302. Ricoeur remarks that this notion of utopia can be linked to Hobbes's mechanics of passions.

86 Ricoeur, *Ideology and Utopia*, 302-304.

'the utopia is an inverted image of what we see in "civilization" (civilization is Fourier's pejorative term for society as a whole). The utopia is an inversion of what is in fact an inverted society. The contrast is between life in civilization, which is bad, and life in harmony, Fourier's utopian world'.[87]

The second point is the idea of social 'attraction' or 'cosmological attraction', which is a 'sign of harmony that must be recovered'.[88] Ricoeur notes that Fourier's passions are social passions that drive a society towards unity and his project is about the resurrection of social passions and emancipation from 'vices'.[89] This call is a call for a return or reversal of vices to virtues/passions. Finally, Ricoeur remarks on Fourier's problematics of passion: '[T]o transpose Habermas' expression, we might say that the problem is no longer discussion without boundary and constraint but fantasy and love'.[90] This relates to Ricoeur's hypothesis that ideology and utopia both deal with 'the opaque nature of power': Ricoeur himself notes this, 'in Fourier the problem of power is undercut by the renaissance of love, a resurrection of love [...] the problem is not how to create the good political state but how either to exist without the state or to create a passion-infused state'.[91]

3.5 Conclusion

To recaptulate what we have been discussing so far, first, we have been able to overcome the dichotomy between the course of things and human action with the notion of interference or intentional intervention. In light of the mutual in-exclusivity of human action and the course of things, we can now see Althusser's and Foucault's *dispositifs* in a new light. Subjects are not simply determined by and respond to material circumstances or conditions. Even though we observe (to some extent) the dissolution of the dichotomy between causation and motivation in Foucault, it is in Ricoeur's action theory we see the overcoming of the dichotomy and a reclaiming of agency lost in what Althusser and Foucault call *dispositifs*. Consequently, we can conclude that subjects are not only formed in and through ideological institutions and their practices but also they act to change and reproduce these institutions.

Then, the subject who is capable of action or agency acts within the framework of temporality. The time of action for the subject is the present in relation

87 Ricoeur, *Ideology and Utopia*, 302.
88 Ricoeur, *Ideology and Utopia*, 304.
89 Ricoeur, *Ideology and Utopia*, 305.
90 Ricoeur, *Ideology and Utopia*, 308.
91 Ricoeur, *Ideology and Utopia*, 309.

to the past and the future – that is, the historical present. From this point we noted that what grasps the notion of temporality is discourse. It is this recognition that led us to the discussion of narrative identity. As we have discussed, narratives, through their configuration of several of events of the past, exhibit temporal unity between the present and the future in a narrative unity. Narratives are crucial in understanding not only the collective self-understanding (identity) of a society but also its motivation for collective action (this has affinities to Foucault's notion of self-writing). From this standpoint, humans, as capable agents, always act and suffer, and they have the capability to act and narrate.

Such capacities of acting and narrating can never be ethically and ideologically neutral. This led to our final discussion on the issue of ideology-critique. We noted that ideology-critique is possible from the position of utopia. Utopia is a vision of *another society, another order*, and it makes possible a transformation of a given social imaginary. The judgment from utopia enables the subject to distance herself from coercive and seductive ideology (whether national or ethnic). In fact, what makes Foucault's practices of freedom possible is utopian imagination or utopian possibilities. Seen from such perspective, utopian imagination can make possible resistance to ideological interpellation (ethnic or national) and *dispositifs*.

Reflections on Part I

The purpose of the theoretical discussion of this part has been to generate a set of conceptual tools that shall be deployed to analyse the Ethiopian case. In such discussion, various theoretical trends have been drawn together in order to address the key philosophical-anthropological question: how do we become subjects? We have already observed why the question of 'identity' needs to be related to the polyvalent notion of the subject. The hermeneutical approach has introduced the element of understanding, how the subject is formed, as well as the element of emancipation, or a critique of the logic of subjection.

I have been able to demonstrate, employing Althusser's theory of ideology, how the subject comes into being as a result of interpellation. The notion of interpellation and the operations of ideological apparatuses have been further developed by Balibar's theoretical analyses of the nation-form. In point of fact, the efficacy of interpellation, in terms of what Althusser calls mastery, has been more elaborated by Foucault's account of ethics and politics: how individuals are constituted as subjects of their own actions, and practices of freedom. The implication of this insight has been that subjects are formed not simply by coercive ideology as such but by their own participation in their subjectification. In this discussion, the contributions of Agamben and Rancière have been used to further support Foucault's account. The notion of *dispositifs,* by both Althusser and Foucault, are central to understanding how objective structures (institutions and their practices or discourses) mediate self-formation. Finally, we concluded with Ricoeur's discussion of narrative identity as a way of reclaiming the sense of agency lost in Althusser's and Foucault's *dispositifs.* This has been done not only by elaborating our narrative constitution and our capability, as agents, to modify them, but also by highlighting the possibility of ideology-critique from the position of utopia or utopian imagination.

From such conceptual discussion of imaginative practices that form the self, I am therefore able to propose the following two protocols for our further investigation of the research context: identity politics in Ethiopia. First, by providing the insight on identity formation mechanisms, the conceptual tools will help to examine the contemporary Ethiopian political context. And secondly, I will deal with the critical element of this conceptual tool, utopian mentality. Let me start with the first one. I will deploy the conceptual tools to shape the question, which will guide the following part: what identity formation mechanisms have been involved in constructing politicised ethnicities? Put differently, through what political technologies have we arrived at *becoming* what we are now? To borrow Foucault's terms, the case will be a genealogical study of the *historical ontology of ourselves.*

I will, then, examine the Ethiopian case in light of the conceptual tools developed in this part. It will be an analysis that will consider the construction of collective identity because of the interplay between objective structures (institutions, technologies, or narratives) and processes of subjectivation (interpellation/mastery, technologies, collective memory). This will involve not only cases of reciprocity between objective traits and processes of subjectivation in identity politics, in which case there is agreement between the ideology of the State and the people, but also cases of disjunction in which there is a relationship of the hegemonic and the counter-hegemonic. As I will explain later, prior to examining the contemporary political condition of Ethiopia, which demands giving sufficient attention to the historical developments that led to the current ethno-politics, I will briefly examine what comes before ethno-politics. In light of the interplay between the two poles, objective structures and processes of subjectivation, mentioned above, the inquiry will aim, particularly, to unfold the historically in-built *dispositifs*. Instances of the processing of the imaginary – nationalist pedagogy, discourses on national identity, or nationalist narratives – embedded in formations of ethno-political subjects will be examined.

The second protocol pertains to the critical element of the hermeneutical approach. As we have already observed, Ricoeur deals with ideology and utopia, thematically, in his *Lectures on Ideology and Utopia*, as twin concepts in his thought on social and cultural imagination. The second strand, utopian imagination, is arguably asserted as that which helps us to transcend ideological circularity or closure. Critique of ideology is made possible from the position of utopia. I have already indicated that Foucault's practices of freedom become more meaningful when informed or synergised by a utopian mentality.

In the light of our previous discussion on the relation between ideology and utopia, we will link the discussions on governmental rationality by Foucault and Weber's analysis of power by Ricoeur to the claim of legitimacy in the multiethnic politics of Ethiopia. The aim is twofold: it is to examine the logic of subjection in the politics of identity in the Ethiopian political context. In addition, it is to inquire if there are any practices of freedom or any movements or sensibilities that counter the *dispositifs*, thereby, challenging the very core of political rationality that justifies the claim(s) for legitimacy. This will set the stage for a transition to the third part, which will outline the theological contribution to the debate on identity politics, which will be exclusively devoted to a construction of theological counter-*dispositifs* informed by a utopian imagination.

Part II

Ethno-political Imagination

Drawing upon various thinkers, the previous part has generated some conceptual tools in order to understand subject formation. In the present part, the different strands of theories shall be deployed to analyse the Ethiopian context. Because of the strong theoretical trajectory in this study one may ask how such a western approach of reading and evaluating material relates to ethno-national political context of Ethiopia. As I have briefly demonstrated in the Introduction, Ethiopian scholarship has been influenced by western thinking and western modes of analysis.[1] To be sure, the socio-political history of Ethiopia had seen much Marxist thinking immersed into its intellectual self-understanding. Due to an anti-Eurocentric sensibility, some may opt for an altogether repudiation of theories or methodologies honed in the West (as we shall see in the 'Theological Introduction' in Part III). Although claiming to be 'non-methodological' may seem viable, some kind of hermeneutics is always unavoidable. Rather, I espouse that a better constructive alternative is an appropriate appropriation of theoretical frameworks. In point of fact, the use of conceptual tools enables us to examine, explicate and critique the historical ideological processes of subject formation, and ultimately prepares the way for a theological critique in the next part.

The main purpose of these chapters is to examine the mechanisms or technologies by which ethno-political identities are constructed in Ethiopia. I shall pursue the analysis in two chapters. Chapter 4, in particular, shall present an account of the process of nationalisation in Ethiopia (the politics of integration): the emergence of what Balibar called *homo nationalis* (*homo Æthiopicus*, in our case) through ideological apparatuses (cf. Chapter 1). In the next chapter

1 For example, see Bahru Zewde, *Documenting the Ethiopian Student Movement: An Exercise in Oral History* (Addis Ababa: Forum for Social Science, 2010), 97-115.

(Chapter 5), we shall look at the imaginative practices that underpin the contemporary politics of identity: the formation of the Ethiopian subject as *homo ethnicus*. We will analyse the contending modes of self-writing in the context of the contemporary ethno-federal politics. I will conclude the chapter by briefly looking at an alternative imagination aiming to transcend ethno-politics, which claims to draw resources from historic Ethiopian traditional values and metaphysical worldviews.

4 The Politics of Integration: The Emergence of *Homo Æthiopicus*

4.1 Introduction

Since it is impossible to say very much coherent about the instrumentalist modes of self-writing and the politics of identity, which emerged out of the experience of Marxism in Ethiopia, without making reference to what comes before them, I shall set out by briefly discussing the functionalist mode of thought: the politics of integration. And since the history of the nation is always presented to us in the form of a narrative (cf. Balibar and Ricoeur on narrative identity in Chapters 1 and 3), I will first outline what is referred to as the narrative of Greater Ethiopia, which is an offshoot of the functionalist mode of thought (4.2). This will lay the ground for a further discussion on the constitution of the diverse people of 'Greater Ethiopia' as Ethiopians.

In light of the conceptual framework, developed in Part I, I will briefly demonstrate that the nationalisation of the people involved the production of fictive ethnicity: fictive Amhara ethnicity (4.3). In 4.4, I will discuss how the process of nationalisation involved the nationalistic absorption of religion, particularly Orthodox Christianity, before I offer a brief remark on the rise of a contending ideology – the imagination of national self-determination (4.5). Finally, I will offer a brief conclusion (4.5).

4.2 The Narrative of Greater Ethiopia

In this narrative, Ethiopia is not only posited as a 'single societal system' but also figures as an ancient polity constituting a historically evolved society.[2] Levine

2 Levine, *Greater Ethiopia*, 69. Levine is an American sociologist in the tradition of the Chicago School who has produced some academic work on Ethiopia that has been of influence on the academic study of Ethiopia. As it has been mentioned in the Introduction, his work is quite representative of functionalist approaches to the study of Ethiopia. And it is for this reason that I prefer to engage his work here. For a brief critique of the Chicago School; cf. Anthony Cohen, *The Symbolic Construction of Community* (London: Tavistock Publications, 1985), 21-38. But here the critique is not methodological.

constructs the evolution of Ethiopian society in five social-evolutionary modalities. First, he begins with the 'assumption that a small number of ethnic stocks settled in Ethiopian plateau in prehistoric times', which had to undergo a series of *adaptive radiations* – drawing analogy from biology – eventually arriving at *holistic specialised cultures.*[3] These are the 'Ethio-Semitic', 'Cushitic', 'Omotic' and 'East Sudanic' or Nilo-Saharan.[4] The differentiation of these groups gave birth to multi-ethnic homogeneous groups whose habitation of different ecological zones created complementarity, which was important for survival in terms of economy, and gave way to further evolutionary developments. In the second modality, the differentiated peoples of historic Ethiopia became interdependent through trade, migration and some other groups entering a stage of *mutualistic specialisation* because of which the circulation of caste groups such as craftsmen in the various ecological zones becomes significant.[5]

The third kind of modality first appeared during the Aksumite era when a political community developed as a result of *internal specialization*: elite formation. The remarkable feature of this period was the introduction of Christianity in the 4th century in Aksum.[6] According to the narrative, the expansion of Islam around the 7th century isolated Aksum from the rest of the Christian world, eventually, leading to its decline. Then, the Aksumites began to look southwards to the central and northern highlands of the present-day Ethiopia. This period is recognised as the 'dark ages', however, out of this darkness, 'a nation' was born, 'which in times of external danger could abandon its centrifugal proclivities and become conscious of its essential unity'.[7] During the 'dark ages', the 'illegitimate' Zagwe dynasty took power until it was overthrown by the 'legitimate' Solomonic dynasty.

---

3 Levine, *Greater Ethiopia*, 167. Here, 'holistic' refers to patters shared by all members of a group and 'specialised' refers to the skills appropriate to a given ecological niche.

4 This kind of classifying people into (fixed) racial categories has been common in historical literature until recently; see for example, Edward Ullendorff, *The Ethiopians* (Oxford: Oxford University Press, 1960). See also Marvin Bender whose work has been foundational in the classification of languages in Ethiopia. He classifies Ethiopia's languages into four groups: 'about a dozen Semitic languages, 22 Cushitic, 18 Omotic, and 18 Nilo-Saharan'; Marvin Bender et al, eds., *Language in Ethiopia* (London: Oxford University Press, 1976), 13.

5 Levine, *Greater Ethiopia*, 169.

6 Levine, *Greater Ethiopia*, 171-174. See Sergew Hable Sellassie, *Ancient and Medieval Ethiopian History to 1270* (Addis Ababa: United Printers, 1972), 89-110.

7 Ullendorff, *The Ethiopians*, 59.

This 'restoration' of the Solomonic dynasty in 1270 ensured the transference of power to the Amhara who consider themselves as the 'true' heirs of the Aksumite Empire. Aksum, (or the 'Tigre'?), became a 'seedbed society'[8] transferring authority to the Amhara, who consolidated the society and the national centre. The medieval period, which was characterised by the growth of Christianity and the relation of the Church and the state, is conceived by the narrative as a golden age.

The fourth kind of modality appeared in the 16th century. The Oromo who newly migrated to the region and who had neither 'a highly specialized local adaptation nor a functionally specialized internal structure' became the anti-thesis to the Amharan thesis.[9] In the 16th century, the golden age of the medieval period was endangered by the jihad of Ahmad Grañ – who had support from the Turks – burnt churches, destroyed historical documents, and islamised people. It was only with the help of the Portuguese, a Christian ally[10], which Ethiopia was able to survive. As a result of the weakening of Christian Ethiopia, the Oromo were able to march into the central and northern highlands of Ethiopia.[11] In the

---

8 Levine, *Greater Ethiopia*, 110; here, Levine supports his argument using Talcott Parsons' characterisation of seedbed societies in *Societies: Evolutionary and Comparative Perspectives* (London: Prentice Hall, 1967).

9 Levine offers a comparative study of the Amhara (hierarchical individualistic) and the Oromo (egalitarian and communistic) systems favouring the former; see Levine, *Greater Ethiopia*, chs. 8 & 9.

10 During the medieval period, there was a myth in Europe of a legendary Christian king called Prester John who was said to have defended his kingdom against Islam. Although the location where this king lived was not known, it was believed to be somewhere in the East. As some have remarked, such imagination expresses Europe's desire for a Christian ally against the Moors and the Portuguese support of Abyssinia is said to be inspired by this desire; see Levine, *Greater Ethiopia*, 8; A.H.M. Jones and Elizabeth Monroe, *A History of Ethiopia* (New York: Negro University Press, 1961), 56-63; John Baur, *2000 Years of Christianity in Africa: An African Church History* (Nairobi: Paulines Publications Africa, 1998), 43-44.

11 Levine alludes to the explanations offered by ecclesiastical Abyssinian chronicler Abba Bahrey who wrote "*A History of Galla*" in 1590s; see Levine, *Greater Ethiopia*, 89. Leaning on such sources, various western *éthiopisant* as well as Ethiopian scholars have depicted the historic Oromo 'movement' as barbaric. For example, Edward Ullendorf construes them as uncivlised and as responsible for the backward state of Ethiopia; Ullendorff, *The Ethiopians*, 73; and cf. Mesfin Wolde-Mariam, *An Introductory Geography of Ethiopia* (Addis Ababa: Berhanena Selam H.S.I. Printing Press, 1972), 16. For an extended discussion, see Jan Hultin, "Perceiving Oromo: 'Galla' in the Great Narrative of Ethiopia," in *Being and Becoming Oromo*, 86-88.

17th and 18th centuries, Ethiopia sank into the *Zamana Masafint* (the Era of Princes) that almost fragmented the state.[12]

The fifth modality explains the transformation that took place during the 19th century. Then, the Amhara gained military excellence and access to firearms and they were able to prove their dominance over others – the Tigre and the Oromo had to follow them – hence, resolving into Greater Ethiopian synthesis.[13] The superiority of the Amhara was already underway before this period because the Amhara had a special or advanced adaptation, an evolutionary modality unachieved by others and for this reason others had to imitate the 'adaptive advantages of the Amhara system' through cultural assimilation to the Amhara.[14] Above all, the sense of its mission embodied in the religious document *Kebrä Nägäst* made the Amhara better candidates for building the modern Ethiopian state: this is linked to resurgence based on the revival of myth, which Levine recounts as 'the return of the repressed'.[15]

Due to the rise of patriotic emperors Tewodros, Yohannes and Menilek who emerged with the projects of centralisation and 'reunification', Ethiopia was saved from disintegration and began heading towards modernisation.This narrative conceives the conquest of southern peoples including the Oromo as an 'ingathering of peoples with deep historical affinities'.[16] Moreover, the narrative

---

12 During this period, mainly four parcellised sovereignties existed: Tigray in the North, Amhara in the Central, Gojjam in the South-West and Shawa in the South; see Teshale Tibebu, *The Making of Modern Ethiopia*, 30; cf. Levine, *Greater Ethiopia*, 78-80, 156.

13 Levine, *Greater Ethiopia*, 184.

14 Levine, *Greater Ethiopia*, 174.

15 Levine, *Greater Ethiopia*, 156. Levine, following Talcott Parsons' notion of 'a complex of *institutive symbolism*', refers to the *Kebrä Nägäst* as 'a societal *script*', which is 'a body of symbols that provides specialized cultural legitimation both for the societal enterprise as a whole and for privileged positions within the society'; Levine, *Greater Ethiopia*, 101. Teshale Tibebu regards it as 'the master text' in postmodernist parlance; see Teshale Tibebu, *The Making of Modern Ethiopia*, 12.

16 What Levine calls the pre-existing 'foundations of unity' are: first, Ethiopia has always been a 'relational network' whose differentiated people groups interacted with each other (and the outside world) through 'trade, warfare, religious activities, migration, intermarriage, and exchange of special services'; Levine, *Greater Ethiopia*, 40-46. Second, the existence of 'pan-Ethiopian traits', which makes it possible to view Ethiopia as a 'culture area': for example, 'beliefs about supernatural beings; ritual practices; food taboos; the cult of masculinity; aspects of social organization; insignia of rank; and customs regarding personal status and the home'; Levine, *Greater Ethiopia*, 47, 46-64. Third, 'creative incorporation' implying that the people of Greater Ethiopia have a mode of relating or responding to 'foreign intrusive influences' through

asserts that the conquests were beneficial because 'they bolstered Ethiopia's position as an independent African power, greatly reduced the intertribal warfare and brigandage that had prevailed in the conquered areas, and paved the way for bringing an end to the slave trade in Ethiopia'.[17] Beyond these five modalities, another historical development characterises the modern Ethiopian society: the evolution from patrimonial to a bureaucratic form. This development is marked by the emergence of ideological 'apparatus of a centralized bureaucracy' through 'modern forms of education and [...] communication', the military, etc.[18] enhancing the integration of people.

Now, more or less, it is this narrative that has served as the state's dominant version of national history until recently.[19] In general, the questions that could be raised against this narrative emanate from its historicist tendency: a historical determinism, a single path of development. This sociological account explains how and why the history of the people described here simply culminates in Greater Ethiopia. Moreover, the view of the Ethiopian society as undergoing a process of differentiation suggests the gradual distinction, or differentiation, of the spheres of the religious from the 'secular' – a logic that culminates in subordinating the religious (and the theological) to the secular (or national), as we noted in the Introduction.

Basically, the narrative has the following basic characteristics: first, it emphasises continuity without break in historical time: the myth of origin of Ethiopia extending back to millennia. As a result, discontinuities or ruptures in the history of Ethiopia are de-emphasised. The second characteristic is its justification of foundational violence, which is regarded as necessary in bringing integration to the Ethiopian society. As a result, the conquest and the modern nation-building process are construed in a positive light. Third, national formation by a dominant *ethnie*, the 'Amhara', and the politics of assimilation are legitimised.

---

absorbing its contents selectively and modifying them to fit or consolidate the native tradition; Levine, *Greater Ethiopia*, 64-68. An example could be 'cultural and literary experience' as Enrico Cerulli observes; see Levine, *Greater Ethiopia*, 64-68.

17 Levine, *Greater Ethiopia*, 26.

18 Levine, *Greater Ethiopia*, 181. Levine describes this as the 'system of modern societies' in Parsonian terms.

19 See for example, Mesfin Woldemariam, *Geography of Ethiopia*. And there have been several political parties whose view on Ethiopian history are shaped by this narrative; see Merera Gudina, "Contradictory Interpretations of Ethiopian History," in *Ethnic Federalism: The Ethiopian Experience in Comparative perspective*, ed. David Turton (Ohio: Ohio University Press, 2006), 121.

Religion, or religious myth, is understood in terms of its functions – legitimation of authority and fostering social cohesion. Its close interrelation with the nation-building is positively construed and even regarded as cathartic.

Seen from a different standpoint, however, the narrative proves to be not only about a national story of integration but also about a moral story that expresses a national ideology that legitimates a particular power structure and social hierarchy. In the subsequent discussion, I wish to demonstrate how the citizen-subject – *homo nationalis* – emerged as a production of fictive ethnicity and how Christian identity was absorbed by national ideology. By doing this, I will be able to identify the historically in-built *dispositif*, which the mode of thought we examined above simply describes in objective sociological terms as natural affinities as though there was a taken for granted consensus (cf. Chapters 1 and 2 for an understanding of *dispositifs* in Althusser and Foucault). In view of what Balibar referred to as 'a history', the above narrative – being a singular history – can itself be regarded as a *dispositif*, a conceptual devise that connects subjects to power structures.

4.3 The Imaginary Singularity of Ethiopians

As noted in the Introduction, the spatial construction of the modern state of Ethiopia, as a territorial state, became a reality during the late 19th century as an outcome of three historical conjunctures: centralisation of the fragmented Abyssinian kingdom; conquests and expansions of regions south of the Abyssinian kingdom; and the various treaties between European and Ethiopian rulers.[20] Such spatial construction was the precondition or the 'prerequisite for the centralization of a socio-economic system and the conspicuous appearance of the state – i.e. the organized apparatus of government' (and as we noted in Althusser, in Chapter 1, the state apparatuses do not operate without ideology).[21] But, since Ethiopia, as a population state, did not possess a 'given' ethnic basis, then, what constituted the model of its unity? Of particular interest, here, is the process of nationalisation by which the diverse people of Greater Ethiopia are ideologically interpellated as Ethiopians – the emergence of *homo Æthiopicus*.

It is known that modernisation has affected, in various ways, every society and Ethiopia is by no means an exception. Christopher Clapham observes that Ethiopia, similar to other ancient empires such as Iran, Thailand and Japan,

20 Addis Hiwet's analysis also confirms that 'the same historical forces' that created the African states created the modern state of Ethiopia; cf. Addis Hiwet, *Ethiopia*, 1.

21 Addis Hiwet, *Ethiopia*, 9.

'responded to the challenge of European encroachment through conversion of its monarchy into a modernising autocracy' to a great extent 'modelled on European lines'.[22] This had significant implications not only on the spatial construction of the modern empire-state but also on the transformation of the loosely-held imperial-form to a centralised nation-form passing a certain threshold in statecraft. During the late 19th and the early 20th centuries, the new Abyssinia or the modern Ethiopian empire-state, could be best described by Conti Rossini's famous aphorism (as indicated in the Introduction): *L'Abissinia èun museo di popoli*. The following quote from Doglas H. Johnson substantiates the diversity, and describes the management of the population, who became subject to a common law under a single polity (Ethiopia), in a lucid manner:

> The administration of the new Ethiopian empire was more flexible and medieval in its recognition of persons who could be regarded as semi-citizens. Within the confines of its territory the empire acknowledged different relationships between subjects and the imperial authority. There were people with whom relations were based almost exclusively on trade; there were those who were obliged to pay tribute and by doing so retained some autonomy; there were some who had rather more onerous obligations and whose own freedom of action was strictly limited; and there were others who were raided. In many ways the degree of 'citizenship' was determined by the degree of exploitation involved and the degree of reciprocity in that exploitation. The degree of exploitation varied not only for those people on the fringes of the empire, but for those in different positions within the hierarchy of the empire.[23]

Implied in this passage is the distinction between the Abyssinian core or centre and its peripheries. 'Abyssinian power' radiates out from this centre to the peripheries primarily to extract economic resources but not necessarily to make the peripheral people Abyssinians by imposition of Abyssinian cultural traits.[24] Also implied in the above text are the different levels of spatial-material relations between the centre and the peripheries. In fact, the three ways of incorporation of the south, which Donald Donham identifies, clarifies Johnson's point, here: these are semi-independent

---

22 See Christopher Clapham, *Transformation and Continuity in Revolutionary Ethiopia* (Cambridge: Cambridge University Press, 1988), 26-27.

23 Doglas H. Johnson, "On the Nilotic frontier: imperial Ethiopia in the southern Sudan, 1898-1936," in *The Southern Marches of Imperial Ethiopia: Essays in History and Social Anthropology*, eds. Wendy James et al. (Cambridge: Cambridge University Press, 1986a), 221.

24 See Donald Donham, "Old Abyssinia," 42. The Christian Abyssinians occupy, what Donham calls the 'core' areas, and from the core 'Abyssinian power' reached out to other spheres (even 'far peripheries') to dominate.

enclaves, *gebbar* areas, and fringe peripheries.[25] To be sure, those who lived within the territorial confines of the empire-state 'were not Abyssinians, but they were reserved for Abyssinian domination'.[26] However, conversely, this does not imply that every Abyssinian living in the Abyssinian core was a citizen, and it does not suggest that every non-Abyssinian living in the periphery was simply a subject.

The Amharic word *zega* originally meant 'subdued', 'subject', 'obedient' and it is only gradually that it took the meaning – 'citizen'.[27] Aleme Eshete's study on the semantic transformation of the word *zĕga* demonstrates the change in the translation of the word that meant 'dependent subject' in the 1920s to adding 'citizen' as its meanings in the late 20th century.[28] Also, as Teshale Tibebu recently argued, there were two categories – the *bala seltan* (the sovereign) and the *zega* (the subject) and this implies that all Christian Abyssinians were not *bala seltan* and hence, not citizens.[29] In fact, in the early 20th century, the common people could not imagine or identify with their nation – Ethiopia – in the same way the nobility or the *literati* did. Included in such group were the indigenous leaders who allied with the central government; for example, an Oromo leader, Gebre Igziabiher of *Nekemte* (in Wellega), in his correspondence with the central government, uses 'agerachin' (our country) 'in the same centralist sense that the Ethiopian crown tended to use'.[30]

---

25 Donham, "Old Abyssinia," 39-43. First, in the so-called semi-independent enclaves, local rulers attained a certain measure of autonomy but made 'tributary to the imperial centre'; in the second type of area called the *gebbar* areas, no direct tributary link was established but rather *gult*-holdings (seignory) were distributed among 'Abyssinian' settlers – the governors and soldiers, *neftennya* ('riflemen'), and the local indigenous leaders called the *balabbat*; thereby, creating a social hierarchy: the *balabbat* became the intermediaries between the new settlers and the southern peasantry.

26 Donham, "Old Abyssinia," 43. Here, the term 'domination' implies governance but the level of autonomy enjoyed by the regions varied from region to region (in some places there was no direct rule).

27 Donham, "Old Abyssinia," 43.

28 See Aleme's paper entitled 'General Examination on Ethiopian Feudalism' was presented at the Ethiopian Feudalism Conference, Addis Ababa, Ethiopia, 1976. For the two dictionary meanings, see Baeteman, Dictionaire, col. 858 and Wolf Leslau, *English-Amharic Context Dictionary* (Wiesbaden: Otto Harrassowitz, 1973), 193 cited in James, *The Southern Marches*, 259, n145.

29 Teshale Tibebu, "Modernity, Eurocentricity, and Radical Politics in Ethiopia, 1961-1991," *African Identities* 6, 4 (November 2008): 364.

30 Alessandro Triulzi, "Nekemte and Addis Abeba: dilemmas of provincial rule," in *The Southern Marches of Imperial Ethiopia: Essays in History and Social Anthropology*, eds. Wendy James et al. (Cambridge: Cambridge University Press, 1986a), 68.

Although he had no policy of integration, emperor Menilek, like his predecessor, emperor Yohannes, 'favoured religious uniformity' in the areas under his 'control'.[31] In every conquered region, the so-called *Ketemmas* (garrison-towns) were established and Orthodox churches were also built that facilitated assimilation, which in the beginning was a selective process.[32] Even during the early years of empire-building, irrespective of their ethnic background, the settlers and the local indigenous leaders who shared the cultural traits of the new settlers were called 'Amhara' by the local indigenous people.[33] Back then, as remarked by Teshale Tibebu, '"Amhara" and "Galla" were not ethnic terms. *Amhara was a metaphor for power, and Galla for the relative lack of it*'.[34]

However, it was under Haile-Selassie I, who emerged out of an 'enlightened wing of the nobility'[35] within the royal court, that the project of building a centralised Ethiopian state by installing the modern state apparatuses was epitomised, which had its implications for the emergence of *homo nationalis*. A discourse on modern governance first broke out among Ethiopia's intellectuals of the early 20th century.[36] Underlying such a discourse was the thematic of civilisation. The discourse accentuated the need for literacy; bureaucratisation and rationalisation of taxation; a monetary system (a national currency); nationalising the army; and promoting international trade if Ethiopia should civilise or recover its old civilisation and catch up with Europe.[37] Part of such reformist agenda was the policy of integration understood as assimilation:

---

31 Negaso Gidada & Donald Crummey, "The Introduction and Expansion of Orthodox Christianity in Qelem Awraja, Western Wallaga, from about 1886 to 1941," *Journal of Ethiopian Studies* X, 1 (1972): 111. He did this through persuasion of the kings or chiefs he subdued (or who willingly surrendered).

32 Addis Hiwet, *Ethiopia*, 4.

33 Alessandro Truilzi, "Competing Views of National Identity in Ethiopia," in *Nationalism and Self-determination in the Horn of Africa*, ed. I. M. Lewis (London: Itheca Press, 1983), 119.

34 Tibebu Teshale, *The Making of Modern Ethiopia*, 45.

35 Addis Hiwet, *Ethiopia*, 62.

36 For example the intellectual pace-setter of his age, Gebre-Heywet Baykadañ, authored two books that became influential: *Ate Menilek-na Ityopya* (Menilek and Ethiopia), published in 1912, and *Mengist-na Yehaezb Astedader* (State and Civil Administration), published in 1924 and in the early 1950s.

37 Richard Caulk, "Dependency, Gebre Heywet Baykedagn and the Birth of Ethiopian Reformism," *Proceedings of the Fifth International Conference on Ethiopian Studies* (1978): 569.

> The policy of assimilation should be at the top of our reforms; for without the union of the Amhara and Galla [*sic*] it is impossible to visualize the future with certainty or enthusiasm [...] It is for the Galla to become Amhara (not the other way round); for the latter possess a written language, a superior religion and superior customs and mores.[38]

Undeniably, such a discourse articulates a grammar of difference between the 'Amhara' and the 'Galla', which served as a loose term to designate the people of the newly incorporated south, as a result of which the latter was required to convert to the cultural and religious norms of the former. Of course, such idea of non-similarity did not have racial connotations. The difference between the Amhara and the non-Amhara was merely cultural: Gebru Tareke argues that there were no racially demarcated settlement areas in the south: 'anyone could become thoroughly Abyssinianized by adopting Amharic and Orthodox Christianity. The French or the Portuguese were far less successful with their policies of assimilation for, in the final analysis, no *assimile* or *assimilado* could ever cross the racial barrier', and he concudes that '[I]n Ethiopia, the "superior-inferior" complex had a cultural connotation only'.[39] Actually, what such recognition of difference accentuated was the necessity for cultural homogeneity deemed important for guaranteeing unity. The notion of unity – conceived as the dissolution of difference – was the principle that underpinned the policy of integration or assimilation:

> The strength of a country lies in its unity, and unity is born of [common] language, customs, and religion. Thus, to safeguard the ancient sovereignty of Ethiopia and to reinforce its unity, our language and our religion should be proclaimed over the whole of Ethiopia. Otherwise, unity will never be attained [...] Amharic and Ge'ez should be decreed official languages for secular as well as religious affairs and all pagan languages should be banned.[40]

In order to transform the heterogeneous Ethiopian museum into a unified homogeneous nation, the production of fictive Amhara ethnicity gave the promise

---

38 Tedla Hailé, "Pourquoi et comment," 88 cited in Bahru Zewde, *Pioneers of Change in Ethiopia: The Reformist Intellectuals of the Early Twentieth Century* (Oxford: James Curry, 2002), 133.

39 Gebru Tareke, *Ethiopia: Power and Protest*, 72.

40 Sahle Tsedalu, Memorandum, Ministry of Pen Archive 29.11.25/1.8.33, quoted in Bahru Zewde, *Society, State and History*, 140. Herein, the 'ban' was not comparable to what happened in other parts of the world such as Spain, for example. Will Kymilcka cites an example from Laitin's book who illustrates that in Spain 'during the Inquisition gypsies who were found guilty of speaking their own language had their tongues cut out'; see Will Kymilcka, "Emerging Western Models of Multination Federalism: Are They Relevant for Africa," in *Ethnic Federalism: The Ethiopian Experience in Comparitive Perspective*, ed., David Turton (Ohio: Ohio University Press, 2006), 61, 28n.

of unity or a singularising strategy (see Chapter 1). Integration was conceived as assimilation into the cultural norms of the Amhara – as Amharisation. Clapham defines Amhara ethnicity by its *plasticity* (see what I said on the plasticity of the linguistic community in Chapter 1).[41] Mandatory to 'participation in national political life', as Clapham observes, was 'assimilation to the cultural values of the Amhara core [or the Abyssinian core]: the Amharic language, Orthodox Christianity and a capacity to operate within the structures and assumptions of a court administration'.[42]

Gerry Saole's remark can also shed some light on the understanding of the term 'Amhara'. To Saole, the term 'Amhara' is quite ambiguous because: '[…] it is effectively robbed of ethnic content'.[43] But does this mean that the Amhara do not exist as a hereditary ethnic group? The debate whether the Amhara exist as an ethnic group featured in post-1991 political scenario in relation to the discourse of federalism. Of course, the crux of Saole's point is not to deny altogether the existence of hereditary Amhara ethnicity but to emphasise the point that '[t]he mere fact that ethnic labels are operative does not necessarily indicate that ethnicity persists […] the question is not "Who are the Amhara" but rather "When and how and why the identification Amhara is the preferred one'.[44] Saole's position is akin to Sevir Chernetsov'sidea of the double-face of the Amhara – existing both as a hereditary ethnic group as a linguistic group (fictive ethnicity).[45]

The policy of integration under Haile-Selassie heightened the place of Amharic as an official language – *pax amharica* – and the government ensured development of the language by building up a large literature in it.[46] (Here, we can recall from our discussion in Chapter 1 how language – the institution of institutions – can be significant in what Althusser calls self-mastery or ideological reproduction

---

41 Clapham, *Revolutionary Ethiopia*, 4.

42 Clapham, *Revolutionary Ethiopia*, 21.

43 Gerry Saole, "Who are the Shoans?" *Horn of Africa* 2, 3 (1979): 27 cited in Heran Sereke-Berhan, "Ethiopia: A Historical Consideration of Amhara Ethnicity," *New Trends in Ethiopian Studies: Papers of the 12th International Conference of Ethiopian Studies* 1 (1994): 754-762.

44 Saole, "Who are the Shoans?" 27.

45 Cf. Siegfried Pausewang, "The Oromo and the CUD," *Oromo Studies Association* XX (2006): 71-73. Siegfried Pausewang, "Political Conflicts in Ethiopia – in View of the Two-Faced Amhara Identity," *Proceedings of the 16th International Conference of Ethiopian Studies* (2009): 550-551.

46 Bahru Zewde, *Society, State and History*, 85-6. On restriction of non-Amharic literatures; see Brian L. Fargher, *The Origins of the New Churches Movement in Southern Ethiopia, 1927-1944* (Leiden: Brill, 1996), 27-29.

for the maintenance of the *status quo*.) For a brief period of time, 1935-1941, the politics of integration through the production of fictive Amhara ethnicity was briefly interrupted by the Italian occupation during which the country was divided into six main administrative regions reflecting ethno-linguistic criteria: Amhara, Oromo-Sidama, Harar including Arsi, Somali, and Eritrea; and, Tigray was administered from Eritrea.[47] The aim was to eclipse the centralist project of the Ethiopian state, which was labelled *politica scionna* – 'a Shawan policy', by challenging Amhara's hegemony through reviving the traditional power game based on provincialism called *politica tigrina* because Tigre was the target for its strategic importance.[48]

After 1941, Haile-Selassie brought reforms partly envisioned by the intellectuals of the early 20th century. His policy of centralisation of administration had both fiscal and political dimensions: politically, it was a strategy of pacifying the regional nobility and administrative-wise, it was an increase in 'rationalization and centralization of land tax and customs dues' ultimately replacing the old, less centralised, order with a more centralised one.[49] In fact, as early as the 1920s, Haile-Selassie's commitment to developing modern educational institutions was so intense and of course, underlying this passion was the development of elites for bureaucratisation of the centralised modern state with the aim of substituting the regional feudal nobility.[50] Haile-Selassie was also committed in developing the military apparatus (first with the support of the British and later the United States). Such transformations made possible the development of modern state apparatuses such as the military and educational apparatuses whose operation facilitated and reinforced the policy of centralisation and integration.

---

47 Alberto Sbacchi, *Ethiopia under Mussolini: Fascism and the Colonial Experience* (London: Zed Books, 1985), 159-161.

48 Cf. Haggai Erlich, *Ethiopia and the Challenge of Independence* (Colorado: Lynne Reinner Publishers, 1986), 141. This exposed subject people to an alternative emperial rule but this experience is not often discussed in the recent federal arrangement in Ethiopia; see Sarah Vaughan, "Ethnicity and Power in Ethiopia," (Ph.D. diss., The University of Edinburgh, 2003), 120.

49 Bahru Zewde, "Hayla-Sellase: From Progressive to Reactionary," in *Ethiopia in Change: Peasantry, Nationalism and Democracy*, eds. Abebe Zegeye and Siegfried Pausewang (London: British Academy Press, 1994), 33-34. After 1941, bureaucratic reform and commercialisation regularised territorial administration. There were some regions (such as Tigray and Wellega; for example) less affected by the centralisation. In the case of the first linkage mentioned by Donham (see above), local rulers retained positions of *awraja* (district) governance in the new arrangement.

50 Bahru Zewde, "Hayla-Sellase," 35.

Such state apparatuses ensured the mastery of Amharic. For example, in his speech to a graduating class at the Holetta Military Academy, Haile-Selassie asserts that: 'claiming to be an Ethiopian without a thorough knowledge of Amharic is tantamount to having no country and to not knowing one's parents'.[51] Through the production of fictive ethnicity diverse people – even such as the Somali who share little with historic Ethiopia in terms of religion and culture – were hailed as Ethiopians: '[W]e remind you [...] that all of you are by race, colour, blood and custom, members of the great Ethiopian family'.[52]

This nationalisation of a diverse people demonstrates that what defines the unity were not objective socio-cultural traits but a projected identity – analogical relations such as the family metaphor employed here producing an imaginary unity that establishes the relation as though it was a natural one (cf. Althusser and Balibar on imaginary relations and symbolic identifications in Chapter 1). But despite the fact that the nationalisation of the diverse people seems to have elevated 'Semitic' language and culture, the process appeared attractive to the assimilated because it was linked to the ascription of status or placements in society (see Chapter 1 for the relation between self-mastery and the distribution of statuses).[53]

Although there was no apartheid-like internal racial caesura between people that confined them in their own culture, customs, language and religion, this does not mean that there was no principle of closure at all. Despite the promise of integration of the diverse people, fictive Amhara ethnicity also naturalised social inequalities. Of course, the principle of closure was not simply posed by hereditary ethnicity (a second-degree fiction as Balibar calls it; see Chapter 1), but it involved several factors (over-determination of factors; in Althusserian terms) whose expressions seek explanations including the structural dimension. Examining the nature of these inequalities is beyond the scope of this book but several studies have shown that the nature of the social inequalities during the *ancien* regime were along class-ethnic lines referred to as class-ethnic cleavages.[54] By and large, it was this production of fictive ethnicity or nationalist ideology that explains the interpellation of subjects as Ethiopians or the emergence of *homo nationalis* (*homo Æthiopicus*).

---

51 Harold Marcus, "Haile Sellassie as a Modernizer," *Journal of Ethiopian Studies* 5-6 cited in Heran Sereke-Berhan, "Ethiopia," 768.

52 Speech given by Haile Selassie I in the Ogaden concerning the inclusion of the Somali into Ethiopia's administration in 1956, *Ethiopian Observer*, December 1956.

53 See John Markakis, *Ethiopia: The Last Two Frontiers* (Oxford: James Currey, 2011), 13.

54 Cf. Addis Hiwot, *Ethiopia*; John Markakis, *National and Class Conflict in the Horn of Africa* (Cambridge: Cambridge University Press, 1987).

4.4 Nationalistic Absorption of Christian Identity

> In the hierarchy of values which sustained the traditional Abyssinian social order, that of the transcendental religious orientation represented by the Orthodox Church may be said to have held the paramount position. This is the sense in which, as has so often remarked, religion has been Abyssinian's only truly unifying factor throughout the centuries. [...] It so penetrated the social system that the basic unit of Abyssinian civil life was in fact a religious one, the parish.[55]

Once, there was no such creature called 'nation'. Instead, in Christian Abyssinia, life was more or less organised around the parish. The Church was a significant link between 'the peasant hamlet and the broader Abyssinian life'.[56] Given the historical role of Christianity as the *raison d'être* of the people, it is obvious that cultural legitimation was deeply connected to Christianity.[57] Although the Church historically sanctified the authority of Abyssinian Christian monarchs, the monarchs, or the state for that matter, would not override the autonomy of the Church. Even, sometimes, the authority of the monarchs was challenged by the Church and the people.[58] Hence, it is quite wrong to understand the history of Orthodox Christianity merely as an instrument of the state.

The integration of the Church and the state involves a complex historical relation that demonstrates not only practices of consent but also dissent. In this regard, the heterogeneous expressions of Orthodoxy in the old Abyssinia could be illuminating. As many would agree, early formation of Christian identity in Abyssinia cannot be understood in mono-linear manner implying that the Church of Alexandria – through the appointed bishops since the days of St Athanasius – was not the only source of influence in Abyssinia.[59] The Judaic dimension cannot be neglected; for example, the *tabot* (Ark) and several other religious beliefs and

---

55 Donald Levine, *Gold and Wax: Tradition and Innovation in Ethiopian Culture* (Chicago: Chicago University Press, 1965), 58.

56 Levine, *Gold and Wax*, 212.

57 Edward Ullendorff remarks, 'Abyssinian Christianity constitutes the storehouse of cultural, political and social life of the people'; see Ullendorff, *The Ethiopians*, 15.

58 A case in point is emperor Susenyos who had to step down (because of his conversion to Catholicism); see Messay Kebede, *Survival and Modernization*, 56.

59 Ralph Lee, "The Conversion of King Caleb and the Religious and Political Dynamics of Sixth-Century Ethiopia," in *An Age of Saints? Power, Conflict and Dissent in Early Medieval Christianity*, eds. Peter Sarris et al. (Leiden: The Netherlands: Brill, 2011), 80.

practices (even if we do not exactly know when these elements were introduced to the Church in history).[60]

What I wish to highlight, here, is the fact that the historical and local expression of Christianity cannot be characterised only as *tabot* Christianity as Teshale Tibebu designates it.[61] Rather, monasticism, first introduced by the so-called 'the Nine Saints' from Antioch/Syria, has also been a characteristic feature of Orthodox Christianity since the 5th century.[62] Even though little is known about the organisation and discipline of the monastic movements, the translation of the Rules of St Pacomius from Greek to *Ge'ez* was completed as early as the Aksumite era. During the medieval period, Abyssinian Christianity experienced a 'revival of monasticism': Christianity's impetus and commitment to evangelism of the 'heathen' in medieval Abyssinia, especially during 13th through to the 15th centuries, which is well accounted in Tadesse Tamrat's influential work: *Church and State* can be attributed to this monastic revival.

Granting the monastic movements had distinctive practices and theological views that typify some differences between them, they were characterised by 'anti-monarchical activity during which their members defied and denied the authority of the Solomonic kings'.[63] Even during the reign of Zara Yacob in the 15th century, who attempted something of an autocratic theocracy, the monastic movements opposed the monarchy. Especially, the Stephanites were considered 'heretics' because they refused to prostate themselves before 'Mary' the mother of Jesus and the 'cross' against the rules of the king. This was not only as a sign of adherence to their faith but also 'symptomatic of their opposition to royal domination of the Church'.[64] It was proper within the monastic circles to deny

---

60 Ullendorff, *The Ethiopians*, 107. Ralph Lee, "Symbolic Interpretation in Ethiopic and Ephremic Literature," (PhD diss., University of London, 2011), 83-116. John McGuckin, "Scholia on the Incarnation of the Only Begotten," in *St. Cyril of Alexandria: The Christological Controversy: Its History, Theology and Texts* (Leiden: Brill, 1994), 303.

61 Tibebu Teshale, *The Making of Modern Ethiopia*, 3.

62 Taddesse Tamrat, *Church and State in Ethiopia, 1270-1527* (Oxford: Clarendon Press, 1972).

63 Steven Kaplan, *The Monastic Holy Man and the Christianization of Early Solomonic Ethiopia* (Stuttgart: Franz Steiner Verlag Wiesbaden GMBH, 1984), 126.

64 Kaplan, *The Monastic Holy Man*, 127-129. See also Elizabeth Isichei, *A History of Christianity in Africa: From Antiquity to the Present* (London: SPCK, 1995), 50 and the Ge'ez text edited by Getachew Haile, *THE GƎʿƎZ ACTS OF ABBA ƎSṬIFANOS OF G^{W}ƎNDAG^{W}ƎNDE* (Louvain: Corpus Scriptorum Christianorum Orientalium, 2006).

'royal jurisdiction over the monasteries'.[65] Even during the era of disintegration or fragmentation of *Zamana Masafint*, 'the main link' between the fragmented 'independent feudatories', according to Richard Greenfield, was not the 'monarchy but the Christian Church'.[66] Thus, the claim that construes the Church as a consistent supportive of monarchy can only be true within a particular viewpoint or specific historical period.

However, some new changes in the sphere of religion – Orthodox Christianity – began to appear during the 19th century with the rise of rulers with a drive towards building a centralised modern state manipulating a religious myth embodied in the *Kebrä Nägäst*.[67] Donald Crummey describes this connection between Christianity and nationhood as the outworking of the myth or ideology of chosen*ness* – an ideology that fulfills both legitimising and integrative functions.[68] Crummey shows how 'pliable and flexible' this ideology is by elaborating how Tewodros set the pattern for a manipulation of this myth and he argues how this ideology has been used to justify the project of statecraft from Tewodros to Haile-Selassie.[69] Even though the use of force or violence was never absent, the process of building the modern state involved the use of this ideology. As Crummey rightly remarks, 'Force of arms could create only the material preconditions for such an authority' but in order to 'create its spiritual foundations aspirant rulers resorted to a neo-Solomonic ideology'.[70] Because of this myth of chosen*ness* both consensus and coercion were 'effectively' combined in regimes from Tewodros to Haile-Selassie.[71] Thus, the historical outcome of this process culminated in the blending of patriotic nationalism and Orthodox Christianity,

---

65 Kaplan, *The Monastic Holy Man*, 126.

66 Richard Greenfield, *Ethiopia* (New York: Frederick A. Praeger Publishers, 1968), 39.

67 See Donald Crummey, "Personality and Political Culture in Ethiopian History: The Case of Emperor Tewodros," in *Personality and Political Culture in Modern Africa*, eds. Malvin E. Page et al. (Boston: Boston University Press, 1998), 85; and Levine, *Greater Ethiopia*, 101.

68 Donald Crummey, "Imperial Legitimacy and the Creation of Neo-Solomonic Ideology in 19th-Century Ethiopia," *Cahiers d'Études africaines* 109, XXVIII-I (1988): 14.

69 Crummey, "Personality and Political Culture," 85.

70 Crummey, "Imperial Legitimacy," 15.

71 He also argues that the ethno-nationalist liberation movements, which we will examine in the next chapter, do also take forward the combination of coercion and ideology. Crummey, "Personality and Political Culture," 85. The conception of God in the Ethiopian chronicles and the *Kebrä Nägäst* is the Old Testament God of war; see Richard Pankhurst, "'Fear God, Honor the King': The Use of Biblical Allusion in Ethiopian Historical Literature, Part I," *Northeast African Studies* 9, 1 (1987): 15-20.

which is the nationalistic absorption of Christian identity or the emergence of *homo nationalis* and the simultaneous formation of *homo religious*.[72]

Due to such historical development, the nature of religious mission (evangelism) and conversion in the newly incorporated south during the so-called *ager maqnat* – the conquest and expansion, and Christianisation – was by and large politically motivated expressing little of the characteristics displayed by the monastic movements of the medieval Christian Abyssinia.[73] Rather what we observe in such a process is a dislodging of the'transcendental values' of Christianity and their substitution with what Levine calls 'system-integrative values' (that is, nationalisation), which made the Church an appendage of the state.[74]

In the context of *ager maqnat*, Christianisation was tantamount to a civilising mission: in order to be 'of times' ('civilised') and become genuinely national (Ethiopian), the newly incorporated people, who previously followed traditional religions, now, fell under a 'very strong pressure [...] towards conversion [to Orthodox Christianity] for only adherence to Christianity could give access to "civilized" status and an equal footing with other Christians who were, in fact, the overlords'.[75]

In some cases the newly incorporated people converted to other alternative religions: Islam and Protestant Christianity.[76] Nevertheless, given the identification of Ethiopian identity with Orthodox Christianity, as Markakis notes, 'it was natural that the adherents of other religions be segregated and penalized'.[77] Islam was accommodated to some extent: Muslims were not identified as truly

72 Markakis, *National and Class Conflict*, 73. Cf. Eyasu Lulseged, "Why Do The Orthodox Christians In Ethiopia Identify Their Faith with Their Nation?" *Proceedings of the First National Conference of Ethiopian Studies* (1990): 7.

73 Tibebe Eshete, *The Evangelical Movement in Ethiopia: Resistance and Resilience* (Waco, Texas: Baylor University Press, 2009), 34. See also Bengt Sundkler and Christopher Steed, *A History of the Church in Africa* (Cambridge: Cambridge University Press, 2000), 694.

74 Levine, *Greater Ethiopia*, 213.

75 Negaso Gidada & Crummey, "Orthodox Christianity in Qelem Awraja," 111. Haile-Selassie's predecessors 'Menilek and Yohannes favoured religious uniformity in the areas under their control'; see Negaso Gidada & Crummey, "Orthodox Christianity in Qelem Awraja," 111. See also Øyvind Eide, *Revolution and Religion in Ethiopia: A Study of Church and Politics with Special Reference to the Ethiopian Evangelical Church Mekane Yesus 1974-1985* (Stavanger: Uppsala: Misjonshøgskolens forlag; Uppsala Universitet, 1996), 97.

76 See J. Trimingham, *Islam in Ethiopia* (London: Frank Cass, 1952).

77 John Markakis and Nega Ayele, *Class and Revolution in Ethiopia* (Nottingham: Spokesman Books (for the 'Review of African political economy', 1978), 33.

Ethiopian but rather as 'Muslims living in Ethiopia'. Protestant churches, some of which were initiated by western missionaries but most of them later spread as indigenous movements, were regarded as 'cultural outsiders' who follow *meté haymanot* (outlandish or imported religion).[78] Especially in the post-war Ethiopia, patriotic nationalism 'demanded that all non-Orthodox Christians could not be counted as "true" Ethiopians' perpetuating and accentuating the crisis of peaceful co-existence or tolerance.[79]

4.5 The Imagination of National Self-determination

The foregoing discussion has briefly elaborated the socio-political corollaries of the politics of integration. Although the production of fictive Amhara ethnicity created ethnic inequalities, the nature of socio-economic and political problems and protests were not limited to the ethnic logic. In fact, prior to the Ethiopian revolution, several 'local resentments'[80] led to rebellions not only in the south but also in the north such as Gojam, now part of the Amhara region, indicating that the revolts cannot be reduced to the ethnic factor or 'Amhara domination'.[81]

To fully grasp the process of revolutionary change, however, we need to look at a tripartite constellation: the state, the people, and in between these two, a third group – the Ethiopian Student Movement who Randi R. Balsvik refers to as the 'bearers of public opinion'.[82] Within this constellation, the state is considered as the static element (Haile-Selassie became no more identified as an icon of progress), the people were the non-political element (politically unmobilised masses), and it is within this context the Student Movement emerged with a strong sense of mission to radicalise progress. Discontented by Haile-Selassie's modernisation and with the state's imagination, the students turned to other radical imaginations.

---

78 Tibebe Eshete, *Evangelical Movement in Ethiopia*, 5, 274.

79 Donham, *Marxist Modern*, 102. See also Arno Tolo, *Sidama and Ethiopian: The Emergence of the Mekane Yesus Church in Sidama* (Uppsala: Uppsala Universitet, 1998), 282.

80 Bahru Zewde, "Hayla-Sellase," 75.

81 Christopher Clapham, "Centralization and Local Response in Southern Ethiopia," *African Affairs* 74, 294 (1975): 81. Of course, the way they were handled differed for in the case of the former the situation was handled with coercion but in the case of the latter the complaint was heeded properly (in fact, because they were not regarded as a threat).

82 Balsvik, preface to *Haile Sellassie's Students*, xiii; see also Hakan Wiberg, "Self-determination as an International Issue," in *Nationalism and Self-determination in the Horn of Africa*, ed. I. M. Lewis (London: Itheca Press, 1983), 61.

Their dream was taking the country out of its 'backwardness' – of course, a theme familiar to early 20th century Ethiopian intellectuals.[83] The Student Movement decided in 1971 that 'Marxism-Leninism was the only possible ideology for Ethiopia'[84] that will eradicate class and national contradictions. Their utopic vision was to 'build an Ethiopia based on equality and consent'[85].

In 'absence of political parties' the Student Movement emerged to function as 'oppositional'.[86] Given the fact that Haile-Selassie's imperial regime could not tolerate any kind of critique from the intellegentsia meant that 'opposition could manifest only in radical form'.[87] Throughout the 1960s and early 1970s, students made a series of demonstrations and strikes and a characteristic feature of the movement was its conscious focus on support and mobilisation of the masses: hence, inventing a tradition of vanguardism.[88] The radical imagination united the ethnically diverse student body in a movement, which eventually made an intentional intervention in the course of history (cf. Ricoeur on the theory of action in Chapter 3).

In such a revolutionary climate or epoch, three observations deserve attention in understanding the rise of national self-determination in Ethiopia. I shall first discuss the Marxian legacy on the issue of national self-determination in order to show how the theoretical ambiguity, rather than theoretical clarity, shaped the discourse on national identity in Ethiopia. Next, I will briefly explain that the 'self' of self-determination is not only a product of discourse but also an ideological construct continually transformed under the conditions of the *practices of war*[89] (as a culture or practices of the self in Foucaultian terms). Finally, a third

83 Addis Hiwet, *Ethiopia*, 76.

84 Balsivik, *Haile Sellassie's Students*, 295. The students' attitude towards religion was quite negative: 'Ethiopia will no longer stretch her hands to the "Deities" that have bestowed her with 3000 years of misery'; see Editorial: The National Democratic Revolution in Ethiopia', *Challenge* 12, 1 (1972): 8. This seems a conscious rejection of conclusion that 'Ethiopia shall hasten to stretch out her hand readily to God' – in fact, a notion persistent in Ethiopia until today (not only among the Orthodox but even among Protestants); see Pankhurst, "Fear God, Honor the King," 15.

85 Pankhurst, "Fear God, Honor the King," 350. The opposition against what the students considered as the 'fake' nationalism and the 'pretentious propoganda' of the regime; cf. Balsvik, *Haile Sellassie's Students*, 266, 279.

86 Addis Hiwet, *Ethiopia*, 96.

87 Bahru Zewde, "Hayla-Sellase," 41. After the failed *coup* of Germame Naway, students tended to be more radical.

88 Bahru Zewde, *Society, State and History*, 248.

89 Achille Mbembe, who analyses African modes of self-writing (from a Foucaultian framework) notes that 'the state of war in contemporary Africa should in fact be

element (related to the previous two) is the crisis of multi-ethnic politics, which set the frame for the understanding and practice of politics as the enactment of identity (cf. Chatper 2 on the logic of subjectivization – the crisis of dis/identification). It is within the context of these overlapping conjunctures that the particular modes of self-writing, which we will discuss in the next chapter, could be understood.

The National Question

As we already noted, in the Introduction, it is the unresolved contradiction of neo-Marxist 'conflict' theories conjoined with the 'principle of self-determination' that informed the discourse on the 'National Question' within the Student Movement in the late 1960s and early 70s. Especially, two strands of neo-Marxist theories – Stalinist and Leninist strands – had an influence on the movement. Two different positions were held by two related organisations: the first upheld the gradual implementation of the 'principle of national self-determination' including secession whereas the other agreed only on 'regional autonomy'.[90] The latter is clearly the Stalinist strand while the former prefers the Stalinist one only for a season before gradually moving to the Leninist position. A third well-articulated stand was held by the Ethiopian Student Union in North America (ESUNA), which was published in its journal, *Combat*: 'The problem of national liberation is inseparably linked with the problem of class emancipation' and therefore 'the national question is essentially one of the emancipation of the broad masses of exploited people of all nationalities'.[91] This strand prefers loyalty to the Marxist priority of class struggle.

Having the presupposition that there were pre-existing 'colonised nations' by Ethiopia, the debate on self-determination within the Student

---

conceived of as a general cultural experience that shapes identities, just as the family, the school, and other social institutions do. And in a still more determinative manner, the state of war invokes regimes of subjectivity'; "African Modes of Self-Writing," 267.

90 Sally Healy "The Changing Idiom of Self-determination in the Horn of Africa," in *Nationalism and Self-determination in the Horn of Africa*, ed. I. M. Lewis (London: Itheca Press, 1983), 113.

91 ESUNA, "The National Question in Ethiopia: Proletarian Internationalism or Bourgeois Nationalism?" *Combat* 2 (1976): IV cited in Healy, "Changing Idiom of Self-determination," 114. Still part of the students who emphasised Ethiopian unity advocated Ethiopianism, which is 'a concept that transcends personal, tribal, and regional loyalties'; see Abdul Mejid Hussein, "Ethiopia and Ethiopianism," *Struggle* 3, 1 (1968): 9.

Movement resonated around the question of 'what is a colony?' without a sufficient critical inquiry into what constitutes the nation. Consequently, this gave rise to certain tendencies which later became problematic.The debate was framed in two forms – the 'National Question' and 'Colonial Question' – but both in one pejorative. Lenin's view on monopoly capitalism[92] became a source to draw from for those who thought Ethiopia (Abyssinia) as a colonial state.[93]

The purpose, here, is not to revive that old debate but to briefly see that what makes the so-called 'the National Question' and its concomitant ideal of national self-determination is neither its theoretical adequacy to resolve the historical quandaries of Ethiopia's subject people nor because of the pre-existence of categorical entities called 'nations' imprisoned within Ethiopia. Rather, the peculiar ways by which such an ideal has come to dominate the imagination of Ethiopians, as I will explain below, proves to be the *states of war* and new ways of death with a revolutionary vision anticipating a new order.[94] This imbued the conception of history as a sacrificial process in which self-sacrifice becomes essential for the redemption of the present and the future. This emphasis on the political agency of ethno-nationalist movements is not to deny the presence of concrete social questions (including ethnic inequalities). Undeniably, there was an ethnicisation of society (due to the production of fictive ethnicity) but such ethnicisation alone cannot explain the manner in which the imagination of national self-determination becomes possible.

Practices of War

Now, with this background in mind, I wish to proceed to the second observation: the Ethiopian self is not only contested in discourse but also in the battlefield. To be sure, as John Sorenson rightly remarks, Ethiopia is 'a warehouse of images, a

92 Smith, *Theories of Nationalism*, 70; Lenin's view - colonies as sources of raw materials - originally, drawn from Marx's assertion in *Capital III*.

93 *Segalee: Oromo Journal of the Union of Oromo Students in Europe*, August 1978 cited in Healy "Changing Idiom of Self-determination," 104.

94 For 'cultural dissension' of the Student Movement; see Teshale Tibebu, "Modernity, Eurocentricity," Teshale observes the absorption of religious motifs such as sacrifice (meswatnet) into revolutionary struggle; Messay Kebede, *Radicalism and Cultural Dislocation in Ethiopia, 1960-1974* (Rochester, NY: University of Rochester Press 2008), 8-36.

repository for obsessions and projections of various identities'[95] and that 'Ethiopian identity' or 'the Ethiopian self' 'has been bitterly contested both on the *battlefields* and in *discourse* with competing versions [representations] of past and future'[96]. Ethno-nationalist movements such as the Tigray People's Liberation Front (TPLF), and the Oromo Liberation Front (OLF) [following the example of the Eritrean People's Liberation Front (EPLF)][97] defined their struggle by the international lexicon of the right to self-determination. In point of fact, the above mentioned struggles with at least the exception of Eritrea do not fit into the 'national' model 'about which the Marxists argued, and in terms of which maps were redrawn' in Europe.[98]

However, these nationalist movements, with 'national consciousness', striving for political self-determination should be understood as 'exercises in programmatic mythology'.[99] It is mythology, which Sorenson also refers to, that provides ethno-nationalists with the authenticity and legitimacy for their nationality claims.[100] In this regard, a new development in the cultural experience of war is the shift from *shiftinet* (banditry; traditional dissidence against authority) to revolutionary struggle (and revolutionary sacrifice), which was heightened by the revolutionary experience during the 1970s.[101] The 'self' of self-determination has been shaped in the acts of war. It is in this context of the practices of war that narratives of the self or self-writing as an important aspect of ethno-nationalist

---

95 Sorenson, *Imagining Ethiopia*, 3.

96 Italics mine. Sorenson, *Imagining Ethiopia*, 17.

97 Even the Eritrean national identity was consolidated through practices of war; cf. Christopher Clapham, "War and State Formation in Ethiopia and Eritrea," *Proceedings, XIVth International Conference of Ethiopian Studies* 3 (c2002): 1433.

98 Cf. Hobsbawm, *Nations and Nationalism*, 160. Hobsbawm makes such a remark in view of the so-called national struggles in the 'third world' are struggles against hegemonies; Hobsbawm, *Nations and Nationalism*, 170-177, 154.

99 Hobsbawm, *Nations and Nationalism*, 154.

100 Myths such as a collective name, a common myth of descent, a shared history, a distinctive shared culture, an association with a specific territory, a shared solidarityare characteristic features of nationalist ideologies; see Anthony Smith, *The Ethnic Origins of Nations* (Oxford: Balckwell, 1986), 13-16, 22-31.

101 See Jenny Hammond, *Fire From the Ashes: A Chronicle of the Revolution in Tigray, 1975-1991* (Lawrenceville N.J. & Asmara: Red Sea Press, 1999), 187. For a brief genealogy of *shiftnet* and peasant outlawry; see Timothy Fernyhough, 'Interpreting Ethiopian Banditry: A Revisionist View', *Ethiopia in Broader Perspectives*, vol. 1, ed. by Katsuyoshi Fukui, Eisei Kurimoto, Masayoshi Shigeta (Kyoto: Shokado Book Sellers, 1997), 57-81.

struggle for national self-determination developed – leading to the process of the transformation of ethnic (cultural) identities and traditional hostilities into modern political identities.[102]

The Crisis of Multi-ethnic Politics

After the 1974 popular upsurge, the Ethiopian state adopted Marxism as its ideology. As Donald Donham notes, the Military Council (the *Därg*) to whose hands power passed *de facto*, 'stole the ideology of its opponent' while, paradoxically, annihilating oppositions.[103] In the process, 'what had been the tortured concern of only a handful of intellectuals eventually became the ideology of the revolutionary state'.[104] The *Därg*, who appropriated the rhetoric of the left in this 'discursive context', attributed to Marxism its own meaning as *hebretesebawinet* (communalism) – a brand of Marxism, which is a melange of state nationalism and Marxism.[105] It accepted the right of nationalities to self-determination in the form of regional autonomy (ideally) while being strongly committed to state nationalism.[106]

---

102 Cf. Kjetil Tronvoll, *War & the Politics of Identity in Ethiopia: Making Enemies & Allies in the Horn of Africa* (Cumbria, UK: James Curry, 2009), 52-55. Past rebellions were linked to the new nationalist struggles: for example, the woyane rebellion of 1943 and the Bale rebellion of the 1960s, which were 'peasant' rebellions without ethno-nationlist consciousness, were considered as the first generation of nationalist fronts.

103 Donham, *Marxist Modern*, 21-27. After deposing Haile Selassie, the Derg encountered a challenge of legitimacy: those civilians who opposed it had to express their opposition from the position of the left and as a result there was a growing attachment to Marxist-Leninist political philosophy; Donham, *Marxist Modern*, 123. Now, the 'Derg realized that it lacked the legitimacy that once surrounded the imperial throne and that it would therefore have to fashion new symbols of authority to replace the old social myth'; Edmond J. Keller, *Revolutionary Ethiopia: From Empire to People's Republic* (Indianapolis: Indiana University Press, 1988), 191.

104 Keller, *Revolutionary Ethiopia*, 127.

105 Bahru Zewde, *Society, State and History*, 255.

106 Bahru Zewde, *Society, State and History*, 255. See also Donham, *Marxist Modern*, 21-27. As a commitment to *hebretesebawinet*, in December 20 1974, *Ityopia tikdem* ('Ethiopia First') was proclaimed and a ten-point programme explaining the 'philosophy' of the new order was issued focusing on 'the indivisibility of Ethiopian unity'; Marina Ottaway and David Ottaway, *Ethiopia: Empire in Revolution* (New York: Africana, 1978), 63. The assumption behind this was that 'political philosophy should spring from the culture and the soil of Ethiopia, and should moreover, emanate

Of course, the revolutionary changes had implications for the transformation of the notion of citizenship.[107] In fact, the ideology of state nationalism developed in a way different from the old politics of integration, which we examined in the previous chapter. The interpellation of subjects by nationalist ideology was carried out even on a greater scale during the socialist regime. Later, in the name of a cultural revolution, the persecution of Protestant Christian churches was legitimised.[108]

A new social imaginary of popular sovereignty began to develop and the state was further centralised. Claiming to be the vanguard of the masses, the revolutionary government, in the name of revolution, asserted itself as the embodiment of the general will of the people. The creation of mass-society was regarded as a drive towards modernity – as progress – in a different way; the myth of progress supplanting the old thematic of civilisation. Consequently, the fusion of the state and society entitled the revolutionary government to mobilise the society and control the subjects' life in general through government organised collectivities – a new technology of domination emerged. Clapham describes this phenomenon of the capture or control of society by the government's mechanisms of control as the project of *encadrement*.[109] State repression expressed in multiple forms from restricting the freedom of expression and association of the nation's subjects to coercive treatments by continual policing and soldiering of territories of its subject population.

During the socialist interlude, Ethiopia's geopolitics was characterised by the Cold War while its internal politics was dominated by practices of war between the state and various ethno-national resurgent fronts. These movements gradually came to relativise the state.[110] The rise of ethno-national resurgent groups

---

from the aspirations of the broad masses; and not to be imported from abroad'; Keller, *Revolutionary Ethiopia,* 193.

107 See Samuel Wolde-Yohannes, "The Vision of Man and Humanity in Ethiopian Culture: A Politico-Philosophical Perspective," in *Faith and Culture in Ethiopia: Towards A Pastoral Approach to Culture* (Addis Ababa: Ethiopian Review of Cultures, 1997), 95.

108 Tibebe Eshete, *Evangelical Movement in Ethiopia*, 248, 277-296. Tibebe Eshete writes that generally the persecution against the Protestant churches had an ideological nature but did not have an ethnic connotation; for the resistance against the regime's ideology and its concept of 'the socialist man' by evangelicals; see Tibebe Eshete, *Evangelical Movement in Ethiopia*, 277-296.

109 Clapham, "Controlling Space in Ethiopia," 14-22.

110 Clapham Christopher, "Degrees of Statehood," *Review of International Studies* (1998): 24, 143-157.

was linked to the crisis of multi-ethnic politics. In light of what I have said in Chapter 2, this crisis is the crisis of impossible identification (the crisis in the logic of subjectivisation; for example, Wallelign Mekonen who challenged fictive Amhara ethnicity writing 'To be an Ethiopian, you will have to wear an Amhara mask'[111] was himself an Amhara).

To be sure, during the early years of the revolution, the two leftist multi-ethnic parties – the Ethiopian People's Revolutionary Party (EPRP) and All Ethiopian Socialist Party (*Ma'ison*) – could not solve their minor political disagreements peacefully and this eventually led to the Red Terror that caused thousands of deaths until the *Därg*, finally, eliminated both.[112] Now, the liquidation of these multi-ethnic parties gave way to the ascendance of ethno-nationalist movements.[113] In the north, TPLF replaced EPRP and similarly, '*Ich'at*, a kindred organization of *Ma'ison*, had been superseded by the Oromo Liberation Front (OLF)'.[114]

The TPLF needed to be in close proximity to the people whose interest it claimed to represent – Tigray – in order to recruit soldiers and draw support from this region. Such dependence of TPLF on the region is said to have led to the politicisation of ethnicity in the region during the socialist regime. However, the politicisation of ethnicity in Tigray, during the years of resistance against the military socialist regime, is quite ambiguous. Even though the proliferation of ethnic-interpellation was intense, it did not necessarily lead to a distinct Tigrean identity, which is 'irrevocably set against any reincorporation into Ethiopia'.[115] In fact, the peasantry could easily shift their allegiance between the two rivals in the region – TPLF and the regime in power.[116] Even in the later years, to TPLF, the nationalities question remained to be 'the best tactic to rally the oppressed peoples of Ethiopia in general and that of Tigray in particular'.[117]

111 Wallelign Mekonnen, quoted in Kiflu Tadesse, *The Generation: The history of the Ethiopian People's Revolutionary* Party, Part 1 (Trenton, NJ: The Red Sea Press, 1993), 54.

112 Bahru Zewde, *Society, State and History*, Bahru reflects on the culture of intolerance between socialist movements whose debates filled the pages of a public press - *Addis Zemen* back in 1976 leading to bloodshed. See also Andargachew Tiruneh, *The Ethiopian Revolution, 1974-1987: A Transformation from an Aristocratic to a Totalitarian Autocracy* (Cambridge: Cambridge University Press, 1993), 205-214.

113 Andargachew Tiruneh, *The Ethiopian Revolution*, 442.

114 Andargachew Tiruneh, *The Ethiopian Revolution*, 442. The acronym *Ich'at* stands for the Revolutionary Struggle of the Ethiopian Oppressed.

115 Clapham, *Revolutionary Ethiopia*, 209.

116 Clapham, *Revolutionary Ethiopia*, 209-210.

117 TPLF Foreign Relations Bureau, "Tigray a Nation in Struggle," (1980): 12.

Similarly, the allegiance of the Oromo people, during the military socialist period, was caught up between the regime and resistance movements such as the OLF.[118] However, unlike the TPLF that occupied substantial areas where its ethnic populations lived, the OLF had a level of access mainly to those refugees living in Sudan and some Western countries. During the time of the previous regime, OLF, as TPLF, accomplished several social services to its refugee population mainly in Sudan.[119] As a 'means of exposure to and communication with the outside world', the migrations of the Oromo opened to OLF political actors new possibilities: global connections of support from Oromo diaspora communities, states (e.g. Sudan), institutions (e.g. *Berliner Missionwerke*).[120] Some such as Van Huer argue that the spatial imagination of Oromia (OLF's version) is 'embedded in diasporic networks' (and this also partly explains its self-exclusion from the Transitional Government of Ethiopia in 1992).[121] Especially, from the 1980s onwards the project of rewriting history has contributed to such version of Oromo identity irrevocably opposed to Ethiopian national identity.

4.6 Conclusion

To sum up the discussion, we began by outlining the narrative of Greater Ethiopia and this was to set the stage for further discussion on the emergence of a singular Ethiopian identity (unity) and the relation of religion to this identity. Analysed in the light of the conceptual categories of the first part, we have noted that despite the assumptions of the narrative of Greater Ethiopia, the achievement of Ethiopian unity was not a matter of objective traits or existing pre-national cultural affinities as much as the production of fictive Amhara ethnicity. And assimilation into this fictive ethnicity required the mastery of Amharic language.

What consolidated Greater Ethiopia was the hailing of individuals of diverse people groups by nationalistic ideology, through the formation of a linguistic community. The process of national integration was tantamount to assimilation

118 Clapham, *Revolutionary Ethiopia*, 218-219.

119 Bulcha, unlike many Oromo nationalists, de-emphasises the forced nature of the refugee crisis but acknowledges that the migration of the Oromo have opened opportunities for international communications; Mekuria Bulcha, *The Making of the Oromo Diaspora: A Historical Sociology of Forced Migration* (Minneapolis: Kirk House Publishers, 2002), 30.

120 Bas van Heur, "The Spatial Imagination of Oromia: The Ethiopian State and Oromo Transnational Politics," (MA thesis, University of Utrecht, 2004), 61.

121 Heur, "Spatial Imagination of Oromia," 61.

into the culture of the nation-builders. Since describing nationalism without making reference to religion is to miss the way the former absorbs the latter, I paid attention to the nationalistic absorption of Christian identity. It was also demonstrated how the sphere of religion (Orthodox Christianity, in particular) was altered by national ideology and how religious forms were themselves embedded in the production of fictive ethnicity.

Generally, during the imperial regime, the historical development was from the empire-form (tolerated diversity) towards the modern nation-form, which is the unfolding of unity-as-sameness or the dissolution of difference. Although the Ethiopian system produced fictive ethnicity (a first degree fiction), it is difficult to definitively conclude that it also produced racial/hereditary ethnicity (a second degree fiction) that led to an internal (ethnic/racial) caesura. In general, the following could be said about the rise of the modern state and the spatial and material relations embedded in its apparatus: 'political centralization negated the legitimate wishes of regions for internal autonomy' reducing the link between the centre and the peripheries into a purely administrative link.[122] Clapham also clearly indicates that this gap between the centre and its peripheries is important to understand the political discontents, which started to rise up during the imperial regime.[123]

Finally, we noted that the development of an alternative imagination did not lead to the negation of fictive ethnicity but rather it paved the way to the enactment of ethnic identity – hereditary ethnicity or fictive genealogy replacing fictive ethnicity. The crisis was the crisis of the logic of heterology or the politics of the self as another, of identification/disidentification, of impossible identification, which concerns the issue of solidarity in politics (*à la* Rancière, cf. Chapter 2).

122 Bahru Zewde, "Hayla-Sellase," 38.
123 Clapham, "Centralization and Local Response," 75.

5 Ethno-politics: The Ethiopian as *Homo Ethnicus*

5.1 Introduction

Having examined the meta-narrative of Greater Ethiopia and its politics of integration, we now can turn to the modes of self-writing (and the politics of identity) that are the products of the instrumentalist mode of thought. The main purpose of this chapter is to demonstrate how contemporary political culture, which aims at establishing an inclusive democratic space for all ethnic groups, tends to replace fictive ethnicity with another fiction, fictive genealogy or hereditary ethnicity and its concomitant politics: ethno-politics. In what follows, I wish to start the discussion briefly describing the narratives of the self that are fundamental to understand contemporary self-formation in Ethiopia (5.2). Herein, I shall contend that both narratives are caught in the tension between 'victimisation' and 'voluntarism'[1]; thereby, legitimising the violent assertion of autonomy or national self-determination. By doing this, I aim to demonstrate the understanding of history, the subject, and the kind of sociality or social order they inscribe and the practices of the self they engender.

After describing the two narratives, I will further the discussion of imaginative practices that institute identity in the structural realities of the federal polity (5.3). Although the practices of the self in contemporary Ethiopia cannot be reduced to ethno-political practices, it is important to note that the pathos of ethno-nationalism and the ethnic logic in politics has not been transcended. As I will argue in 5.5, the way out of the current political dead-end, which is produced by the identification of identity with politics, cannot be found in the emerging mode of thought I designated as the trope of nativism before the conclusion (5.6).

5.2 Modes of Self-Writing and Polarised Subjectivities

It is over against the background of the historical context briefly elaborated at the end of the previous chapter (4.5) that the rewriting of history in Ethiopia emerged. These historical discourses endeavor to 'correct' the historical

1 Herein, I borrow Achille Mbembe's expressions 'the cult of victimization' and 'voluntarism'; cf. "African Modes of Self-Writing," 239-240.

imbalances of the narrative of Greater Ethiopia from different standpoints – as history always proceeds from history (as we noted in Ricoeur, Chapter 3). Since they are acts of truth that fashion discourses such as national self-determination and identity into a rational principle of action, such projects of rewriting history can be correctly regarded as modern ascetic social practices (cf. Foucault's understanding of the human/social sciences as modern ascetic practices in Chapter 2).

As we will see later, they exhibit characteristic features of modes of self-writing that attempt to define the 'self' of national self-determination. As narratives of the self, they narrate the decline of a certain historical golden age, which is lost or degraded, as a consequence of the historical emergence of the modern state of Ethiopia and the outcomes of that statecraft. The meanings they attribute to such historical phenomena of modern state-building vary according to their particular views on the nature of historical wrong-doing whether domination, or colonisation. But two ideas are equally shared by both: that are, the historic construction of the modern state of Ethiopia led to the economic exploitation of subject people; and the cultures of these people were subjected to historical degradation (this is the space of experience [see Chapter 3] articulated in the narratives). In order for subjects to represent themselves as agents or persons of will, they must assert their ethnic identity (understood as the horizon of expectatio'; cf. again Chapter 3). Being modes of writing that inform and connect the self to the field of action, such historical narratives can be understood as what was described as self-writing in Chapter 2.

The Narrative of Colonisation (Oromia)

First, the narrative construction draws attention to an imagined historical polis of the Oromo, in times immemorial, within the Horn of Africa – 'Biiya Oromoo'[2], which has become the basis for the 'spatial imagination of Oromia' since the late 1970s. Asafa Jalata writes,

---

2 Asafa Jalata, *Oromia & Ethiopia*, 3. The name 'Ormania' first appeared in a map drawn by Lewis Krapf between 1837 and 1855. The vagueness of the map has been criticised by Bahru Zewde and Sorenson; Bahru Zewde comments on Asafa's use of Krapf's map: 'Asafa [...] reproduces a map by the nineteenth century German missionary, Krapf, showing a region called "Ormonia" which is presumed to be a corruption of "Oromia". Rather inconveniently, this entity is located south of Kafa and Walayta, an area that is not commonly associated with Oromo settlement'; see Bahru Zewde, *A History of Modern Ethiopia* (London: James Currey, 1991), 34.

> The Habasha people evolved through the children of Arab immigrants and Africans in the Horn of Africa, probably in the first half of the first millennium B. C. They later differentiated mainly into the Amhara and Tigrayan peoples. [...] Even before the Arab elements immigrated to the Horn of Africa and mixed with some Cushitic groups and developed into the Abyssinians or Habasha, the region was the home of the so-called Cushitic and negroid peoples.[3]

After asserting the claim for a distinguishable identity of the Oromo (what is regarded as the proper *ethnonyme*) and that the Oromo are the true 'sons of the soil'; then (secondly), the narrative proceeds to substantiate this claim offering a construction of an idealised pre-colonial Oromo ethnic past. The narrative employs the logic of difference to idealise pre-colonial 'Oromia' as radically distinguished from Ethiopia. The latter is portrayed as a class differentiated hierarchic society[4] while the former is conceived as an egalitarian 'nation' with a democratic system of governance called the *gada*.[5] This contrast between the 'democratic' egalitarianism of Oromia and the authoritarian hierarchism of Ethiopia is meant to serve as a rhetorical device against Ethiopian 'colonialism'.

But similar to the narrative of Greater Ethiopia that exalts the culture of patriotism (*arbañoč*), this narrative alludes to the Oromo conquest, heroism or patriotism of the glorious days of *gada*. It makes reference to the *butta* wars, which the Oromo conducted, ritually every eight years. For example, they conducted twelve major *butta* against both Muslims and Abyssinians between 1522 and 1618 prior to establishing their present homeland.[6] Like the story of integration, or Amharisation, in the narrative of Greater Ethiopia, this discourse offers an account of 'Oromoization': the Oromo were able to greatly increase their numbers

---

3 Asafa Jalata, *Oromia & Ethiopia*, 6, 17-18.

4 This is observed in the Amhara worldview that authority is good and beneficial for society and without it any people can go astray; see Levine, *Greater Ethiopia*, 122-124.

5 Asafa Jalata, *Oromia & Ethiopia*, 7. The *gada*-system is comprised of the *gada*-sets (age-sets) and *gada*-grades. The former are age-homogeneous classes of people who (together) undergo the same rites of passage and, thus, share the same status while the latter refer to the duties (activities) the groups undertake throughout their successive stages of development; Asafa Jalata, *Oromia & Ethiopia*, 51. Each *gada* period lasts for eight years; see Asafa Jalata, *Oromia & Ethiopia*, 20.

6 Asafa Jalata, *Oromia & Ethiopia*, 21. *Butta* used to be conducted ritually every eight years. In recent years, the Oromo in diaspora have began commemorating patriots' day; see Asafa Jalata, "Celebrating Oromo Heroism and Commemorating the Oromo Martyrs' Day (Guyya Gootota Oromiyaa)," The University of Tennessee, Sociology Publications and Other Works, n.p., Accessed 24 April 2010, http://trace.tennessee.edu/utk_socopubs/12

by 'adopting' conquered people to the *qomo* (clan) through an integrative process called *mogassa* or *gudifacha*.[7] Initially, Oromoised people 'had limited cultural and political rights' and since the integration was efficient '[I]t is impossible today to tell the difference between the so-called Oromo-proper and the assimilated groups'.[8] Again, as a discourse of inversion it expresses the superiority of Oromoisation over the Ethiopian 'failed' project of integration but it is never critical of the logic of fictive ethnicity.

Third, due to the brutality of Ethiopia's conquest of Oromia, the Oromo subject has been exposed to an economically exploitative system and even dispossession of land. The narrative holds Ethiopia's hostility and brutality towards the Oromo responsible for the decline of this golden age leading to the ultimate 'colonisation' of 'Oromia'.[9] Consequently, due to the cultural imposition by the coloniser, the Oromo are said to have undergone a cultural degradation and the experience of self-alienation. Following the Ethiopian settler colonialism, five kinds of social arrangements detrimental to the Oromo developed: the *ketemmas* (garrisons that later developed into towns), slavery, the *balabbat*-system (the local intermediary class), the *neftennya*-gebbar system (expropriation of surplus, taxing), and the colonial landholding system.[10] The narrative claims:

> The major contradictions in Oromia revolved around nation-class, with the Oromo identifying the main enemies as the Ethiopian colonial ruling class, its Euro-American supporters, and a few Oromo collaborators who helped in perpetuating the colonial system. [...] The Oromo paid educational and health taxes to educate the children of the colonial settlers and build clinics and hospitals to prolong the lives of their enemies.[11]

The narrative does not place Oromo subjects under equal levels of exploitation within the broad 'masses' of Ethiopia but rather it gives the impression that the social and economic privileges were exclusively restricted to the Ethiopian

---

7 Asafa Jalata, *Oromia & Ethiopia*, 16.

8 Asafa Jalata, *Oromia & Ethiopia*, 16.

9 The story goes back to the 16th century; Asafa Jalata, *Oromia & Ethiopia*, 42-48.

10 Asafa Jalata, *Oromia & Ethiopia*, 62ff. Central to these arrangements (except slavery) was the issue of land: Oromo land was confiscated by the Ethiopians and was divided among thirty one Menelik's officials, moreover, Oromo land was sold as a commodity to foreign landlords as a result of which many Oromo were evicted, dislocated and massacred; Asafa Jalata, *Oromia & Ethiopia*, 63-4. The Ethiopian colonial state 'claimed absolute rights over three-fourth of the Oromo lands and provided portions for its officials in lieu of salary. The remaining one fourth of the colonized land was divided among the Oromo collaborators; Asafa Jalata, *Oromia & Ethiopia*, 70.

11 Asafa Jalata, *Oromia & Ethiopia*, 102.

settlers while denied to the Oromo.[12] Furthermore, it overlooks or denies the fact that the conquest and the 'colonial' administration – the *balabbat*-system in particular – were co-inventions of Menilek and his chief Oromo collaborators such as *Ras* Gobana Daachu and the Oromo intermediate class that was created later. The discourse employs 'Gobanites' and 'neo-Gobanites' as a metonymy for quislingism of historic and contemporary Oromo allies with the central Ethiopian government.[13]

Fourth, the narrative inscribes the Oromo subject as being caught in a series of conspiracies and subjugations by successive regimes. In this narrative, we encounter a reading that the 1974 Ethiopian revolution was a revolt of the Oromo and other 'colonised nations', referring to the southern people of Ethiopia 'against Ethiopian settlers and their state, the rich merchants, and the Oromo intermediate class'.[14] Nevertheless, the narrative asserts that the changes of the revolution were not radical enough to change the fate of colonised nations. It criticizes the collectivisation of urban dwellers and rural peasants in associations, which is regarded to have served the revolutionary regime only as mechanisms of control. Moreover, the regime, in the name of the famine crisis in 1984, implemented a resettlement and villagisation projects that moved Ethiopian populations to Oromo places with the aim of 'militarizing the Oromo population in order to isolate them from Oromo guerrillas': that is, in order to 'crush the Oromo Liberation Front'.[15] Generally, the narrative laments that the Oromo are treated as secondary citizens under successive regimes (first under the 'Amhara' and now under the 'Tigre', TPLF).

A few remarks can be forwarded, here. In this narrative, old racial categories – Habasha (Ethio-Semitic groups) versus the Oromo (the Cushitic groups) – are evoked not to challenge fictive ethnicity but rather to assert the authenticity of the Oromo-self invoking another fiction: fictive genealogy.[16] In doing so, the

---

12 Asafa Jalata, *Oromia & Ethiopia*, 87.

13 Asafa Jalata, *Oromia & Ethiopia*, 53.

14 Asafa Jalata, *Oromia & Ethiopia*, 103.

15 Asafa Jalata, *Oromia & Ethiopia*, 117-119, 139-143. The basic contention is that the resettlement villages became 'security villages' and the settlers were armed by the regime to fight the OLF.

16 The primordiality of thdisce ethnic group 'Oromo' was simply taken for granted but 'the term Oromo was simply unknown to many ordinary people. One was Borana or Gerri or Gabbra'; Günther Schlee and Abdulahi A. Shongolo, "Local War and Its Impact on Ethnic and Religious Identification in Southern Ethiopia," *GeoJournal* 36, 1 (1995): 11.

narrative does not only construct essential difference between the two quasi-racial or ethnic categories but also conflates racial/ethnic identity with territory; thereby, drawing an ideal boundary between the authentic native and the illegitimate non-native. But, echoing Alessandro Triulzi, one may ask: in order to assert that the Oromo are native to the region, should the Oromo ethno-nationalists create 'new images of racialized differences and essentialized traits'[17]? The political implication of this claim of territorial authenticity is not only to justify that the Oromo are native to the region (contra the old myth that they immigrated from elsewhere) but obviously 'to deny the alleged "Arab" descendants (Abyssinians) the right to declare themselves part of the same "belonging", a shared territory'.[18] This spatial imagination has served to justify the use of violence to attain national independence and also has been a factor in the crisis of the civic body, resulting even in ethnic cleansing, in post-1991 federal politics. Thus, the moral question of violence associated with the question of land is ignored and even justified by this discourse.

We also find a reading of the Oromo self as victimised and vulnerably exposed to a series of brutal systemic socio-economic and political subjections under successive regimes. It is claimed that the culture of Oromo, and its potential as a system of governance, has been historically degraded by Ethiopian colonialism. In the struggle for the 'decolonisation' of Oromia, two categories are being mobilised: the figure of the Oromo-self as victimised and the assertion of Oromo culture –*Oromumma*, which is regarded as uniquely egalitarian and democratic (contra the socio-political systems of the 'coloniser').

---

17 Triulzi, "Battling with the Past," 286.

18 Triulzi, "Battling with the Past," 286. While acknowledging the role of the spatial imagination of Oromia as a rhetorical device in power-struggle, Sorenson is wary of the 'strong quasi-mystic connection' of the Oromo nationalist discourse with land; he cites Sabboontuu Jiilchaa's writing in *Qunnamtii Oromia* against the Transitional Government of Ethiopia (TGE): 'The beautiful mountains of Oromia have begun to spit out their volcanoes in violent storming eruptions, protesting against you. [...] The terrain of Oromia has turned itself into quicksand to you intruders. [...] They are more than glad to give you your eternal burial ground, for all they care, and because it's what you deserve'; see Sorenson, "Ethiopian Discourse and Oromo Nationalism," in *Oromo Nationalism and the Ethiopian Discourse: The Search for Freedom and Democracy*, ed. Asafa Jalata (Lawrenceville, NJ: Red Sea Press, c1998), 237. In some places, the Oromo encouraged other people groups living in their areas to go back to their original places; see Gideon Cohen, "Identity and Opportunity: the Introduction of Local Languages for the Purpose of Primary Education in the SNNPR, Ethiopia," (Ph.D. diss., University of London, 2000), 8.

As a discourse of inversion, this narrative draws its categories from the narrative it claims to oppose (the narrative of Greater Ethiopia). In doing so, the discourse replicates old opposed binaries (Amhara-Galla or Abyssinia-Oromia) and re-establishes polemical relationship with the Ethiopian-*Other*. In view of what we said about the selective function of narratives (cf. Ricoeur in Chapter 3), we notice that such a narrative makes certain aspects remembered as others are systematically forgotten or muted.[19] For example, the narrative makes Oromo victimisation remembered, but Oromo political participation in the Ethiopian state apparatus – even participating in the domination of other people – and Oromo integration and interaction with the various people of Ethiopia are systematically explained away, de-emphasised or sometimes denied and muted.[20]

The Narrative of Domination

Adhana Haile Adhana's historical narrative aims at demonstrating a discontinuity in the history of Ethiopian statehood as Christian Abyssinia transformed itself into Greater Ethiopia under the Shawan aristocracy.[21] He argues that understanding this rapture, which he calls 'mutation' in statehood, has a direct

19 Difference is idealised – what we have already noted as a negative construction of identity, as inversions and oppositions, are simultaneously productions of broken and muted objective similarities. Without the existence of a relationship, in the first place, between the two entities, the desire or necessity to distinguish the Oromo-self from Ethiopian-Other could not have been meaningful or even appealing.

20 See Fikre Tolossa, "A Historical Explanation as to Why Members & Supporters of the TPLF are Ethnocentric," Jan.-Feb. 1997 (Ethiopian Review), n.p. Accessed 20 March 2012, http://www.ethiopic.com/Fikre1er.htm

21 Methodologically, he follows Christopher Clapham, who employs a historical approach rather than Marxist universal categories because the latter, as he argues, reduces 'the past from a series of complex interactions into a two-dimensional backcloth from which appropriate figures – feudalism, imperialism, exploitation – [...]'. Even though, he adopts Clapham's methodology, Adhana criticises Clapham for limiting his analysis to Haile Selassie's regime only and he prefers to stretch his own analysis back to the medieval period insofar as he is able to locate the mutation in Ethiopian statehood; cf. Christopher Clapham, *Revolutionary Ethiopia*, 14, and Adhana Haile, "Mutation of Statehood and Contemporary Politics," in *Ethiopia in Change: Peasantry, Nationalism and Democracy*, eds. Abebe Zegeye and Siegfried Pausewang (London: British Academy Press, 1994), 12-13.

implication for understanding contemporary Ethiopian politics.[22] The narrative fulfils three major purposes.

First, it constructs an idealised pre-Menilekan socio-political order, especially the medieval golden age, as non-coercive and non-dominating order, in which Tigray had a privileged status. Adhana asserts that Tigray was marginalised during the post-Menilekan era. Next, the narrative describes the post-Menilekan order as one marked by coercion and domination resulting in the alienation of subject peoples including Tigray. Finally, the narrative concludes by justifying the current Ethiopian socio-political order as a radical reconstruction of the pre-Menilekan non-dominating order – 'a new brave world', an Ethiopian polity where not only Tigray emerged as a 'nation' but also other 'nations, nationalities and peoples' become liberated to exercise of their freedom of national self-determination.[23]

Adhana agrees with Gebru Tareke in distinguishing between 'Christian Abyssinia' and the post-Menelik 'Ethiopia' and delineates the difference between the two entities to unfold the basic contradictions in Ethiopian statehood. He affirms that the former is 'a direct offspring of Aksum' while the latter is an independent development in spite of the fact that the former 'certainly manifests itself in the economic, social and political institutions of Ethiopia'.[24] The narrative conceives the medieval state, Christian Abyssinia, as both an empire and a Christian nation. According to the narrative, monarchy, the Ethiopic script, Christianity, and architecture of the Christian nation are all legacies of Aksum.[25] A 'common history' and Christianity were the unifying 'core culture' (of Abyssinia), but not

---

22 Adhana strongly suggests that 'history, more than any other discipline, must inform our understanding of contemporary Ethiopian politics'; Adhana Haile, "Mutation of Statehood," 12. He cites Jesman, who in the early 1960s alluded to Ethiopia as a country 'burdened with its past', and he refers to Gebru Tareke as well who recognises the burden of history; see 1963:1 cited in Adhana Haile, "Mutation of Statehood," 12. Adhana's methodological choice and focus on historical reconstruction reminds us of the debate on the nation-class contradiction and quite obviously Adhana's ideological position seems in support of the primacy of the national question over that of class struggle (that reflects TPLF's, and by extension EPRDF's [Ethiopian People's Revolutionary Democratic Front], view); Adhana Haile, "Mutation of Statehood," 12.

23 Adhana Haile Adhana, "Tigray-The Birth of a Nation within the Ethiopian Polity," in *Ethnicity and the State in Eastern Africa*, ed. by M.A. Mohamed Salih and John Markakis (Uppsala: Nordiska Afrikainstitutet,1998), 42, 49.

24 Adhana Haile,"Mutation of Statehood," 16.

25 Levine regards Aksum (the Tigre) as a seedbed; cf. Levine, *Greater Ethiopia*, 110.

'Amhara core culture' (as Clapham argues).[26] Further, Adhana's narrative indicates that the 'monarchy was a common institution of the nation – i.e. it was not an instrument of political domination of the elite of one linguistic group over the others. The political system rested on a balance of interests of the monarchy (the royal court) and the regional or local ruling houses': the nobility (*mekuanint*) possessed 'the double traits of centripetality and centrifugality'.[27]

Here, what the narrative constructs is an account of a non-dominating and unifying hierarchy regulated by a balance of power and that the diverse linguistic groups were not maintained by force. In this idealised non-dominating Christian nation Tigray had a well recognised and respected status: Tigray 'had long been the cradle of Ethiopian Christendom' and as late as the 18th century, royal rule of protocol had it that the governor of the heartland of Tigray was *primus inter pares* in matters of state.[28] The purpose of such projection into the past (idealised past) is obviously for pragmatic goals – that is, to construct normativity for contemporary political arrangements based on the model of unity in diversity as opposed to the unitary system of the previous regimes (more of this to come later).

After such an account of the Christian nation, Adhana goes on to assert that this historic state was also an empire. In the empire, he claims that 'the nation was a builder, a core, or a component of the empire'.[29] His core argument is that 'the Shawan dynasty *empirized* the state-nation-state and, hence, worked towards *denationalization* of the state-nation' the result of which is that 'the

26 Adhana Haile, "Mutation of Statehood," 19.

27 Adhana Haile, "Mutation of Statehood," 19. 'Political and religious identity is counterbalanced by linguistic (and secular) cultural diversity' and this was a 'cultural rather than a political centrifugality'; see Adhana Haile, "Mutation of Statehood," 21.

28 Adhana Haile, "Mutation of Statehood," 21.

29 Adhana Haile, "Mutation of Statehood," 17. The historic Ethiopian state 'spread and contracted spatially depending on its own inner capacities. It created the empire without dissolving itself through empire-building and reeled inwards into its core without disintegrating or disappearing. Reversals had always been temporary, thanks to the absence of lasting or better organized other polities in the horn'; Adhana Haile, "Mutation of Statehood," 21. The Abyssinian polity attained its nationhood through noncoercive means and even the expansion to form the empire was through a mechanism of 'evangelisation and subsequent full political integration, portions of the empire into integral parts of the state-nation and its state'; Adhana Haile, "Mutation of Statehood," 21. In such cases, the 'contradictory feature of the state was positively resolved' but during 'adverse historical circumstances (as during 1529-1543) the contradiction found resolution in collapse of the empire element, that is to say, negative resolution'; Adhana Haile, "Mutation of Statehood," 21.

historic contradiction of the state-nation-empire-state had now resolved itself into an *empire-state*, with northern Shawa alone occupying the status of state-nationhood'.[30] Thus, the Ethiopian statehood had *mutated*, and of course, following the mutation of statehood, two major socio-political changes occurred: first, since the reign of Menilek '*Shawan monopoly of power*', and as a result '*complete political domination*' of the components of the empire began.[31] During the reign of Haile-Selassie, especially after 1941, this monopoly of power was further consolidated through centralisation that led to the pacification and replacement of the regional nobility by Shawan governors.[32]

The narrative, then, goes on to state that after 'Amharic and Amhara culture became the essential attributes of being an Ethiopian', cultural domination further contributed to the denationalisation of the state-nation and marginalisation of Tigray, in particular.[33] Moreover, despite the ideological manoeuvre of the regime that Ethiopia was inclusive of all ethnic and religious groups, there was internal exclusion or discrimination based on such differences.[34] Thus, this 'Amhara-dominated state' but never 'Abyssinian'-dominated state '[...] cannot really be reduced to the north versus the south, nor to the Amhara ruling class (let alone Amhara) versus the rest, but stems largely from the nature of the Shawan aristocracy itself'.[35]

After a clear account that identifies the crisis of fictive Amhara ethnicity, then, Adhana describes contemporary Ethiopian politics since 1991 as the 'Shakespearian "to be or not to be"', which he elaborates as follows: first, the first three decades of the 20th century proved to be a time when Ethiopia's survival was at stake in view of its backwardness as compared to its European counterparts, which led to 'patriotic reformism' 'from above' 'in order to catch up with Europe'.[36] But this, in the 1950s and 1960s, gave rise to 'patriotic revolt' 'now propelled by the perception of Ethiopian backwardness compared with emerging independent Africa', which 'culminated in the Ethiopian Student Movement, 1960-1974.[37] This movement struggled against class and national oppression, which, finally, brought the 'popular democratic upsurge' (in 1974); nevertheless, this 'democratic upsurge

30 Adhana Haile, "Mutation of Statehood," 24.
31 Adhana Haile, "Mutation of Statehood," 24, 26.
32 Adhana Haile, "Mutation of Statehood," 26.
33 Adhana Haile, "Mutation of Statehood," 27.
34 Adhana Haile, "Mutation of Statehood," 26.
35 Adhana Haile, "Mutation of Statehood," 27.
36 Adhana Haile, "Mutation of Statehood," 27.
37 Adhana Haile, "Mutation of Statehood," 27.

in turn ended in a military dictatorship (1974-91)' because 'the historical contradiction of Ethiopian statehood was, in practice, wrongly reduced to the land question alone'.[38] In practice, then, the previous regime continued 'the politics of the Shawan aristocracy'.[39] Nonetheless, the overcome of this regime by EPRDF in 1991:

> [M]arks a complete break with the 100-year-old dominant politics (i.e. a negation of the traditions and political and ideological legacies of the Shawan aristocracy – a negation of the negation) and offers a new hope of the survival (affirmation) of Ethiopian statehood on democratic foundations: complete respect, in practice as in word, for the democratic rights of the *nations* and *nationalities* that constitute the state, as well as the democratic rights of individual citizens, social groups and productive social classes. The agenda is not thus to resurrect the historic state-nation, let alone the historic contradiction of the state-nation-empire-state. The agenda is to create the broadest possible democratic conditions that would provide for the emergence, through democratic practice, of an all-inclusive state-nation: a new unity in diversity. This is the politics of 'to be' (revolutionary democracy) in contemporary Ethiopia.[40]

The politics of 'not to be' constitutes two varieties: 'chauvinistic nationalism' (Greater Ethiopian nationalism), which is a 'positive offshoot' of the one-hundred year Shawan aristocracy, and the 'nationalism of withdrawal' such as the Oromo and Somali nationalisms, which is a reaction to the former. These two variants are seen as duos that need and reinforce each other. These two are opposing and irreconcilable political postures that are incompatible with the politics of 'to be' or revolutionary democracy and they are geared towards the disintegration of Ethiopia.[41] The former is associated with the urban elites who are regarded as hostile to the 'labouring masses' who EPRDF (Ethiopian People's Revolutionary Democratic Front) assumes to liberate and represent. However, the positive legacy of the Shawan aristocracy is that it became the cause for the rise of EPRDF and its allies – the co-belligerence of various ethnic groups – to overthrow this hegemony:

38 Adhana Haile, "Mutation of Statehood," 27.

39 Adhana Haile, "Mutation of Statehood," 28.

40 Adhana Haile, "Mutation of Statehood," 28. Others such as Christopher Clapham also regard such historic rapture as an outcome of the crisis of the project of the modern state and its apparatuses; see Christopher Clapham, "Ethnicity and the National Question in Ethiopia," in *Conflict and Peace in the Horn of Africa: Federalism and Its Alternatives*, ed. Peter Woodward and Murray Forsyth (Aldershot, UK: Dartmouth Publishing Company, 1994), 27-40.

41 Adhana Haile, "Mutation of Statehood," 28.

> The Shawan aristocracy has left one basic legacy. It brought together various peoples and subjected them, over a period of 100 years, to historical experiences emanating from a single centre. These common experiences have enabled, for example, the Amhara, the Oromo, the Agaw, the Tigray and the Afar to join hands under a single front (EPRDF) to negate the political and ideological traditions of the Shawan aristocracy.[42]

Finally, the narrative affirms that the liberation of Tigray, and Ethiopia as a whole, was realised removing 'all the constraints that had stood in the way of Tigray becoming a nation' and consequently, 'Tigray finally emerged as a 'nation' within the Ethiopian polity, not only after a struggle against incredible odds, but because it had to struggle against such odds'.[43] This implies that Tigray as a nation was not formed through ethno-national ideology under the context of practices of war but that it was already, or perennially, a nation that endured through historical odds.

In conclusion, Adhana's narrative construction achieves two major things, here. First, with the phenomenon he termed 'denationalization' Adhana strategically dissociates Tigray, or the Tigre, from the Amhara-Tigre complex, thereby subtly arguing, that Tigray cannot be regarded as an oppressor 'nation' with the 'Amhara'. Second, by emphasising the marginality of Tigray, Adhana defines the figure of the Tigrean, and also other subject peoples of Ethiopia, as victim and, thus, justifies the struggle of this 'wounded subject' for the right of self-determination – voluntarism.[44] In order to highlight the marginalisation of Tigray, and hence, the illegitimacy of the post-Menilekan political order, Adhana downplays the fact that Tigray was less affected by the erosion of the regional nobility as compared to other regions because of Haile-Selassie's centralisation.[45] By way of contrasting the political status of Tigray and non-Shawan Amhara in post-Menilekan era to the (idealised) pre-Menilekan socio-political order, the narrative demonstrates how Tigray including all non-Shawan peoples were victimised under socio-political and economic exploitation of the political centre. What follows from this discussion of the figure of the victim is its mobilisation in the struggle for national self-determination: the solidarity of the *ethnos*, the proliferation of ethnic-interpellation. The belligerent impetus of subjects mobilised

42 Adhana Haile, "Mutation of Statehood," 28-29. In Kinfe Abraham's expression Ethiopian statehood evolved from the empire-form to federation; Kinfe Abraham, *Ethiopia from Empire to Federation* (London: Ethiopian International Institute for Peace and Development, 2001).

43 Adhana Haile, "Tigray-The Birth of a Nation," 49.

44 Adhana Haile, "Tigray-The Birth of a Nation," 47-49.

45 See Bahru Zewde, "Hayla-Sellase," 34.

'under a single front (EPRDF)' is said to have negated the dominating hegemony and resulted in a 'brave new world': the enactment of ethnic identity, the supplanting of fictive ethnicity by fictive genealogy.[46]

Truth Regimes and War of Memories

The modes of self-writing examined above exhibit some common characteristics. They exhibit greater conscientiousness to the instrumental conception of knowledge albeit, and ironically, they lack self-reflexivity. They simplify the complex historical processes by reifying history. As we have already noted, the privileging of victimhood has led to the mobilisation of the categories of the figure of the victim – whether Oromo or Tigrean or others – and the assertion of cultural uniqueness in the struggle for the right of self-determination. Both narratives we have examined legitimise liberation movements whose mechanistic view of history fuels the use of violence to acquire the right to self-determination. Such movements display paradoxical features – they are ideological and coercive (violent), they act for (in the name of) and against humanity (others) ultimately building 'democracy' on undemocratic bases – war/violence and a tradition of vanguardism. In this regard, this paradigm not only lacks self-reflexivity but also proves that its formulation of national self-determination is founded on a lean philosophical basis.

As narratives of the self (cf. Chapter 3), they synthesise heterogenous elements – discordant concordance (see Chapter 3). For example, the self, whether Oromo, or Tigrean, is said to have suffered or victimised while at the same time patriotism or violent struggle – either historic or recent – is positively asserted. Such modes of self-writing, as I have mentioned above, are caught up by the tension between voluntarism and the cult of victimhood, thereby, legitimising ethno-national struggle for liberation through the instrumentality of violence. Here, the fragilities of identity and memory become evident as the selective function of narratives lead to the manipulation of collective memory (see Ricoeur on the selective function of narratives; Chapter 3). As ideological projects or programmatic mythologies, they foster the construction of polarised subjectivities (ethno-political mobilisation) and legitimise particular truth regimes or power structures (see Chapter 2 for the construction of

46 It is also a supplanting of one hegemony with another (in the name of the masses), see TPLF/EPRDF, 'TPLF/EPRDF's Strategies for Establishing its Hegemony & Perpetuating its Rule', English translation of TPLF/EPRDF document originally published in June 1993, cf. *Ethiopian Register* 3 (June 1996): 20-9.

subjectivities and truth regimes; and cf. Chapter 3 for what I have said on ideology as legitimation of power). Triulzi rightly describes this situation as 'war of memories'.[47]

In both narratives, the subject is seen as an effect of material relations based on ethnic distinctions. The narrative of colonisation portrays the Oromo self as a victim of Ethiopian colonialism while from the Tigrean perspective the subject is seen as a victim of Shawan aristocracy, its tradition and ideological legacies. Both emphasise the notion of historical degradation and cultural imposition by the oppressor or colonial nation whether Abyssinia or the Amhara. To the Oromo ethno-nationalist discourse, which highly stresses this notion, cultural alienation is deep and the subject is said to have encountered derogation. By privileging victimhood, it calls the subject to refashion herself by reclaiming lost or marginalised or undignified culture and the right for national self-determination.

Both narratives are founded on and reproduce polemical relationships accentuating the thematic of identity and difference. The dream is obviously totalising or singularising ethnic selves insofar as they produce solidarity of the *ethnos* through ethnic-interpellation (cf. Chapter 1). The narrative of colonisation is a narrative not only of the Oromo-self but also about the Ethiopian-*Other* who becomes the cathartic object of hate (in Mbembe's terms). The dream entertained, here, is simply an oblivious dream of living without others: non-Oromo Ethiopians. The narrative of domination not only recounts about allies but also about enemies whose objectives it holds as irreconcilable and a threat to the kind of politics – Revolutionary Democracy – it legitimises. In general, such modes of self-writing employ abstract categories – 'nations' and 'nationalities' – to explain the historical process within the Ethiopian society; reduces economic activity to the history of mere exploitation or utter utility; and history as a sacrificial process.

In such modes of thought, identity is conflated with geography (time as space); the subject is conceived as merely dialectical; and political practice as the assertion and enactment of identity, which legitimises violence (practices of war). Therefore, ultimately, such modes of self-writing cannot avoid reproducing opposed subjectivities, racialised binaries, and economies of in/exclusion. In a nutshell, they prove to be the contemporary *dispositifs* that capture and form – as *ascesis* – Ethiopian subjects: the technologies or the cultivation of the self.

---

47 Brossat 1990 cited in Triulzi, "Battling with the Past," 282.

5.3 Self, Federal Polity and the Global Order

Where are we today? What kind of technologies of the self are in operation? And what kind of social practices are produced? In preface to my answer, I must note that the modes of the self-writing are not yet exhausted. Although political developments have led to a gradual decline in the high spirits of the rhetoric of national self-determination as was in the early years of the inauguration of ethnic-federalism in the early 1990s, the pathos of ethno-nationalism and the ethnic logic in politics are not yet transcended.

To understand the practices of the self in the context of the federal polity, we need to follow the political developments in three phases.[48] The first (earliest) phase, in the early 1990s, was a season of empowering ethnic groups insofar as they identify themselves as 'nations, nationalities and peoples' (*beher, behereseboch, hezboch*), and that they 'freely' exercise their right for national self-determination. In the second and third (later) phases, the emphasis turns to be reversing the decentralising gesture of the early years; however, as noted above, the centralising trend is not due to greater integration of people or the taming of ethno-nationalism for the pathos of ethno-nationalism is still strong and will remain to be so not only because of the ideological commitment of the incumbent government but also on the tenacity of ethnic based parties and opposition movements both at home and the diaspora.[49]

Enacting the Federal Body Politic

In the first phase of ethnic-federalism, the focus was on translating ethnic identity into territorial boundaries and the empowering of ethno-political categories or identities through the rhetoric of national self-determination. In post-socialist

---

48 See Assefa Fiseha, "Theory versus Practice in the Implementation of Ethiopia's Ethnic Federalsim," in *Ethnic Federalism: The Ethiopian Experience in Comparative perspective*, ed. David Turton (Ohio: Ohio University Press, 2006), 147.

49 The tenacity of ethnic-based parties (within the EPRDF coalition, its affiliates and other opposition parties) has contributed to 'the most serious blow to multi-ethnic politics in Ethiopia'; Merera Gudina "Contradictory Interpretation of Ethiopian History: The Need for a New Consensus," in *Ethnic Federalism: The Ethiopian Experience in Comparative perspective*, ed. David Turton (Ohio: Ohio University Press, 2006), 127.This has also ensured the absence of credible opposition (at least until 2005); Bahru Zewde, *Society, State and History*, 443. For the tenacity of ethno-political imagination among the diaspora see Semir Yusuf, "Contending Nationalisms in a Transnational Era: The Case of Ethiopianist and Oromo Nationalisms," *Journal of Asian and African Studies*, No. 44 (June 2009): 299-318.

era, Ethiopia is re-imagined as an 'assemblage of distinct ethnicities'.[50] Such imagination entailed restructuring Ethiopia by elevating the category of the *ethnos* – 'nations, nationalities, and peoples' that substituted the 'people' in the previous Constitutions of 1987 and 1955. The new Constitution defines 'nations, nationalities and peoples' as 'group(s) of people who have or share a large measure of a common culture, or similar customs, mutual intelligibility of language, belief in a common or related identities, and who predominantly inhabit an identifiable contiguous territory' and grants them 'unconditional right to self-determination, including the right to secession'.[51] Each of these categories – nations, nationalities, and peoples – are not elaborated but only vaguely defined by the new Constitution.

The translation of ethno-linguistic identity into identifiable territorial boundaries – by drawing an ethnic map – reconstructed Ethiopia.[52] Such spatial reconstruction produced and transformed regional identities into ethno-political ones and constituting parts of the federal body politic: for example, old provinces of Gojam, Gondar, Wollo, parts of Shawa, etc. are now totalised as 'Amhara' and in the same manner Oromia is created out of provinces such as Jimma, Arsi, Bale, Illubabor and parts of Shawa, Wellega, and Hararge.[53] People

50 Clapham, "Controlling Space in Ethiopia," 27, 35.

51 Federal Democratic Republic of Ethiopia (1994) *Constitution*, ratified by the National Constituent Assembly, 8 December 1994. Art. 46, 47. The federal arrangement based on ethno-linguistic criteria has been considered as 'fundamentally suicidal' by Ehrlich and a 'recipe for disaster' by Brietzke; see Charles Ehrlich, "Ethnicity and Constitutional Reform: the Case of Ethiopia," *Journal of International and Comparative Law* 6 (1999): 62; and Paul Brietzke, "Ethiopia's 'Leap in the Dark': Federalism and Self-determination in the new Constitution," *Journal of African Law* 39 (1) (1995): 35. Fasil Nahum who drafted the Constitution remarks that the Constitution is meant to create an equilibrium between the historically 'centripetal and centrifugal forces'; *Constitution for a Nation of Nations: the Ethiopian Prospect* (Lawrenceville, NJ: Red Sea Press, 1997), 45.

52 Vaughan, "Ethnicity and Power in Ethiopia," 28. The Commission did not find the task simple as they had to consider language-use, than history, as they were afraid that this could lead to endless dispute. Vaughan, "Ethnicity and Power in Ethiopia," 34-35.

53 See Bahru Zewde, *Society, State and History*, 355. This is a disjuncture from the experiences of the previous two regimes. In the previous regime, there were fourteen provinces and most of them did not reflect ethnicity: Shawa, Wellega, Illubabor, Kefa, Gamo Gofa, Sidamo, Bale, Harrerghe, Wello, Gojam, Gonder, Tigray and Eritrea. The new regional states are Oromia, Amhara, Tigray, Afar, Somali, Benishangul-Gumuz, Gambella, Harari, and SNNP (Southern Nations, Nationalities and Peoples). The ambiguities are not only the difficulty of aligning political identities with ethnic ones in

who used to identify themselves as Gojjamé, Gondaré, Wolloyé, Shawan must identify themselves as Amhara but there has never been a region called by this name except briefly during the Medieval period as there has never been a region called Oromia except on the pamphlets of OLF.[54] Moreover, the translation of the term 'nation' into Amharic/*Ge'ez* as '*Beher*' is inappropriate:

> *Beher* denotes not people, but the land they live on. *Beher* is the land of a people, not the people of a land. When people identify their *beher*, they mean to refer to the land they are from, not the language they speak, the culture they follow, or the religion they practise. *Beher* is regional, trans-ethnic, trans-religious identity. [...] a related word [is] *agar*. In Amharic, the word *agar* is used in three different ways: as country, region, and locality.[55]

This conflation of ethnic identity with territory (or in other words, of time and space) is a new ethno-political experiment.[56] The fact that the government preferred to bestow the right of self-determination to all territorially demarcated ethno-linguistic groups, rather than limiting this right to those who clearly had shown the desire, as some have argued, reveals the government's 'complex political strategies' (i.e., divide and rule) and 'ideological commitments' (Marxist left-over).[57] As a proof of this commitment, the government intensively engaged in hailing these groups to identify themselves as 'nations' or 'peoples' with 'rights of self-determination'.[58] This entails that the solidarity of the *ethnos* through ethnic-interpellation become central to political processes – a new processing of

---

a country with around eighty ethnic groups but also in many cases people identified themselves differently (religion, region, local, etc.).

54 Bahru Zewde, *Society, State and History*, 355.

55 Teshale Tibebu, "Modernity, Eurocentricity," 366.

56 Arnoult Serra-Horguelin has written on "The Federal Experiment in Ethiopia: A Socio-Political Analysis," n.p. Institut d'etudes politiques de Bordeaux, Université Montesquieu-Bordeaux IV, 1999. Accessed 27 January 2009. Centre D'etude D 'Afrique Noire. See aslo Bahru Zewde, *Society, State and History*, 334.

57 Will Kymlicka, "Emerging Western Models," 56. Such move has never escaped the critique of those who are even sympathetic examiners of the TPLF such as John Young: 'Constitutional making under the EPRDF has little in common with the bargaining, trade-offs, and compromises that usually typify such process; rather it reflects the weakness of the country's democratic institutions, the political objectives of the governing party, and its position of dominance with a state where serious opposition had been crushed or marginalized'; John Young, *Peasant Revolution in Ethiopia: The Tigray People's Liberation Front, 1975-1991* (Cambridge: Cambridge University Press, 1998), 195.

58 Young, *Peasant Revolution in Ethiopia*, 57.

the imaginary. The myth of ethnic-conflict and the manipulation of fear underpinned the justification for this new political rationality, which resulted in the ethnicisation of the party apparatus. The following speech by the leader of TPLF, the late Prime Minister of Ethiopia, Meles Zenawi, reveals this:

> From a purely legal point of view, what we were trying to do was to stop the war, and start the process of peaceful competition, peaceful expression of political opinion, and so forth. The key cause of the war all over the country was the issue of nationalities. Any solution that did not address them did not address the issue of peace and war. [...] People were fighting for the right to use their language, to use their culture, to administer themselves. So without guaranteeing these rights it was not possible to stop the war, or prevent another one coming up.The other dimension is that of democratisation of society. [...] People were already expressing themselves even at the early stage before the conference in terms of nationalities. There were so many nationality-based organisations. That is representation of a certain sentiment.[59]

In an attempt to generate territorially-defined identities, through aligning political identities with territories, the state created new economies of in/exclusion. This can be supported by three important observations. First, the institutionalisation of ethnicity transformed traditional small-scale and traditionally manageable enmities into conflicts between demarcated 'adjacent regional states'.[60] Assefa Fiseha cites the examples of the contentious claim over the town of Babile by Oromia and Somali regional states; between Borana and Gari; between Afar of Afar and Somali of Somali regional states.[61]

Second, in regional states where there is no significantly dominant ethnic majority, the minority exercise local tyranny over against the majority and exactly this is the case, for example, in the regional states of Beneshangul-Gumuz, Gambella and Harar.[62] As Eisei Kurimoto has observed, the Anywaa of Gambella

59 Sarah Vaughan, "The Addis Ababa Transitional Conference of July 1991: Its Origins, History, and Significance," *Occasional Papers* 51 (University of Edinburgh: Centre of African Studies, 1994), 56. The Oromo People's Democratic Organisation (OPDO) is example.

60 Assefa Fiseha, "Theory versus Practice," 136. This is more evident in pastoralist areas.

61 Assefa Fiseha, "Theory versus Practice," 136. Moreover opposition forces in these 'hot spots' are supported by neighbouring states – what Kymlicka calls 'securitization of ethnic relations', cf. Assefa Fiseha, "Theory versus Practice," 40.

62 Assefa Fiseha, "Theory versus Practice," 137. But this growing hostility is not only restricted between the political elites of the two competing groups Benishangul and Gumuz, but it also involves their subjects; see Berhanu Gutema Balcha, "Ethnicity and restructuring of the state in Ethiopia," Working Paper no.6 (Denmark: Aalborg University DIIPER & Department of History, International and Social Studies, 2008), 8.

call the new political situation as *girrgirr* (an Amharic word implying rebellious outbreak or riot – distinct from *abyot* or revolution) implying a state of extreme confusion, a kind of Hobbesian 'war of all against all'.[63]

Third, out of the nine regional states, only five of them, Afar, Amhara, Oromia, Somali and Tigray, have states of their own but none of them are internally homogenous because of minorities living within these states.[64] The fate of minorities, including those who do not wish to identify with a single ethnic group, in multi-ethnic regional states where the dominant group claims to own the 'mother state' proves to be economic and political exclusion and sometimes subject to ethnic cleansing.[65] The Constitution is completely silent, or excludes, the rights of mixed groups and individuals whose identification cannot be restricted to a single ethnic group.[66] The consequence has been the uprooting of micro processes, which disturbs inter-ethnic harmony.

New Trends and Federal Politics

Due to a sudden outbreak of war between Ethiopia and Eritrea between 1998 and 2001, patriotic nationalism was revitalised leading to the 're-channelling of resources and manpower to the center and hence to a more centralized federation'.[67] This is the second phase. And the third phase started in the aftermath of the war. This relates to the internal party crisis in the TPLF, which resulted in the expulsion of dissidents from the TPLF and the coalition EPRDF (Southern, Tigrean and Oromo states). The crisis affected not only 'the autonomy of the states' but also 'contributed to a shift in the balance of power' from the states to the federal government.[68] Soon, the discourse shifted from national self-determination to the dangers of 'narrow nationalism' and the 'manipulation of

---

See also Dereje Feyissa, "The Experience of Gambella Regional State," in *Ethnic Federalism*, 215-228.

63 Eisei Kurimoto, "Fear & Anger: Female versus Male Narratives among the Anywaa," in *Remapping Ethiopia: Socialism and After*, eds. Wendy James et al. (Oxford: James Currey, 2002), 230.

64 Assefa Fiseha, "Theory versus Practice," 136.

65 Assefa Fiseha, "Theory versus Practice," 136. For ethnic cleansing, see Schlee and Abdulahi A. Shongolo, "Local War," 8-9.

66 Cf. Gideon Cohen, "The Development of Regional and Local Languages in Ethiopia's Federal System," in *Ethnic Federalism: The Ethiopian Experience in Comparative perspective*, ed. David Turton (Ohio: Ohio University Press, 2006), 170-172.

67 Assefa Fiseha, "Theory versus Practice," 147.

68 Assefa Fiseha, "Theory versus Practice," 147.

ethnic identity for parochial purposes'.[69] However, this does not imply a change in the political rationality of EPRDF, which still upholds the principle of national self-determination and that there will be the danger of 'disintegration' and 'fragmentation' (*yemebetaten adega*) if this principle, or more correctly, if a political organisation that supports this principle – the EPRDF itself – is not governing.[70] In 2002, Prime Minister Meles Zenawi – resorting to 'alarmist rhetoric' – claimed that 'Ethiopia could be worse than Somalia and Rwanda'.[71] And during 2005 post-election bedlam, this warning was repeated when the 'opposition leaders were accused of plotting Rwanda-style genocide in Ethiopia'.[72]

This rhetoric shift to the discourse of peace and stability also coincided with the fight against terrorism, which eventually led to the labelling of any dissident group as terrorist. Such political developments suggest that those living in regions such as Oromia and Ogaden, for example, where liberation fronts – labeled as narrow nationalists (formerly) or terrorists (now) – fight against the state are exposed to extremely fragile living conditions defined/characterised by the state of emergency. Political repression is justified by the governing party in the name of the fight against terrorism.[73]

Human Rights Watch continually reports on the crisis that include detention, torture, mutilations, extra-judicial killings, corporate punishments, forced displacement of people from their homes, and material devastation of territorial frameworks such as villages and districts by the state and sometimes by the

69 Assefa Fiseha, "Theory versus Practice," 147.

70 Tronvoll, *War & the Politics of Identity*, 213.

71 Tronvoll, *War & the Politics of Identity*, 213.

72 Tronvoll, *War & the Politics of Identity*, 213. Recently, the Charities and Societies Law that regulates and restricts the activities of civil society or non-governmental organizations and the law that restricts political parties from receiving foreign funding have been issued. Such laws aim to contain oppositions and guarantee the hegemony of the incumbent government. Although these laws have strong implications on Islamic organisations, they are meant for imposing tight control on opposition parties. See Adem Abebe, "Rule *by* Law in Ethiopia: Rendering Constitutional Limits on Government Power Nonsensical," Working Paper 1 (April 2012): 6-9.

73 This has been accentuated by the authoritarian political culture; see Paulos Milkias, "Authoritarianism and the Ethiopian Body Politic Dissonance between Democratization and Elite Political subculture," *Proceedings of the 16th International Conference of Ethiopian Studies* (2009): 692-696. Such authoritarianism implies a 'monopoly of power by a ruling class of Abyssinian origin' relegating others such as the lowlands at the margin of the state; see John Markakis, *Ethiopia: The Last Two Frontiers* (Cumbria, UK: James Currey, 2011), 345, 357.

combined actions of the state and rebels place unprecedented burden and uncertainty in the lives of subjects.[74] Indeed, this presents a condition to subjects where the possibility of fulfilling themselves as 'continuous subjects' gradually becomes exhausted.[75] In conclusion, the practices of the self in the context of the federal polity and in the face of the new global order proves to exacerbate the the polarisation of subjectivities of citizens.

5.4 A Turn to Metaphysics: Re-enchanting Tradition

In the previous sub-chapters, I have mapped out the various modes of self-writing in Ethiopia and we have noted that the contradiction between contending constructions of historical narratives and their implications for the contemporary conception of politics as a contest over and an enactment of identity. The conclusion drawn in the foregoing discussion was that the identification of politics with the self or identity of the community has led Ethiopian politics to a dead-end. At this juncture, I wish to inquire if there are other alternative imaginations or utopian

---

74 The political repression includes the denial of rights such as the right to freedom of speech, placing restrictions on the physical movement of residents, control of/through voluntary institutions for farmers, and the imprisonment and torture of students (including expulsion from schools); see "Country Reports on Human Rights Practices," 2001 (Washington: Department of State), n.p. Accessed 20 March 2012, http://www.state.gov/j/drl/rls/hrrpt/2001/af/8372.htm; Human Rights Watch, "Suppressing Dissent: Human Rights Abuses and Political Repression in Ethiopia's Oromia Region," May 2005, Vol. 17, No. 7 (A); Human Rights Watch, "Collective Punishment War Crimes and Crimes against Humanity in the Ogaden area of Ethiopia's Somali Regional State," June 2008. Political repression and the suppression of the freedom of expression has been noted by scholars such as Balsvik and Theodore Vestal; see Theodore Vestal, *Ethiopia: A Post-Cold War African State* (Westport, Conn.: Praeger, 1999), 132-135; Randi Rønning Balsvik, *The Quest for Expression: State and the University in Ethiopia under Three Regimes, 1952-2005* (Addis Ababa: Addis Ababa University Press, 2007), 143-176. For the crisis of academic freedom (i.e., limiting the role of educational institutions in generating knowledge and making them political centres of ideological dissemination), in particular, see Baye Yimam, "Academic Freedom at Addis Ababa University: An Overview of Its Past and Current Experiences," in *Academic Freedom in Ethiopia: Perspectives of Teaching Personnel*, ed. Taye Assefa (Addis Ababa: Forum for Social Studies, 2008), 19-57. Such a political paradigm seems more akin to what Achille Mbembe termed 'necropilitics'; cf. "Necropolitics," *Public Culture* 15, 1 (2003): 11–40.

75 Compare with Achille Mbembe's analysis of the states of war in Africa; "African Modes of Self-Writing," 267.

projections, which transcend the dominance of identitarian ideology. To this end, I will briefly examine below the mode of thought I designated as the trope of nativism by drawing attention to the work of Messay Kebede and I will restrict my engagement mainly with his book entitled *Survival and Modernization: Ethiopia's Enigmatic Present: A Philosophical Discourse* to ethno-national considerations.

The Traditional Matrix

Messay Kebede attributes the survival of Ethiopia to its unique (native) system of power: the trinity of the Church, the imperial throne, and the regional nobility.[76] He begins elaborating such traditional matrix (which is much the same as Adhana). He understands the relation between Ethiopia's Orthodox Christianity and the Ethiopian state (in imperial Ethiopia) – a relation which he articulates employing the notion of 'symphonic unity'[77]. From the standpoint of such 'principle of fusion', both entities – the Church and the State – work towards the same goal and this implies that the latter cannot have a secular goal separate from the sacred and the former should serve as a source of legitimation.[78] Such teleological singularity resulted, in the past, in a theocracy whereby 'divine guidance' 'descends upon the state'.[79] Moreover, in the principle of fusion, the autonomy of both the Church and the state is respected: one should not intervene in the other.

Messay warns that the conception of this unity should not give the impression that the Church involves as a 'king-maker' or 'king-confirmer' or become a 'tool of factions'; the Church only consecrates or legitimises the one who emerges as a victor of the power struggle but the Church always remains above central and regional factions. Given the fact that succession in Ethiopia was not hereditary (primogeniture), unlike in the case of Catholicism, the Orthodox Church has never conceived the king as incarnating 'spiritual as well as temporal powers'.[80] The principle of fusion enabled the Church to transcend 'ethnic particularism' and this can be further confirmed by the myth found in the *Kebrä Nägäst*, the secret of which 'was to ensure the fusion of the Church and state only at the national level'.[81]

---

76 Messay Kebede, *Survival and Modernization*, 67.

77 Messay Kebede, *Survival and Modernization*, 72. This kind of conceptualising is akin to Levine's discussion under what he described as 'functional specializations', see Levine, *Greater Ethiopia*, 122.

78 Messay Kebede, *Survival and Modernization*, 71.

79 Messay Kebede, *Survival and Modernization*, 71-74.

80 Messay Kebede, *Survival and Modernization*, 72-74.

81 Messay Kebede, *Survival and Modernization*, 81, 93-97.

As Messay argues for the *Kebrä Nägäst* 'imparted both dispersion and unification', 'whereby the choice of God was given centerstage', and he rejects the standpoint that views the dialectics between 'centripetal' (the monarchy) and 'centrifugal' (the regional nobility) forces as an 'anomaly'.[82] Rather, he argues that the struggle between the two 'should illuminate how imperial and regional powers were so arrayed as to mutually reinforce each other and realize a balance of power'.[83] Further, he argues that regionalism and ethnicity should not be conceived as anomaly – as is evident in most scholarly works – but rather they should be understood as significant elements that helped to counter-balance central imperial power.[84] However, he argues that such a struggle was not a disposition against 'or a rejection of Ethiopian nationhood'.[85]

Messay conceives Ethiopian nationhood 'whether it applied to Abyssinia or modern Ethiopia' as *historical* and *cultural* and 'it has never been ethnic and would not have been so without an essential corruption of its essence'.[86] This definition of the essence of Ethiopian identity or Ethiopian*ness* as cultural rather than genealogical draws Messay's attention to the role played by the Amhara in bringing together the diverse people of Ethiopia through a 'supra-ethnic consciousness'. He validates this by reiterating Clapham's explanation of Ethiopian identity by the notion of the plasticity of Amhara (cf. Chapter 4 on fictice Amhara ethnicity).

Messay argues that the cultural nature of Ethiopian identity is a modernising asset, 'an impersonal and normative order'[87], which he claims to be best described in terms of Jean-Jacques Rousseau's social contract.[88] What gave rise to 'the religious nationalism of Ethiopia'[89], according to Messay, was not simply the principle of fusion because Christianity is a universal religion. Rather, he alludes to the particularising role of the *Kebrä Nägäst*, which unified the political and the religious – emphasising the submission to earthly sovereignty.[90] This kind of

82 Messay Kebede, *Survival and Modernization*, 86-87.

83 Messay Kebede, *Survival and Modernization*, 88.

84 Messay Kebede, *Survival and Modernization*, 93-97.

85 Messay Kebede, *Survival and Modernization*, 101.

86 Messay Kebede, *Survival and Modernization*, 106. This is a stance in opposition with the conception of Ethiopia as a loosely-held empire by Addis Hiwet, Gebru Tareke and Adhana Haile Adhana; Addis Hiwet, *Ethiopia*; Gebru Tareke, *Ethiopia*; Adhana Haile, "Mutation of Statehood," 12-13.

87 Messay Kebede, *Survival and Modernization*, 259.

88 Messay Kebede, *Survival and Modernization*, 259.

89 Messay Kebede, *Survival and Modernization*, 71-72.

90 Messay Kebede, *Survival and Modernization*, 116.

nationalist absorption of Christian identity – 'national religion' – is conceived as an important aspect of Ethiopian survival.[91]

Such traditional matrix characterised by a high degree of survival and cohesion – consensus society – is claimed to be grounded in and supported by distinct Ethiopian metaphysical world views. For Messay, *semna worq* (literally translated as wax and gold), which is a poetic expression deemed as the 'Amhara genius' and contribution to Greater Ethiopian culture by Levine, exhibits not only a literary style but a metaphysics deeply rooted in Ethiopian religiosity.[92] With a certain Platonism, the metaphysics of wax and gold distinguishes between appearance and essence (the former often veiling the latter) in such a way that it displays the former that veils, than expresses, the latter. Appearance is regarded as a usurpation of reality or truth (the essence).[93] This maintains the antinomy of wax and gold. The movement from the wax to the gold is ascent to a higher, true and absolute reality. The implications of such metaphysics are not only limited to epistemology but also extends to ontology.

God is not only conceived as mystery but the utter dependence of the created order on its creator is affirmed and the denial of this dependence is regarded as the greatest of all sins: *tigab* (satiety).[94] Nature cannot be regarded as an autonomous field governed by natural laws and the metaphysics of wax and gold stands in opposition to such dualism between the divine and the created world. Attributing autonomy to the created world is tantamount to limiting the divinity of God. What best characterises the Ethiopians' attitude is, then, neither ritualisation of nature, which is a dominant African attitude to maintain the equilibrium of nature through performing systems of rituals nor objectification or scientific manipulation, which is predominantly Western. But rather it favours submission to God's will: a teleological attitude that nature awaits the fulfillment of God's plan.[95]

Based on the metaphysics of wax and gold is the notion of *idil* ('fortune' or 'fate').[96] *Idil*, which explains the Ethiopian myth of social mobility, and which

91 Messay Kebede, *Survival and Modernization*, 109-110.

92 Messay Kebede, *Survival and Modernization*, 181.

93 This is contrasted to a Western conception that holds the view that appearance expresses the essence; see Messay Kebede, *Survival and Modernization*, 191.

94 Messay Kebede, *Survival and Modernization*, 182-184.

95 Messay Kebede, *Survival and Modernization*, 190-191.

96 However, Messay distinguishes *idil* from fatalism: *idil* 'is at the antipodes of fatalism and resignation, since fate is not so much certitude as a constant quest'. Here, the understanding of *idil* he presents contradicts Levine's description, which has to do with

should not be negatively understood (as mere fatalism). Messay argues that *idil* is connected to the theological notions of covenant and election: *idil* turns every acquired thing into God's gift.[97] Not only economic merits but also ascent to or descent from can be understood in light of such metaphysical outlook (we will see this below). A topographical metaphor goes with the wisdom of wax and gold, which upholds a hierarchical worldview of higher and lower positions. Although these positions are fated but the hierarchy is a flexible one that alternates people implying that the hierarchical system remains without change while only the people occupying the positions alternate. The social mobility operates in both directions – upward and downward mobility. Even if the agency of individual persons is required to maintain or acquire a position, it is the will of God that is regarded as the ultimate determinant. Certain similarities are drawn between the notion of *idil*, which involves the reversal of positions, and the Heracletian view of the reversal of superiors and subordinates.[98]

Such view construes being as dialectical and practices of war as having the determinate power to decide hierarchical positioning or effect the reversal of positions. Messay cites: 'war is the father of all and king of all [...] some he makes slaves, others free'.[99] The wisdom of wax and gold, as a unity of opposites, binds together those who are fated to the higher and lower positions based on the acceptance of reversal of positions for God gives and takes away. This perfectly agrees with the Ethiopian notion of time (*gize*), which is not a linear progression but a reversal of positions.[100] From this metaphysical notion derives the understanding of authority or power as open field for competition or struggle.

Despite views that claim the traditional Ethiopian system as feudal, Messay conceives traditional Ethiopia as a meritocratic society with a flexible social mobility. And it was only under Haile-Selassie, due to the establishment of hereditary monarchy that resulted in the blockage of this social mobility (a distortion of the traditional system), that the Ethiopian system appeared to be a feudal or a dependent capitalist mode of production.[101] The impact of modernisation – wrongly

---

docility or lack of hope or motivation to change; cf. Levine, *Wax and Gold*, 86-87. But Messay cites from Plowden to validate his interpretation: 'Each man considers himself as born to great destinies, and the smallest spark sets fire to his ambition'; see Messay Kebede, *Survival and Modernization*, 185.

97 Messay Kebede, *Survival and Modernization*, 183.

98 Messay Kebede, *Survival and Modernization*, 186.

99 Messay Kebede, *Survival and Modernization*, 186.

100 Messay Kebede, *Survival and Modernization*, 192-3.

101 Messay Kebede, *Survival and Modernization*, Chaps. 5 and 6, 243-345.

understood as westernization – has greatly uprooted and dislocated the Ethiopian 'traditional personality' – which can be noted in the rise of radical politics since the 1960s. This can be attributed to Euro-centric mode of thought caused by modernisation. Due to ill effects of modernisation, Ethiopians have left their unique tradition behind them and from this follows that the Ethiopian self, on the basis of Ethiopia's distinctness, should reinvent its relation to itself and rethink modernisation in order to get away from the place historical developments relegated to it. Thus, the need to 'return to the source' should be strong in order to recover their tradition.

A Return to the Source

In this mode, he casts a projection of a new social order – a utopia of reconstruction (see Chapter 3 on utopian imagination). His projection encompasses the restoration of a unified order that maintains a fair distribution of power that will also be a just society with unrestrained or unblocked social mobility. Overall, Messay's projection of a new order constitutes a 'monarchic' and a meritocratic society and takes into account what he calls the modernising assets of Ethiopia's traditional values such as the myth or the notion of *idil*. For Messay, the revitalisation of the monarchic order and the role of the regional nobility become essential because, in the first place, the monarchic order will fill the void created by the loss of an important but missing national point of reference.

Whilst he does not wish to dismiss completely the 'possibility of the restoration of the monarchy' in the literal sense, but his reference to it implies a figurative sense.[102] Such monarchic vision holds that the 'modern presidential figure' 'must be the resultant of all Ethiopia's regional, ethnic, religious, class, and professional diversity, the center of consensus of all particularism'.[103] Furthermore, he asserts that neither electoral democracy nor parliamentarian nomination suffice for creating this centre. To create the new monarchy a 'voluntary renunciation of power' by the current authorities is expected and if this occurs, then, this act, according to Messay's vision, will create a 'mythical event' out of which will emerge 'a mythical meaning'.[104] Messay claims that the 'extraordinary event of sacrifice of power' will lead to 'a new legitimacy and universality (cross-ethnic, religious, etc.)' resulting in a 'popular attachment'.[105] The restoration of

---

102 Messay Kebede, *Survival and Modernization*, 364.
103 Messay Kebede, *Survival and Modernization*, 365.
104 Messay Kebede, *Survival and Modernization*, 365.
105 Messay Kebede, *Survival and Modernization*, 365-366.

the monarchic point of national reference is indispensable for Messay if the 'nation' has to recapture its unifying imaginary.

Messay envisions the new order not as exclusively monarchic but rather as a form of a mixed government: a political system with two poles; namely, the mythical-national and the parliamentarian.[106] This implies that the monarchic order embraces a parliamentarism whose role will be representing 'regional and ethnic interests' in order to maintain the balance of power as was in traditional Ethiopia between the monarchy and the regional nobility. In reconstructing such normativity, Messay attempts to resolve some contradictions although he does not reach a constructive synthesis. For example, he speaks of the desirability of 'a new' *Kebrä Nägäst*, which is an expression of not only Christianity but also that of Islam; and such a discourse of inclusion also extends to the integration of the 'democratic' ethos of the Oromo (*gada* system) to the hierarchically oriented culture of Ethiopia through practices of syncretism.[107] This narrative, in contrast to ethno-nationalist narratives, which privilege the collective over the individual subject, seems to hold the promise of resisting divisive ethnic-interpellations.[108] However, although this narrative has a drive for a usable, or serviceable, social imaginary for a renewed social bond, it is entangled in the same logic and rhetoric that works in ethno-national ideologies.

Back to the Stalemate?

To argue that this nostalgic thesis – not to say that nostalgia, as an exercise in political pragmatics, is always a bad thing – only brings us back to the stalemate, I should perhaps first draw out some of the philosophical premises and the political implications of this discourse. First, this narrative conceives politics as a reclaiming of a lost, but an essential, identity – 'the traditional personality' or Ethiopian*ness* – only proves that the language of its pragmatics being duplicitous. Despite declared difference, this narrative shares the substantialist illusion of the previous ethno-national narratives. Put differently, what this project exhibits is the assumption that it is possible to define identity in an essentialist manner or by a set of historically fixed values. In doing so, it veils the fact that

106 Messay Kebede, *Survival and Modernization*, 367.

107 Messay Kebede, *Survival and Modernization*, 379-396.

108 Especially for individual subjects who do not wish to identify themselves with any ethnic group it offers a possibility of directly identifying themselves (directly) with the greater symbolic group (Ethiopia), which the revolutionary politics (liberation) in Ethiopia has not made possible.

identity is not a substance (fixed) and, most importantly, that it is constituted through a series of diverse *practices of the self*.[109] Thus, it inevitably indulges in the same fragilities of temporality and of collective memory we noted in the previous narratives.

Again, this narrative shares the same *episteme* with the previous ethno-nationalist narratives. As the previous narratives relied on a moral economy – the idea of 'good' and 'evil' – expressed as domination (the oppressor vs. the oppressed) and colonisation (the coloniser vs. the colonised) in order to highlight suffering and victimisation, this narrative articulates a moral economy in terms of the erosion of tradition or failed modernisation – essentially Ethiopian vs. non-Ethiopian or Western – and yet he is relying upon Rousseau. In addition, all of them assert that unless the suspended morality is bridged through the negation of what negates the self-asserted identity the Ethiopian subject cannot express herself positively thereby perpetuating resentment or wounded attachment. Consequently, this implies that to construct a new future, one should first look to the past (a return to the past) that is imagined as the only legitimate repository of the truth about self – Ethiopian identity – overlooking the interruption of fictive ethnicity during the past regimes.

Such logical similarity leads us to question the place of this narrative in contemporary ideological constellations in Ethiopia: divergent and contending views (propounded by ethno-nationalist groups). Messay himself alludes to these groups as sharing the same 'national urge' for renaissance: a return to the source.[110] His idea is that as long as they excise their pathological excesses, the combination of 'the Oromo search for self-assertion', 'the Amhara longing for resurgence', and 'the Tigrean restorationist drive' can have a constructive contribution to modernising Ethiopia.[111] Whatever positive picture Messay might attribute to this constellation, what sustains the logic of this obsessive back-ward looking is the same logic of reclaiming an essential identity. This takes us back to the problem of the identification of identity or the self with politics.

What Messay identifies as a desire or resurgence for tradition rightly fits in with narratives concerning the 'trajectory of decline' (what he refers to as the

---

109 These include not only the ones mentioned in the previous chapters – the state of war, manipulation of collective memory, narratives of identity, language and territoriality/senses of place and their mastery – but also religious practices other that Ethiopian Orthodox Christianity (such as Islam, the Ethiopian Catholic Church and the 'Evangelical' (generally Protestant) churches of Ethiopia).

110 Messay Kebede, *Survival and Modernization*, 361-362.

111 Messay Kebede, *Survival and Modernization*, 398.

'withdrawal of status')[112] of Amhara and its dilemma in defining itself in ethnic terms.[113] For that matter, it may not be a mistake to regard this nostalgia as 'Amhara comeback'.[114] Actually, we cannot set apart this narrative from the contemporary mood of ideological war between competing political mythologies including political elites and their respective ethnic groups whom they claim to represent. On this ground, the claim of this narrative of objectivity and universality becomes rhetorical. This narrative makes subjectivity the basis for politics in the same way the other narratives, we examined in the previous chapter, do.

Moreover, apart from showing some concern over the blockage of social mobility, Messay's analysis overlooks important ethical issues in the history of the political culture of Ethiopia.[115] Above all, the question that whether these practices can be applicable in a global market economy simply goes unquestioned. Although the myth of social mobility, the Ethiopian notion of *idil*, is not a bad thing as such, the question is how critique is possible against a corrupted meritocratic system. Given the fact that there will always be people whose place in the social hierarchy is never commensurate with the merit they deserve; and that everyone does not start equal because of birth, migration, etc. which may create inequalities. Most importantly, if tradition and religion are evoked simply as something that liberate desire or motivation and something that controls personal greed but never as posing a serious challenge to materialism and institutional exploitation, then, the whole course of the subject's life becomes assimilated to *idil* as fate or

112 Cressida Marcus, "Imperial Nostalgia: Christian Restoration & Civic Decay in Gondar," in *Remapping Ethiopia: Socialism and After*, eds. Wendy James et al. (Oxford: James Currey, 2002), 239, 243.

113 In this context, therefore, 'The construction of churches and quasi-ecclesiastical buildings' is not simply an exclusively religious or pious devotion, but Marcus claims, 'is arguably more pertinent in terms of Amhara nationalism than the commanding castles or administrative buildings'. Hence, according to Marcus, what we see as a resurgence of tradition in the construction of churches is an attempt 'to recapture... [a] moral and ideological universe' and 'Christian activity can be understood to be a site of resistance'. See Marcus, "Imperial Nostalgia," 244.

114 Kostas Loukeris, "Contending Political Ideologies in Ethiopia: After 1991: The Role of Intellectuals," *Polis, Revue Camerounaise De Science Politique* 12 (Numero Special 2004 - 2005): 7.

115 The problem of rules of succession constitutes a positive thematic for Messay. He portrays the history of war in positive light. He argues this power struggle inhibited the development of a hereditary feudal aristocracy but fortunately in Ethiopia due to this absence Ethiopia is said to have remained an open society with a free social mobility.

fatalism.[116] In his desire to translate secular notions such as meritocracy and consensus society into the metaphysics of *idil* and the theological notion of covenant, unfortunately, Messay empties Christianity of its critical capacity.

Even though Messay seems critical of Ethiopia's authoritarian tradition (especially Haile-Selassie's), his model of the relation between society and the state still remains opaque. Given the history of Ethiopia's political culture, we note that there is a permanent trend of fusion between society and the state representing the general will in the name of, first, the myth of the chosen people, then the revolution, and now liberation. The state mobilises, guides and controls its subjects from a single centre. Such disposition, identified as *identikit* by Vaughan and also by Clapham (who calls it *encadrement*, see Chapter 4), to impose rules from above without a meaningful participation of baseline communities is an issue overlooked by Messay.[117] In fact, even for the kind of projection he propounds he greatly values the importance of a 'government' that might inject it to the society 'in a forceful manner'.[118] In fact, he explicitly praises authoritarianism as a *technique of the self* to nurture 'an achieving' spirit.[119]

5.5 Conclusion

By way of analysing the historical narratives of identity, against the historical background in which they emerged, I have been able to show how Ethiopia's past has become a 'contested terrain' and that these narratives exhibit 'a process of retrospective projection that defines the national self'.[120] The problem of ideologised or manipulated memory has become a challenge in such a contested situation. The narrative constructions are contending ethnicised or 'nationalised truths' producing their own subjects. In the political environment dominated by ethno-political imagination, as Triulzi has appropriately remarked, 'one fears

116 Its vision of a meritocratic society is less about tradition than a political project of liberalism, which is said to be opposed to the Revolutionary Democracy of incumbent party. To argue for a meritocratic society, it is not that important to re-enchant tradition. After all, what is unique about this Ethiopian value? Does it differ from the American dream?

117 Vaughan, "Ethnicity and Power in Ethiopia," 203. Cf. also SarahVaughan, "Responses to Ethnic Federalism in Ethiopia's Southern Region," in *Ethnic Federalism: The Ethiopian Experience in Comparative perspective*, ed. David Turton (Ohio: Ohio University Press, 2006), 187-188.

118 Messay Kebede, *Survival and Modernization*, 361.

119 Messay Kebede, *Survival and Modernization*, 263.

120 Sorenson, *Imagining Ethiopia*, 38.

that an ethnic over-reaction risks being self-damaging to the very cause it allegedly propounding'[121]. The contending modes of self-writing keep on fuelling or reinvigorating ethno-political imagination with its mechanism of ex/inclusion of neighbours either as friends or enemies.[122] As we already noted, despite Adhana's optimistic appraisal of the present post-1991 political dispensation as 'a brave new world', it can be regarded as *girrgirr* (war of all against all).

The contested past, according to Merera Gudina, characterises the ethnic (and non-ethnic) based political parties whose 'contradictory mobilization strategies have immensely contributed to the foundering of the struggle for democracy since 1991'.[123] According to him, it is because of such contradiction that 'the search for a common political vision' has been undermined.[124] What Merera, and many others, express is the public wish 'to move out of the present impasse: the abandoning of hegemonic aspirations and zero-sum game politics by the ruling elite and of extravagant claims to the right of secession by certain other elites'.[125] While lamenting over the decline of multi- or non-ethnic political parties in Ethiopia, Merera demonstrates the longing for transcending ethno-political imagination:

> [D]emocratizing multi-ethnic states need carefully constructed political structures and institutions which are able to mediate and accommodate diversities rather than *exacerbate differences*. To accomplish these tasks we need political leaders *who think and act bigger than their own ethnic groups* reach a national consensus, leading to a new 'social charter' for a New Ethiopia, where inter-elite competition is democratically regulated and ordinary citizens are empowered.[126]

Of all attempts to deal with the collective representation of society, Messay has shown a remarkable concern with what binds society. By demonstrating that Christianity was a source of cohesion, Messay argues that it (Christianity) should not be regarded as factional (ethnic; ideological) in nature. His account of what Ethiopian identity entails has an apologetic tone that nation-building by the dominant *ethnie* (Amhara) was not a project to annihilate or dissolve other

---

121 Triulzi, "Battling with the Past," 287.

122 Schlee and Shongolo, "Local war," 8.

123 Merera Gudina "Contradictory Interpretation," 128.

124 Merera Gudina "Contradictory Interpretation," 128.

125 Merera Gudina "Contradictory Interpretation," 129.

126 Merera Gudina "Contradictory Interpretation," 129. 'Despite some signs of the revival of multi-ethnic parties and the creation of new ones, ethnic-based political movements seem set to dominate the country's politics, in one way or another, for years to come'; see Merera Gudina "Contradictory Interpretation," 127.

ethnic groups but rather to unite them with a supra-ethnic consciousness. From this standpoint, Messay attempts to portray the nation-form in a positive manner. He concludes that there should be a need to revive and modernise it insofar an impersonal civic order evolves.

However, this narrative, which evinces a utopia from Ethiopia's historical past (a utopia of reconstruction), manifests the same logic when it comes to its conception of identity and politics. Even though Messay dissects the anatomy of past and contemporary melancholy in Ethiopian socio-political life, in order that we realise the reality and the pervasiveness of the alienation caused by the erosion of tradition, his failure to fully conceive the crisis of the nation-form is not adequate enough to take note of the ethnicisation of society (the production of fictive ethnicity). In the end, his proposed return to the source (re-enchantment of tradition) takes us back to the same fragilities of temporality and memory: to the war of memories, to a politics of settling scores, to a 'psychology of distrust'.[127] Thus, the hope of transcendence out of the ideological closure due to the identification of identity with politics is not to be found in this narrative, which simply whitewashes the past and overlooks the production of fictive ethnicity. Rather, this narrative brings us back to the dead-end.

Reflections on Part II

Since the history of a nation is always presented to us in the form of narrative, I began my analyses on Ethiopia by outlining the so-called the narrative of Greater Ethiopia. As we already noted, the main characteristic feature of this narrative is the legitimation of a single path of historical development – a singular history affirming a singularising or totalising project that I considered as a *dispositif*. In the discussion that followed, I further elaborated this standpoint by drawing attention to how the imaginary singularity of Ethiopia developed through the production of fictive Amhara ethnicity. We also looked at the nationalistic absorption of Christian identity.

And what we concluded from that discussion was that the production of fictive ethnicity was not only an open process fostering and shaping the understanding of national unity. It did also harbore, to some extent, a principle of closure (not along racial lines) effecting of social hierarchy and reproduction of socio-economic inequalities. Obviously, such analysis comes closer to the instrumentalist mode of thought at some points. However, despite the instrumentalist

127 Triulzi, "Battling with the Past," 285.

mode of thought that places ethnic sentience prior to the emergence of the nation-form and modern state apparatuses, I argue that it was after the production of fictive Amhara ethnicity that led to the emergence of *homo nationalis* (*homo Æthiopicus*).

Granted, the discourse on the 'nationalities' question was a legitimate counter-*dispositif* strategy to enact equality; I contend that the emphasis on the assertion of identity has led to the crisis of multi-ethnic politics. In Rancière's terms, this demonstrates 'impossible identification' (see Chapter 2 on the logic of subjectivisation). Such political failure consolidated by the practices of war, which is partly responsible for the present political scenario in which national self-determination has become the *raison d'être* of the state. What is at stake, here, is that difference was not conceived as the *topos* of an argument to enact equality but rather it was conceived simply in ethnic terms. In consequence, the ethnic category is given the place of determinacy – the single determining factor in political and structural arrangement – identification instead of disidentification (the crisis of the logic of heterology). Hence, instead of equality, (ethnic) identity is being asserted or enacted. It is this identification of politics with the identity of the (ethnic) community that has led contemporary Ethiopian politics to a dead-end.

As we have already examined, the contemporary practices of the self are not free of the opposed subjectivities and movements of images of hate or hostility between essentialised ethnic identities. The ethno-federal structure installed in post-1991 political dispensation did not tame ethno-nationalism. Rather, it resulted in consequences (that might not be intended by the state from the beginning) leading to reversal of decentralisation (while maintaining the outward form of decentralised federal structure). Such move will certainly create a tension in the relation between the centre and the regions hindering the political participation of the regions vis-à-vis the central government. In this case, we can recall the relation between the centre-periphery relations during the imperial regime in which the link was simply administrative without the political participation of the peripheries.

Now, the question becomes, is it possible to consider the contemporary political development under ethnic-federalism as the resolving of the old centre-periphery dialectic into a sort of centre-centre dialectic; or in a different idiom: can there be a balance between centripetal and centrifugal forces? From what we have discussed at the end of the fifth chapter, the current trend proves to head in the direction of greater centralisation (centralised federal structure) and the effect of such development does not only hamper the political participation of the regions (vis-à-vis the central government) but also the civil society at large. If we take what Foucault calls the practices of freedom to be the litmus test for any liberative vision or action, contemporary political developments are far from being liberating.

How is, then, the way out of this dead-end to be articulated? The way out of such impasse cannot be sought in the projection we briefly analysed in Chapter 5 – the trope of nativism. As I have already argued, such projection cannot take us beyond the stalemate since it shares the same ethnic logic (despite declared differences). The contention was that it lacks the sensitivity to the intervention of fictive ethnicity. Moreover, its vision of a meritocratic Ethiopian society is highly governed by pragmatic liberalism. The account of the emergence of *homo nationalis*, we examined in Chapter 4, also dovetails the formation of subjects as *homo religious*. The transcendent values of religion were reduced to systems-integration. Due to such nationalistic absorption, religion, without a self-criticism, cannot yield as a possible site for resisting ideological *dispositifs* that has captured Ethiopians at present. In the dispensation dominated by ethno-political ideology, the suspicion that Christian identity can be manipulated (instrumentalised) by politics (especially the old order or political paradigm) still lingers; thereby, depoliticising religion and marginalising its teachings (the theological). Even in the trope of nativism religion (i.e., Christianity) figures as an identity that should be secularised (being tamed and governed by impersonal institutions of the state) and its naturalisation is taken to be an asset significantly important for national life (i.e., Ethiopian nationalism) – inappropriately positioning the theological and emptying Christianity of its critical capacity (as I mentioned above).

As I have suggested in the Introduction, such understanding of religion (Christianity) is reductionistic. Christianity can neither be reduced to its functions, such as integrative aspects (social bond), nor to being an ideological intermediary. The arguments that will follow in the next part will make it clear that emancipatory vision is inherent in Christianity. It will be argued that the way out of the political impasse can be theologically articulated – a new culture of the self and the re-invention of politics. Such theological articulation will also re-position the theological that has been inappropriately positioned by secular social views. Prior to proceeding straight into the theological discourse, however, I wish to introduce or clear the ground for this theological turn.

Part III

Theo-political Imagination

Leaning on the work of the Russian philosopher-theologian, Sergie Bulgakov, I aim to articulate a political theology that addresses the Ethiopian context. Prior to the theological discourse, however, I wish to defend myself from a possible objection on my use of external sources (but whose contents are not completely foreign) to Ethiopia (Chapter 6). In the following chapter, I will clarify on my choice of the Russian theologian and the compatibility between Russian and Ethiopian Orthodoxies, which I succinctly justified in the Introduction to this book. Employing the three-fold (overlapping) theological task of cultural hermeneutics (self-criticism, critique and construction), I will pursue my argument in three stages.

First, I shall argue for a Christian account of agency as a protocol against Christian tendencies that do not avail for resistance against ethno-political ideology. This chapter, Chapter 7, will be more or less a theological self-criticism (of the Church). In Chapter 8, I shall argue for a distinct Christian ontology the aim of which is to counter the social ontology underpinned by ethno-political ideology. After such theological critique, in Chapter 9, I will announce the politics of metanoia as a political theology, which offers an account of an alternative social order.

6 Theological Introduction

Prior to undertaking the theological task, I wish to offer a brief explanation on my theological sources. The nature of the theological construct, which will be the focus of this part, is contextual in a double sense. First, it is contextual in the sense that it is a construct that aims to address the agenda presented by the analyses of the preceding part. Herein, what contextualises theology is the socio-political context. Second, it is contextual in that it displays considerable sensitivity to the worldview of the interlocutors, which the theological construct intends to address. It is in view of the latter that the question on the origin of sources becomes legitimate. Thus, in order to ensure the contextual posture of this theological work, its sources must have certain affinities with the local context (if not essentially be local).

In this case, I am confronted with a situation whereby there are rarely local theological works that can adequately and appropriately serve as sources for the kind of theological work I envision, here. Let me explain this briefly. Often political theology in Ethiopia seems synonymous with the myth of election (covenant), which is embodied in the document called the *Kebrä Nägäst*. We have already seen how Messay Kebede recently alluded to the significance of this myth albeit to whitewash the history of the involvement of the Ethiopian Orthodox Church in imperial politics. Reviving this myth would be tantamount to affirming Greater Ethiopian nationalism, which has been subjected to critique (see discussion in Part II, Chapter 4). A post-nationalistic political theology cannot be blind of the production of fictive ethnicity.

The Orientalist school in Ethiopian studies has generally focused on Ethiopian Orthodox Christianity and there is in fact little theological content in the works it has produced thus far.[1] The repression of religion and the exclusion of

1 For example, see Claude Sumner, *Ethiopian Philosophy* (Addis Ababa: University of Addis Ababa, 1974); Getachew Haile, *The Faith of the Unctionists in the Ethiopian Church* (Haymanot Masihawit) (Louvain, 1990); Donald Brake, *Historical Investigation of Monophysitism in the Ethiopian Orthdoox Chruch* (Ph.D. diss. Dallas: Dallas Theological Seminary, 1977); Mebratu Kiros Gebru, *Miaphysite Christology: An Ethiopian Perspective* (Gorgias Press, 2010).

theological studies from the university by the military socialist regime (since 1974) are also significant factors that explain the under-development of theological research. Whilst theological works on dogmatic or biblical issues pertinent to Christianity in Ethiopia are not lacking, few works attempt to address socio-political issues. Thus, what is available constitutes works that are either inappropriate (because they exhibit a socio-politically partisan tendency) or inadequate (because they are limited by ecclesiastical or confessional boundaries) to what I conceive as necessary for the task in hand. (We can refer to some of these materials later).

Although there are a large number of literatures on the topic of 'nation', 'state', and 'ecclesia', they have limited relevance to the Ethiopian situation. What has been said about the theories of nationhood must also be taken to apply to most theological literature on the topic. For example, we can refer to the most recent theological literature in relation to nationhood drawing upon the works of Karl Barth and Søren Kierkegaard, which offer a theological critique of state-nationalism and Christian nationalism.[2] However, analyses of contending ethno-national self-determinations and theological resources that can address such complexities are beyond the scopes of such works.

In view of this, the theological discourse of this part will draw upon non-local sources. Based on the considerations stated above, the theological work of Sergie Bulgakov[3] seems most appropriate for my task. Of course, as I have acknowledged, a legitimate question or possible objection can be raised. One could ask: 'to what extent can the theological construct be regarded as 'Ethiopian' (or appropriate to Ethiopia) while it draws from non-local sources?' Given the rise of anti-Eurocentric sensibility among some contemporary Ethiopian intellectuals,

2 Stephen Backhouse, "Nationalism and Patriotism," in *The Oxford Handbook of Theology and Modern European Thought*, eds. Nicholas Adams, George Pattison, Graham Ward (Oxford: Oxford University Press, 2013), 41-58. Carys Moseley, *Nations and Nationalism in the Theology of Karl Barth* (Oxford: Oxford University Press, 2013).

3 Bulgakov (1871-1944) was a political economist who turned from Marxism to Idealism. Though, he was born into a priestly family (6th generation), he abandoned his faith for Marxism during his young age. After his conversion, he was ordained as a priest. Following his expulsion from Russia by the command of Lenin, he was exiled in Paris where he served as the Dean of St Sergius Theological Seminary. Only some of his philosophical and theological works were first translated into French and later into English. In recent years, Bulgakov's popularity both in the West (as well as East) is increasing. See Rowan Williams, "Eastern Orthodox Theology," in *The Modern Theologians An Introduction to Christian Theology Since 1918*, ed. David F. Ford (Oxford: Blackwell Publishing, 2005), 572-578.

drawing upon external sources may easily be misunderstood as an instrument of intellectual colonialism (oftentimes expressed metaphorically as the 'Eucalyptus effect'[4] in local idiom). By highlighting the concerns expressed through this line of thinking and the possible dangers it harbours, I wish to offer a brief rationale in order to show that my preference is not simply arbitrary.

As we have already noted in the previous part, the development of anti-Eurocentric mode of thought among Ethiopian scholars relates to the contemporary shift from an 'acultural' to 'cultural' theories of modernity.[5] Such scholars are highly critical of the Eurocentric form of modernisation – modernisation as Westernisation – that Ethiopia is thought to have undergone since the regime of Haile-Selassie and the Euro-centric radical Marxist politics of Ethiopia's 'organic intelligentsia'[6] since the 1960s. While the concern for and sensitivity to the local context seems to have its inspiration from cultural theories of modernity, its proponents tend to express their views in a distinctly African post-colonial idiom (though unusual to Ethiopians who, historically, have displayed little identification with black Africa in racial terms). For example, echoing a prominent figure of Negritude, Aimé Césaire, Ethiopian scholars such as Teshale Tibebu and Messay Kebede have recently advanced the imperative: 'return to the source'.[7] The need to establish local knowledge appears to be reminiscent of ethno-philosophy.

In order to draw out the implications of this line of thinking for theology, let me briefly outline the concerns of ethno-philosophy and African theology, which are, in fact, offshoots of the movement of negritude.[8] In

4 Eucalyptus trees were first introduced to Ethiopia from Australia at the end of the 19th century to solve the problem of wood shortage but recently their benefit has been questioned because of their draining effect.

5 This is akin to multiple-modernities paradigm. The logic is that in order to develop 'traditional societies' must undergo 'modernisation', which is tantamount to eradicating traditional beliefs, customs, or values that impede modernity. Cf. for example, Charles Taylor, *Modern Social Imaginaries* (Duke University Press, 2005).

6 Teshale Tibebu, "Modernity, Eurocentricity," 345.

7 See Teshale Tibebu, 'Modernity, Eurocentricity," 345; Messay Kebede, "The Rehabilitation of Violence and the Violence of Rehabilitation: Fanon and Colonialism," *Journal of Black Studies* 31, 5 (May 2001): 540-541.

8 The negritude movement was initiated by three Africans - Césaire, Léopold Senghor and Léon Contran - studying at Sorbonne in Paris in the 1930s; see Bénézet Bujo, *African Theology in Its Social Context*, trans. John O'Donohou (Maryknoll, NY: Orbis Books, 1992), 50-56.

Africa, ethno-philosophy developed as an intellectual resistance to Eurocentrism.[9] For instance, Senghor argued that 'black people had a particular way of knowing, determined by their psychophysiology, which may be described as knowing by participation'. Furthermore, '[...] In contrast to Western ways of knowing, which, [...] analyzes the object, breaking it into pieces, so to speak, African cognition proceeded by embracing the object'.[10] The purpose of such an argument – that bases racial difference on epistemological difference – was to account for the technological backwardness of 'Africans' without agreeing upon their inferiority.[11] Indeed, this philosophy of black identity was a response to the thematic of 'civilisation' promoted by the legacy of the enlightenment and colonialism in light of which the black race was recognised as primitive.

The birth of black African theology is often associated with names such as Vincent Mulango and Tharcisse Tshibangu.[12] In the works of such scholars, the dominant theological discourse was that of Africanisation or the indigenisation of Christianity in Africa (but inculturation or incarnation was never mentioned at such early stage). The purpose of this theology was not only the indigenisation of Christianity but also a reactionary gesture meant to show the West how African culture is distinct, authentic and dignified. Recently, there has been much criticism that such theologians could never move 'beyond the theology of the negritude movement' to a form of constructive 'theological synthesis'.[13]

In response to this, among several others, John Mbiti and Bénézet Bujo have embarked upon constructive theologies. Especially, the latter has taken the theology of ancestors as the starting-point for his Christology (Christ as a proto-ancestor), which also lays the basis for an African ecclesiology.[14] In general, the inclination of African theology is towards the recognition of the African past not just as a 'chronological past' but rather as an 'ontological past' – implying that African Christianity and its theological task should be informed by African

---

9 Cf. J. O. Sodipo, "Some Philosophical Aspects of the African Historical Experience," in *African Philosophy*, ed. Claude Sumner (Addis Ababa: University of Addis Ababa, 1998), 346-354.

10 Kwasi Wiredu, "Introduction: African Philosophy in Our Time," in *A Companion to African Philosophy*, ed. Kwasi Wiredu (Oxford: Blackwell Publishing, 2004), 6.

11 Messay Kebede, "The Rehabilitation of Violence," 540-541.

12 Bujo, *African Theology*, 58-66.

13 Bujo, *African Theology*, 66.

14 Bujo, *African Theology*, 75-114.

culture.[15] There is now little interest and emphasis in themes such as inculturation, but contemporary African theology is being challenged to move beyond inculturation (to address liberation, for example).[16]

Similarly, the contemporary relevance of ethno-philosophy has been questioned recently. The main critique of the project of ethno-philosophy concerns its emphasis on the metaphysics of difference between Africa and the West (which also applies to African theology). For instance, Achille Mbembe argues that despite that 'the work of difference has performed important functions in the scholarly practice that sought to undercut imperial paradigms, it is clearly time, in the case of Africa, to revisit the frontiers of commonality'.[17] Mbembe also discusses problems in the discourse of Africanity in which Africanness becomes associated with blackness; hence, implicitly denying the possibility of 'multiple ancestry'.[18] Moreover, Africanity tends to be statically defined by its past experience (whether slavery or colonial).

Therefore, if any theological discourse in Ethiopia must be contextual, the following two caveats must be taken into account. First, any theological reckoning must consider the limits of the logic of difference and the concomitant project of rehabilitation or the re-enchantment of tradition for it can lead to a form of reverse racism/ethnicism. The second caveat can be seen as an extension of the first: that is, the emphasis on difference between the local (national) and the West can be a mere intellectual exercise to whitewash past injustice. In the case of Ethio-centricity there can be a danger of defining Ethiopianness by a fixed and limited set of values. To be more precise, the danger can be recourse to Ethiopianism, to fictive ethnicity; thereby, putting a distinction between the genuinely national and the falsely national.

---

15 Kwame Bediako, *Theology and Identity: The Impact of Culture upon Christian Thought in the Second Century and in Modern Africa* (Oxford: Regnum Books, 1999), 4.

16 Bujo, *African Theology*, 70-73. Bujo has attempted to develop a constructive theology and ethics (Palaver ethics) drawing upon an African notion of community; cf. Bénézet Bujo, *The Ethical Dimension of Community: The African Model and the Dialogue between North and South* (Nairobi: Paulines Publications Africa, 1997).

17 Mbembe and Nuttall, "Writing the World," 351. Achille Mbembe also remarks on the fact that Africa has not been able to develop a philosophic-theological meditation (on human suffering and wrongdoing in a single theoretical framework) that transgresses the boundaries of the divine and the human, which is comparable to German philosophy (from Luther to Heidegger) and Jewish Messianism. Mbembe argues against the inadequacy of ethnophilosophy; cf. "African Modes of Self-Writing," 239-240.

18 Mbembe, "African Modes of Self-Writing," 256.

With these caveats in mind, then, we can attend to some basic differences of worldview between Ethiopia and the West that needs to be taken into account when constructing a theology that is contextual. To quote from Messay Kebede, who draws attention to the difference in metaphysics between the two:

> While it is true to say that both forms of thinking [Western and Ethiopian] had in common the distinction between essence and appearance, divergent evolutions caused them to move apart. Especially after the Renaissance, Western thinking tended to recognize greater consistency to appearance, thereby generating a dualistic conception of being. [...] Be it the Cartesian notion of material substance and its mechanical movement or Kant's concept of phenomena, nature was increasingly conceived of as autonomous. As was foreseen by Aristotle, God became progressively the prime mover: One who sets the machine once and for all, after which the world functions by itself and according to fixed laws, which are the object of scientific knowledge. [...] The Ethiopian metaphysics never followed this course of thinking. It clung to distinction between essence and appearance and made no attempt to inject a bit of reality and autonomy into appearance.[19]

Although a very broad sketch, the above remark very roughly represents the conceptual difference between the West and Ethiopia.[20] According to Messay, the conception of nature as an autonomous and a self-sufficient field, or a notion of law-governed nature, which humans could make an object of knowledge, is lacking in Ethiopia. Rather, as Levine has pointed out, the Ethiopian 'has no drive to conquer or master over nature; he has no inclination to fuse or lose himself in nature; he has no need to keep nature in equilibrium through a system of rituals'.[21] As a matter of fact, 'there is no word for "nature" in his [Ethiopian's] vocabulary ... [N]or is there a sense that the things of nature have minds or laws of their own'[22]. Thus, unlike 'Western rationalism' that

---

19 Messay Kebede, *Survival and Modernization*, 186-187.

20 But here, when we compare the cultural differences stated above, we need to remember that such differences are deeply connected to religious traditions. Though what is represented as 'Ethiopian culture' is specifically relatesdto Christian Ethiopia (by way of generalisation), the other cultures are not profoundly different from this. The metaphysics of difference illustrated here must be conceived in terms of religious conceptions rather than race. And it should be noted that there have been thinkers in the West whose philosophies or theologies cannot fit in such a generalisation.

21 Levine, *Gold and Wax*, 66.

22 The immense labour invested to translate Marxist-Leninist terminologies into Amharic failed because some words such as 'Nature' could only be translated as 'creation'; Samuel Wolde-Yohannes, "The Vision of Man and Humanity," 96-97.

'represents the will to dominate'[23], the Ethiopian 'system of thought is "mystical" i.e. it tends to be in union with Nature and does not try to dominate Nature from outside.[24]

Levine claims that 'the Abyssinian clergy have tended to avoid systematic theology, believing that to probe too deeply into the nature of God verges on blasphemy' and thus, he concludes that 'Abyssinians view God above all as *mystery*'.[25] Here, unfortunately, Levine associates 'mystery' with 'ignorance' (a negative attitude towards knowledge). However, the notion 'mystery' links to what is known as the apophatic approach to theology in the Orthodox tradition. Apophatic or mystical theology, according Vladimir Lossky, is the notion that 'God no longer presents Himself as object, for it is no more a question of knowledge but of union'.[26] Such theology is also called 'negative theology': 'a way towards mystical union with God, whose nature remains incomprehensible to us'.[27] Nevertheless, this does not imply any prohibition on the pursuit of knowledge of God through any systematic-theological way. Lossky argues that the 'negative (apophatic) way attempts to know God not in what He is (that is to say, in relation to our experience as creatures) but in what He is not. [...] Thus, side by side with the negative way the positive way, "cataphatic," open out'.[28]

For this reason, the dominant attitude towards knowledge is that of 'participation' rather than 'pure' interest in theological knowledge as a matter of description and information. In its emphasis on the inseparability of knowledge and right living (or love), the Ethiopian monastic tradition is a strong witness to this fact.[29] In general, the characteristic feature of the dominant worldview that shapes religious and cultural life in Ethiopia is one that does not create a separation between the realms of nature and grace. The interplay or exchange between the supernatural and the natural is quite a familiar conception. Of course,

---

23 Leopold Sedar Senghor, *Liberté – Négritude et humanisme*, (Paris: Seuil, 1964), 84 cited in Claude Sumner, ed., *African Philosophy* (Addis Ababa: University of Addis Ababa, 1998), 319.

24 Messay Kebede, *Survival and Modernization*, 319.

25 Levine, *Wax and Gold*, 67.

26 Vladimir Lossky, *The Mystical Theology of the Eastern Church* (Cambridge: James Clarke, 1991), 28.

27 Lossky, *Mystical Theology*, 28.

28 Lossky, *Mystical Theology*, 32.

29 See John Meyendorff, *Imperial Unity and Christian Divisions: The Church 450-680 A.D.* (Crestwood, NY: St Vladimir's Seminary Press, 1989), 119.

Walther Plowden was correct when he remarked that Ethiopians 'imagine a special interference in every act of their lives'.[30]

Thus, it can be asserted that there is no absolute distinction, and complete conflation, between nature and grace; reason and revelation (in the theological sense) in the cultural realm of Ethiopia. Even in the rationalistic approaches of the 17th century Ethiopian philosophers such as Zar'a Ya'eqob whom Claude Sumner parallels with René Descartes reason never becomes a substitute for revelation.[31] As Sumner describes Zar'a Ya'eqob's approach in philosophy, he writes, 'Criticism is the initial condition of his method, division the occasion for his inquiry, and the *hatata* [treatise] its principle'.[32] Zar'a Ya'eqob's method of knowing God, as Teodros Kiros suggests, can more or less be defined as 'a discursive subjection of faith, any faith, to a critical examination by intelligence or natural reason'[33]; however, this does not imply that Zar'a Ya'eqob has no place for revelation. Rather, as Sumner argues, Zar'a Ya'eqob does not accept the self-sufficiency of reason for he upholds that 'reason is not complete without God's guidance'.[34] Even though Zar'a Ya'eqob argues that there are two kinds of law – God's law and human law, he never ascribes autonomy to the latter. Rather he grasps that human law is always insufficient and its deficiency needs to be completed by divine law. For humanity, divine law should always be the guide to right living and appropriate act. According to Zar'a Ya'eqob, the divorce of humanity from divine

---

30 Walther C. Plowden, *Travels in Abyssinia* (Westmead: Gregg International Publishers Limited, 1972), 91 cited in Messay Kebede, *Survival and Modernization*, 183.

31 See Sumner, *Ethiopian Philosophy*, 70-2, 104-111. Sumner's initiative has made it possible to have some works on Zar'a Ya'eqob in English but otherwise his (Zar'a Ya'eqob's) work has been analysed by Italian, French and German scholars; to mention but a few: Zera Yacob was born in Aksum in 1599 (in the northern part of present day Ethiopia). Zar'a Ya'eqob wrote his *Hatata* (Treatise) in 1667 in which he recorded his life and his thought. Sumner adds the following evaluative remark on Zera Yacob "the glow of an enlightenment in the shadows of the African past"; See *A Companion to African Philosophy*, ed. Kwasi Wiredu (Oxford: Blackwell Publishing, 2004),172. Zar'a Ya'eqob's work is judged as 'a real contribution to the history of human thought' (Enno Littmann (1909) "Geschichte der athiopischen literature," in *Geschichte der christlichen Literaturen des Orients*, vol. II (ed. Carl Brockelmann. Leipzig: C. F. Zmelangs Verlag), 202.

32 Sumner, "The Light and the Shadow: Zera Yacob and Walda Heywat: Two Ethiopian Philosophers of the Seventeenth Century," in *African Philosophy*, 176.

33 Teodros Kiros, "Zera Yacob and Ethiopian Traditional Philosophy," in *African Philosophy*, 183-184.

34 Claude Sumner, "The Light and the Shadow," 174.

truth will only result in the destruction of human souls and the corruption of moral fibre.[35]

Then, what are the implications of these dissimilarities in metaphysics for constructing political theology in Ethiopia? In passing, Messay Kebede spells out the significant implication of metaphysical differences for the theological conception of the distinction/relation between God and the world. He makes an interesting point that the Christological belief (the union of the two natures in Christ) of Orthodox Christianity, in Ethiopia, shows the 'rejection of metaphysical dualism' (of the West) and this, he continues, 'shows the sympathy of the Ethiopians for the conception advocating the utter dependence of the created world'.[36] Although brief, Messay's allusion to Christology in relation to the rejection of metaphysical dualism serves him to elucidate the historic relation of religion and politics, or rather Church and State.

By examining some of the differences between Ethiopian and Western metaphysics, we come much closer to the Eastern Orthodox perspective from which Bulgakov constructs his theological system. In point of fact, the attribution of metaphysical dualism between nature and grace (or reason and revelation) to the West is simply a crude generalisation. The important point in the recognition of difference – I emphasise – must be a discovery of commonality. What is interesting, here, is Messay's recognition of a problematic in theology: the problem of mediation. In the West, this problematic was profoundly examined by theologians such as Henri de Lubac and von Balthassar.[37] But, the Eastern Tradition had never conceived a gap between nature and grace or between reason and revelation without indorsing monism (more of this in the next chapter).[38] Particularly,

35 See Teodros Kiros, "Zera Yacob," 185. Sumner notes the influence of neo-Platonism upon Zera Yacob's and Ethiopia's philosophy in general; cf. "The Notion of the Human Being in Ethiopian Written Philosophy and in Oromo Wisdom Literature," in *Faith and Culture in Ethiopia*, 191.

36 Messay refers to the Christological position of the EOTC as 'monophysite'; see Messay Kebede, *Survival and Modernization*, 193. This conception of the relation/distinction between God and the world, according to Messay, is concomitant to the relation of Church and State after the model of Byzantine ('symphonic unity'); cf. Messay Kebede, *Survival and Modernization*, 71.

37 See John Milbank, *The Suspended Middle: Henri de Lubac and the Debate Concerning the Supernatural* (Grand Rapids, MI: Wm. Eerdmans, 2005).

38 Cf. John Milbank, "Sophiology and Theurgy: the New Theological Horizon," 1. Accessed 12 June 2012, http://www.theologyphilosophycentre.co.uk/papers/Milbank_SophiologyTheurgy.pdf Since they did not undergo through the series of events called 'the Reformation, Counter-Reformation, Enlightenment, Romanticism, Modernity',

thinkers such as Vladimir Soloviev and (later) Bulgakov developed a tradition of thinking on divine-human communion that addresses the issue of mediation. In this regard, the preference for Bulgakov clearly proves to be an advantage over Soloviev because the former developed (and corrected) the views of the latter.

Having concluded that there should be no disparity between the worldview embedded in the theological sources and that of the interlocutors, I have demonstrated how my preference of theological resources is compatible with the metaphysical outlook predominant in Ethiopia. But the recourse to the doctrine of Christology may raise another problem concerning the Christological position of the Ethiopian Orthodox Church, which is non-Chalcedonian. (Here, the question is not directed towards the Christological positions of Protestants or Catholics that are, Chalcedonian). Allow me to briefly show why this will not be a problem. Since it is known that the legacy of St Cyril of Alexandria has shaped the Christological position of the Orthodox Church in Ethiopia, let us take our cue from Cyril's Christology in order to understand the Ethiopian Orthodox Church's ambiguous Christological position.[39] Cyril's anti-Nestorian teachings were translated from Greek to *Ge'ez* and this version is preserved as *Qerellos*. The Cyrillian Christological formula, which was accepted by the Council of Ephesus in 431, emphasises the 'one [*Mia*] incarnate nature [*Physis*] of God the Word' (and according to this formula, divinity does not absorb but perfects the humanity of Christ).[40] Rather than negatively 'opposing the *physis* of the logos to the *physis* of manhood', as (later) in the Chalcedonian definition: 'one person in two natures', 'Cyril concentrates on a historical event that has occurred to the *physis* of the Godhead of the logos, namely that it has taken flesh (cf. Jn.1:14)' and hence, consequently he stresses the union of the divine and the human in Christ.[41]

During the 17th century, Christological debates in the context of Trinitarian controversies (the encounter with Catholic Jesuit mission certainly played a catalytic factor) led to factions.[42] The position, which abides by the Cyrillian for-

---

the Eastern Orthodox can easily 'thinking as a tradition'; see Aristotle Papanikolaou, "Orthodoxy, Post-Modernity, and Ecumenism: The Difference that Divine-Human Communion Makes," *Journal of Ecumenical Studies* 42, 4 (Fall 2007): 527.

39 José L. Bandrés and Ugo Zanetti, "Christology," in *Encyclopaedia Aethiopica*, ed. Siegbert Uhlig (Wiesbaden: Harrassowitz Verlag, 2003), 729.

40 See John Meyendorff, *Byzantine Theology: Historical Trends and Doctrinal Themes* (New York: Fordham University Press, 1974), 32-35.

41 Bandrés and Zanetti, "Christology," 729.

42 In the argument on whether one accepts the duality of natures in Christ or not, historically, these three views have been competing perspectives; see Getachew Haile,

mula, later known as the *tewahdo*, was taken as the position of the Ethiopian Orthodox Church since the Council of Boru Meda (1878), and consequently, the Church was recognised as the Ethiopian Orthodox *Tewahdo* Church (hereafter, EOTC).[43] Historically, the EOTC rejected the Council of Chalcedon on the one hand, and it anathematised Nestorius as well as Apollinarius and Eutyches, on the other hand.[44] This seems paradoxical (apparently contradictory) because how can the EOTC remain 'monophysite' while rejecting Eutychianism?

Recent theological works affirm that EOTC's Christology should be understood as 'miaphysite' rather than 'monophysite'.[45] According to Pope Shenouda III, miaphysite Christology is a mid-way between dyophysite and Monophysite Christologies.[46] At present, theological consultations and theological works tend to affirm that there are no major differences between the Eastern Orthodox (Chalcedonian) and Oriental Orthodox Churches apart from some terminological differences.[47] Although the anathemas (by both Churches) are not yet revoked; the most recent document of EOTC affirms the readiness for full communion.[48]

Generally, the concerns on both sides cannot create a gulf between them. From the Chalcedonian standpoint, the danger of 'monophysite' Christology is

---

The Faith of the Unctionists in the Ethiopian Church, ix cited in Bandrés and Zanetti, "Christology," 730; Tesfazghi Uqbit, *Current Christological Positions of Ethiopian Orthodox Theologians* (Roma: Ponitificium Insitutum Studiorum Orientalium, 1973), 88; Brake, *Monophysitism in the Ethiopian Orthdoox Chruch*, 153.

43 The Church rejects Eutyches, accepts Dioscorus, abides by the Cyrillian formula; see Aymro Wondmagegnehu and Motovu Joachim, *The Ethiopian Orthodox Church* (Addis Ababa: The Ethiopian Orthodox Mission, 1970), 96-100.

44 Nestorius emphasises the distinction between the two natures of Christ and his teaching was condemned as the heresy of dyophysitism in 431; the Christological formulae by Cyril helped to refute Nestorius' view (which spread in the Antiochene Church); later Eutyches' interpretation of Cyril's Christology was also condemned as the heresy of 'monophysitism', which confused the divine and the human natures of Christ (the absorption of the latter by the former); while Apollinarius held that there are two natures in Christ, he denied that Christ as man had a soul of his own; see Meyendorff, *Byzantine Theology*, 32-5, 94-5.

45 Mebratu Kiros, *Miaphysite Christology*, 77-98; also cf. Abba Hailemariam Melese Ayanew, "Influence of Cyrillian Christology in the Ethiopian Orthodox Anaphora," (Th.D. diss. University of South Africa, 2009), 224-253.

45 Cf. H. H. Pope Shenouda III, *The Nature of Christ* (St Mark Coptic Orthodox Church, 1999).

46 Mebratu Kiros, *Miaphysite Christology*, 102-6.

47 Bandrés and Zanetti, "Christology," 732.

48 See Aymro Wondmagegnehu, and Joachim, *Ethiopian Orthodox Church*, 95-98.

the total absorption or assimilation of Christ's human nature by his divine nature eventually leading to docetic understanding of the former. Contrary to this concern, however, the EOTC holds that 'neither of the natures was assimilated by the other' and the 'manhood of Christ was absolutely real and perfect'.[49] The other accusation against the union of the two natures is that monophysitism embraces the heresy of 'monothelitism' (one will). But again to the contrary, 'monophysites' (more appropriately, miaphysites) embrace 'miathelites' (that the two wills were united to one end without opposition), which is the same position as the Chalcedonian Churches.[50]

From the point of view of the non-Chalcedonians, the emphasis on unity of divinity and humanity in Christ is not 'a sign of monophysite tendency' but rather a concern with the soteriological implications.[51] As a matter of fact, 'the central issue' in the Christological debates, as John Meyendorff reminds us, 'was the ultimate fate of *man*'.[52] This is the reason for the high regard given to the pre-Chalcedonian Cyrillian legacy. The two consequences of this tradition are the conception of Mary as Theotokos and the conception of Christian salvation as divinisation (deification).[53]

What such debate indicates is the inadequacy of the Chalcedonian formula. This is also noted by Ethiopian Protestants (evangelicals, as they prefer to call themselves) who realise this inadequacy and attempt to understand the miaphysite position as different from the Chalcedonian position (but in effect affirming 'the perfect union of Christ's full deity and full humanity', which sounds perfectly Chalcedonian).[54] This position is akin to the position of 'Cyrillian Chalcedonians' who 'never admitted that there was a contradiction between Cyril and Chalcedon'.[55] In brief, such Christological issue is an open (never a closed) question and it is possible to think of new theological developments: *theologoumena*.

---

49 Aymro Wondmagegnehu, and Joachim, *Ethiopian Orthodox Church*, 95-98.

50 Meyendorff, *Byzantine Theology*, 36-37.

51 Bandrés and Zanetti, "Christology," 729.

52 Meyendorff, *Byzantine Theology*, 32.

53 Bandrés and Zanetti, "Christology," 729.

54 Steve Strauss, "Creeds, Confessions, and Global Theologizing: A Case Study in Comparative Christologies," in *Globalizing Theology: Belief and Practice in an Era of World Christianity* (eds. Craig Ott and Harold A. Netland. Grand Rapids, MI: Baker Academic, 2006), Ch. 6.

55 Strauss, "Creeds, Confessions," 34. It is only the strict interpretation of Eutyches that can be charged of "Cyrillian fundamentalism" (monophysitism); cf. Meyendorff, *Imperial Unity*, 192-193.

This does not imply a disclosure of new dogmas but the development of new lines of theological thinking through interpretation of the dogmas (Christology/Trinity) 'by applying to it the philosophical and theological categories of our present age'.[56] Bulgakov regards the two dogmas – Christology and Trinity – as significant for ecumenical dialogue and thus, the perspective I am going to draw from his work will not only be Orthodox but profoundly ecumenical.

In what follows, then, I wish to explain briefly how I am going to appropriate Bulgakov's work. In the following chapter, I shall start by examining Bulgakov's two-Sophias Christology that will lay the basis for an account of agency.[57] The main purpose of this discussion is to derive a theological anthropology from Bulgakov's Sophiology. In the subsequent chapter, I will argue for a distinct Christian social ontology based on Trinitarian theology. This will be important to address the question of difference, labour and peace/violence. After articulating a Christian anthropology, ontology and also ecclesiology, I will announce the politics of metanoia that reverberates a comprehensive questioning and transformation.

---

56 Sergie Bulgakov, *The Orthodox Church* (London: The Centenary Press, 1935), 119-120.

57 As we will see later, Bulgakov gives the name 'Sophia' (rather than using the abstract term *ousia*) as the self-manifestation of God. Sophia has its content the 'All' of the 'All-unity' of the Divine World, which is the pattern of 'multiplicity and unity in the created world'; see *Charles Lee Graves*, *The Holy Spirit in the Theology of Sergius Bulgakov* (Geneva: World Council of Churches, 1972), 8. James Pain and Nicolas Zernov, eds., *A Bulgakov Anthology* (Philadelphia: The Westminster Press, 1976), 144-156. As elaborated above the Ethiopian context is not unfamiliar to certain notions that will be raised by Bulgakov and 'extra-canonical texts' that do 'more justice to these Biblical elements than that which hitherto has passed for mainline orthodoxy' (such as for example, the Book of Enoch which exists in its Ethiopic version only expresses the messiah as wisdom); cf. John Milbank, "Sophiology and Theurgy," 5-6.

7 Divine-Humanity and Agency

7.1 Introduction

What is central to the following theological discussion is the same problematic articulated in the first two parts of this book; namely, the formation of the subject. The aim of this chapter is to provide a theological account of human *agency*[1], which counters the rival anthropological articulation by ethno-political ideology. To accomplish this, as announced in the Introduction, Christian theology must reject the negative social ontology and the practices of the self engendered by this rival ideology. As we may recall from the discussion of the previous part, the functionalist paradigm conflates Christianity (understanding it as a natural religion) with the social order (understood as a cohesive force); and the instrumentalist paradigm associates Christianity (and its practices) with the *status quo* and charges it as an 'intermediary' or 'ideological', which is a 'false' mediation of 'reality'.

This leads us to the consideration that such a counter-*dispositif* strategy, envisioned here, requires, first of all, a theological self-criticism. This implies that we need a theological account of a Christian *askesis*[2] that can correct tendencies within Christianity that cannot yield as possible 'sites' of resistance against ideological *dispositifs*.[3] Once this question on the discursive Christian practices

1 To be an agent or 'to act is fundamental to being political'; see Graham Ward, *The Politics of Discipleship: Becoming Postmaterial Citizens* (Grand Rapids, MI: Baker Academic, 2009), 181.

2 As we will observe later, Bulgakov's use of the term *askesis* can be understood in relation to both praxis (political/ethical activity/action) and *poiesis* (creative making/intentional action) and it resists any division between thought and action. For the elaboration of these terms; see Ward, *Cultural Transformation and Religious Practice*, 6-8 and Giorgio Agamben, "Poiesis and Praxis," in *The Man Without Content*, trans. Georgio Albert (Stanford: University of Stanford Press, 1999), 68-93.

3 This is not simply accepting the charges as 'true' and they, of course, misconstrue Christianity. Christianity allows self-criticism; however, I do not think it important that one should whitewash Christianity of its past failures before Christian theology suggests a liberating vision. See, for example, Kathryn Tanner, *The Politics of God: Christian Theologies and Social Justice* (Minneapolis: Fortress Press, 1992), 35-74.

is satisfactorily answered, then the way will be clear for the more constructive proposals of the next two chapters.

In this chapter, I will contend that Bulgakov's theological articulation of divine-humanity (a differentiated-unity of Christology) can inform Christian *askesis* that paves the way for a liberating politics. Since Christian theology deals with the transcendental (i.e. a reality with a metaphysical hierarchy), the operation of Christian *askesis* requires a principle of mediation. The discussion on Bulgakov's 'Two-Sophias Christology'[4] aims at providing an account of cosmic-mediation as a protocol against monism (cosmism) and deism (a-cosmism) (7.2). Then, I shall discuss the political significance of Christ's incarnation, which is both 'event' and 'task', to Christian *askesis* (7.3) before the conclusion of the discussion in 7.4.

7.2 Two-Sophias Christology and Cosmic-mediation

The recognition of the necessity for a certain mediating principle can be traced back to the time of Philo.[5] In search of a unifying principle between the two, theologians such as Tertullian, Origen, and later on, Arius, ended up in articulating a Christology of 'subordinationism': thereby, establishing a Trinitarian heresy.[6] Bulgakov acknowledges the necessity of a unifying principle. Recognising that this question remained unsolved during the Arian controversy and the Christological debates, he argues that the mediating principle should not 'be sought in the Person of God at all, but in his Nature', and more precisely, in the divine-human union: Godmanhood.[7] And Bulgakov insists that it is only divine-humanity that can safeguard Christianity against the dangers of monism, which conflates God and the world, and deism, which creates an 'impassable gulf'.[8]

The Problem of Divine-Human Unity and Chalcedon

According to Bulgakov, among the early Church Fathers, the first theologian who identified the problem of the unity of both natures in Christ, the God-Man,

4 I borrowed this descriptive terminology from Brandon Gallaher, "The Christological Focus of Vladimir Solovi'ev's Sophiology," *Modern Theology* 25 (4 October 2009): 634.

5 Sergius Bulgakov, *The Wisdom of God: A Brief Summary of Sophiology* (London: Williams and Norgate, 1937), 112.

6 Bulgakov, *The Wisdom of God*, 112.

7 Bulgakov, *The Wisdom of God*, 112. Hereafter, instead of 'Godmanhood', I will use the term 'divine-humanity' - a term Boris Jakim, Bulgakov's prominent translator, prefers.

8 Bulgakov, "The Wisdom of God," in *A Bulgakov Anthology* (eds. James Pain and Nicolas Zernov. Philadelphia: The Westminster Press, 1976), 150.

was Apollinarius.[9] For Apollinarius, as for the theologians of Chalcedon, the basic axiom applied to the propositions on Christology (the Incarnation) was that 'two perfect (complete) principles cannot become one'.[10] Based on such an axiom, then, Apollinarius understood the question of the unity of the two essences – divine and human – in the person of Christ as an anthropological problem (since human nature is changeable, it cannot be trusted for our salvation). To solve the quandary, Apollinarius argued that the human nature, which is 'changeable (*treptos*)' (its changeability is due to the freedom proper to it), must be absorbed into the divine nature 'unchangeable (*atreptos*).[11] Bulgakov remarks that the rejection of human nature or the devaluation of 'the *human* feat of Christ' characterises the weak point in Apollinarius's Christology, which gave rise to monophysitism and a mechanical conception of salvation (*deux ex machina*).[12]

Apollinarian Christology, Bulgakov notes, marks the beginning of a 'dialectical' Christology between two Christological positions that eventually culminated in the Chalcedonian synthesis.[13] The first position or the thesis belongs to the Alexandrians, which was represented by St. Cyril (later in monophysitism, one-nature Christology and monothelitism, one will in Christ): '*the unity* of the God-Man' in Christology.[14] The second position, the antithesis, which was

---

9 Sergius Bulgakov, *The Lamb of God*, trans. Boris Jakim (Grand Rapids, MI: Wm. B. Eerdmans, 2008), 2-18.

10 Bulgakov, *The Lamb of God*, 5.

11 Bulgakov, *The Lamb of God*, 5.

12 Bulgakov, *The Lamb of God*, 281. Of course, as Bulgakov notes, Apollinarius's view concerning the correspondence of the '*pneuma* or *nous*' to 'the divine hypostasis, which is inseparably united with the divine nature' is an aspect that has been misunderstood; see Bulgakov, *The Lamb of God*, 11.

13 Bulgakov, *The Lamb of God*, 19.

14 Cyrillian Christology, according to Bulgakov, formally rejects Apollinarianism, but it neither 'inwardly' overcomes Apollinarianism nor develops 'the postulate of *unity* in Christology' further beyond Apollinarianism; Bulgakov, *The Lamb of God*, 21-25. St. Cyril insisted upon the 'the truth of the unchangeability of Divinity in the Incarnation', arguing that 'the Word was united with the flesh *unfathomably and ineffably and only He knows how*', however, his opponents were unwilling 'to accept this antinomy clothed in apophatics'; Bulgakov, *The Lamb of God*, 25. To St. Cyril, 'Christ is one of two natures [...] the two natures before Incarnation are opposed there to the unity after Incarnation' and accordingly the duality of Christ can only be discerned in 'contemplation'; thus, St. Cyril exhibits a resonance to the unity of the two natures but his Christology remains questioned on grounds of whether the human freedom is preserved in Christ. See Bulgakov, *The Lamb of God*, 26.

represented by the Antiochene Christology of Diodore of Tarsus, Theodore of Mopseustia, Theodoret, Nestorius, the dithelites, and the adoptionists: '*the duality of the natures in the God-Man*'.[15] As we shall see later, the dogmatic formulations of the fourth and the sixth ecumenical councils proved the inadequacy or the 'one-sidedness' of both positions and that they could express 'the truth of the Church' only in 'the dialectical whole'.[16]

Finally, by 'suppressing' the excesses of the two positions, the council of Chalcedon synthesised the two: the thesis of the unity of Christology and the antithesis of the bi-unity of Christology. However, Bulgakov argues that what Chalcedon accomplished was merely a dogmatic resolution, which provided a 'principle of equilibrium', while the theological synthesis remained incomplete. What we find in the Chalcedonian definition on the two natures in Christ, according to Bulgakov, is a series of negatives: '*without* separation, *without* confusion, *without* change, *without* division', which spell out the 'no' of Chalcedon but not the 'yes'.[17] For example, 'without separation' excludes '*total* separation' and 'without confusion' eliminates '*total* fusion' but the positive interrelation remains unelaborated and for this reason, he argues that the Chalcedonian definition can only be understood as 'a *preliminary* definition' but never as a '*prohibition*' against 'positive definitions'.[18]

Bulgakov remarks that further theological developments after Chalcedon, even the sixth ecumenical council on 'the two wills and energies', could simply expound the negative definition of Chalcedon but did not offer any positive elaboration of the dogma.[19] A valuable clue for the elaboration of the dogma in post-Chalcedonian theology is that of the theology of Leontius of Byzantium who explains the Manhood of the God-man as 'enhypostatic' in the Word – that is, 'the divine person of the Word became that of a human nature as well'.[20] But still this elaboration leaves an important question unanswered: What metaphysical ground provides the condition for the possibility for the Word to become

15 Bulgakov, *The Lamb of God*, 18-19. Nestorius, indeed, recognised an important issue that remained unanswered by patristic theology: his 'Christology thus exhibited a *dialectically* important aspect of the fundamental Christological antinomy: he attempted to understand the bi-unity as a unity not of natures possible without personal centers, and how the union of the natures in the form of the union of these centers possible in the case of the full reality of each of them?'; see Bulgakov, *The Lamb of God*, 46.

16 Bulgakov, *The Lamb of God*, 19.

17 Bulgakov, *The Lamb of God*, 194. Italics added.

18 Bulgakov, *The Lamb of God*, 195-6. Italics in the original.

19 Bulgakov, *The Lamb of God*, 195.

20 Bulgakov, *The Wisdom of God*, 128.

human? Briefly, the notion of enhypostatisation or in-hypostatization poses the ontological challenge in a manner that defines what the conditions for the Incarnation have to be, which Bulgakov presents as follows:

> insofar as it hypostatizes the human nature, the hypostasis of the Logos is, in a special sense, a human hypostasis too, that is proper not only to God but also to Man, that is, to the God-Man. In order to be a human hypostasis, the hypostasis of the Logos must be human or, more precisely, *co-human*; and for this reason the hypostatization of man's nature by this hypostasis does not destroy or coerce it but corresponds to a primordial interrelation between the two. On the other hand, man must also be capable of *receiving* and *encompassing* within himself, in the capacity of the human hypostasis, the divine hypostasis. In other words, by his initial essence man must already be divine-human in this sense; he must bear hypostatic divine-humanity within himself and represent, in this capacity, an ontological "site" for the hypostasis of the Logos.[21]

Then, how can the above condition – that the Logos, in order to assume human nature, must, originally, be akin to humanity and that human nature, in order to unite with the divine nature, must have the capacity to receive divine nature – be fulfilled? What Bulgakov regards as a hope 'future Christology' was kindled by a single term/concept: 'theandric energy' (theandric means divine-human) contained in a letter from pseudo-Dionysius to Gaius.[22] It is this idea, which received only a partial application in the notion of 'the "communication of properties" (*perichoresis, communicatio idiomatum*)'[23], which provides the insight for Bulgakov to artiuclate

---

21 Bulgakov, *The Lamb of God*, 186; here, it should also be noted that *enhypostasis* unlike the negative notion of *anhypostasis* presupposes commensurability between the human and the divine and hence, defines a theological anthropology of relationality; for debates on *anhypostasis- enhypostasis*, see Graham Ward, *Christ and Culture* (Oxford: Blackwell, 2005), 7-12; F. LeRon Schults, *Reforming Theological Anthropology: After the Philosophical Turn to Relationality* (Grand Rapidds, Mich.: Eerdmans, 2003), 147-50.

22 St. John of Damascus received this term as 'an indispensable and self-evident doctrine' and he devotes a paragraph in his book 3 of *Critical Exposition of the Orthodox Faith*; see Bulgakov, *The Lamb of God*, 209.

23 Bulgakov, *The Lamb of God*, 248. The two terms seem to be at odds because the former term is now commonly used in Trinitarian theology rather than Christology. Bulgakov does not offer an explanation for this, but the scholar of patristics, G.L. Prestige argues that 'contrary to what is frequently stated, it [*perichoresis*] did not historically belong to all the trinitarian cycle of ideas at all. Its only theological use, until pseudo-Cyril, was Christological and it meant, until pseudo-Cyril, something quite different from co-inherence' but as 'encircling or encompassing' or 'interchange' understood as 'reciprocity of action' very close to the communication of properties ('*communicatio idiomatum*'); G.L. Prestige, *God in Patristic Thought* (London: SPCK, 1952), 291. For a recent discussion on the usage of *perichoresis* for Christology and

the positive interrelation between the two natures. For Bulgakov, the theological implications of this concept – 'theandrism' – for Christology is immense for the reason that it conjoins the two fundamental conditions in Christology: on the one hand, the hypostasis of the Logos must be compatible to human nature, and on the other, the human must have the ontological capability to receive the divine hypostasis.

The Sophianicity of the Divine and the Human

Based on the idea of theandrism, Bulgakov conceives a 'primordial identity' or inner commensurability between the two natures: the Divine I of the Logos and the human I (yet, without denying differences).[24] Here, Bulgakov employs a tripartite anthropology that 'man' 'consists of an uncreated, divine spirit, hypostatized by a creaturely I, and of a created soul and body' and the spirit is 'a spark of Divinity that is endowed by God with a creaturely – hypostatic face in the image of the Logos and, through Him, in the image of the entire Holy Trinity, insofar as the trihypostatic Face can be reflected in the creaturely consciousness of self'.[25]

Bulgakov further elaborates the relation between the two natures in light of the two variants of Wisdom (Sophia): Divine Sophia and created Sophia, in which case, 'manhood' is conceived as 'the created form of divine Wisdom, which is simply God's nature revealing itself'.[26] Man, according to Bulgakov, contains the 'creaturely Sophia'; hence, he is a 'sophianic being' (and he is the 'sophianic hypostasis of the world') and this 'creaturely hypostasis' is already 'supernatural'.[27] Therefore, man has the ontological capability for hypostatization by the divine Logos.

Without such identity, he insists, we cannot speak of the '*in-humanization* of God' or the 'in-hypostatization of the Logos' for this depends on the idea that the hypostasis of the Logos becomes the 'proper hypostasis' also of human nature.[28]

---

the relation between '*perichoresis*'and '*communicatio idiomatum*', cf. Oliver D. Crisp, "Problem with Perichoresis," *Tyndale Bulletin* 56, 1 (2005): 119-40.

24 Bulgakov, *The Lamb of God*, 186.

25 Bulgakov, *The Lamb of God*, 186.

26 Bulgakov, *The Wisdom of God*, 132. The doctrine of Sophia will be explained in the next chapter that deals with the Trinitarian ontology. But at this juncture, I simply want to remind that Bulgakov's use of Sophia in place of the Greek abstract term *ousia*, as the principle of God's self-revelation and consubstantiality, should not suggest that it is a fourth hypostasis. It has only the capacity for 'hypostasiety'. Cf. Bulgakov, *The Lamb of God*, 89-156.

27 Bulgakov, *The Lamb of God*, 188.

28 Bulgakov, *The Lamb of God*, 185.

On this basis, Bulgakov insists that 'from all eternity the person of the Word was somehow human' and due to his 'becoming the person of the created human nature' elevated the human nature without destroying it'.[29] The relation that unites this identity is like a relation of 'image to the Proto-Image' and the difference – between 'eternity and temporality, between the creator and creation'.[30] This 'original analogy', for Bulgakov, is congruent with Apostle Paul's anthropological view that draws a parallel between the 'first man' who is 'of the earth, earthy' and the 'second man' who is 'the Lord from heaven' (cf. 1 Cor. 15:47-49).[31] Thus, Bulgakov argues that, in light of sophiology (two Sophias), what appears to the 'rationalist' a 'metaphysical absurdity' turns to be a metaphysical possibility.[32]

The sophianicity of human nature remains 'ontologically indestructible' and sin (or the original sin) could only deprive him of the fullness of the sophianic nature: '[T]his state [sin] makes him subject to the elements of the world, which appears before him not as Sophia but only as *natura* (which is to become itself, to engender itself) or as the elementally chaotic Achamoth'.[33] Due to sin, the world became 'asophianic and even partly antisophianic in the mode of its being'.[34] Nevertheless, Bulgakov asserts, the assumption of the human nature by the second Adam did not include sin and hence, it was 'so adequate to its divine Prototype'.[35]

Therefore the mediating principle that unites the two natures, divine and human, uncreated and created, for Bulgakov, lies in the '*sophianicity* of both the Divine world (i.e., of Christ's divine nature) and of the creaturely world (i.e., of His human nature)'.[36] Sophia is on both sides – on the two poles of divinity and humanity simultaneously. The relation of identity between the two Sophias (Divine and creaturely) is like the relationship that exists between that of image to its Proto-Image. The latter, as a creaturely becoming being, has to 'become itself' – that is 'become identified with its Proto-Image' and achieve 'the fullness of its sophianization or deification'.[37]

Sophia is also the principle of mediation between the Godhead and humanity: '[T]he Logos is the demiurgic hypostasis whose face is imprinted in the Divine

29 Bulgakov, *The Wisdom of God*, 130-1.
30 Bulgakov, *The Lamb of God*, 186.
31 Bulgakov, *The Wisdom of God*, 115, 130.
32 Bulgakov, *The Wisdom of God*, 133.
33 Bulgakov, *The Lamb of God*, 187.
34 Bulgakov, *The Lamb of God*, 199.
35 Bulgakov, *The Wisdom of God*, 133.
36 Bulgakov, *The Lamb of God*, 197.
37 Bulgakov, *The Lamb of God*, 197.

world, as in the Divine Sophia, by the self-revelation of Divinity through the Logos'.[38] In such schema, the Logos is the second Person of the Trinity as well as the 'pre-eternal God-Man as the Proto-Image': 'Sophia is also the heavenly humanity as the proto-image of the creaturely humanity; inasmuch as she is eternally hypostatized in the Logos, she is His pre-eternal Divine-Humanity' and the creaturely world is created on the basis of the proto-images of the Divine world as the creaturely image of Divine Sophia in her becoming, but this Divine Sophia is the divine nature of the Logos.

Double Kenosis

Given the fact that analogical relation established between the two natures is based on the ontological commensurability of the two natures and that these natures are different in their modes of being, then, how can we give account of the unity of life in the God-Man? Bulgakov finds the answer in the doctrine of kenosis. He argues that a full understanding of *communicatio idiomatum*, which patristic theology partially understood, entails accepting a double kenosis of the two natures: the self-renouncement of both the divine and human.[39] On the one hand, the Logos descends into the world (renouncing his glory) so that it re-unites humanity with God while, on the other, the human will of Christ submits itself to the divine will in order to ascend (by participation in the divine).[40] This implies,

---

38 Bulgakov, *The Lamb of God*, 187. Sophia is both what safeguards the consubstantiality of the Logos with the Godhead: 'The hypostasis of the Logos is *directly* connected with Sophia. In this sense the Logos *is* Sophia as the self-revelation of Divinity; He is her direct (although not sole) hypostasis. The Logos is Sophia in the sense that He *has* Sophia as His proper content and life, for in Divinity, Sophia is not only the totality of ideal and nonliving images but also the organism of living and intelligent essences that manifest in themselves the life of Divinity'; Bulgakov, *The Lamb of God*, 187.

39 While a proper/full understanding entails understanding the influence as working both ways, patristic theology knows only the kenosis of the divine nature.

40 Though kenotic ideas exist in the works of Vladimir Soloviev, Fiodor Dostoevskii, Nikolai Berdiaev and Pavel Florenskii, by contrast, Bulgakov's theory of kenosis is quite comprehensive; cf. Paul L. Gavrilyuk, "The kenotic theology of Sergius Bulgakov," *Scottish Journal of Theology* 58, 3 (2005): 252-254. His view is neither kenotic minimalism nor kenotic radicalism. Unlike the views of the former, he does not relegate the kenosis to a particular event such as death on the cross momentary. In contrast to the latter, he argues that the Son of God did not abandon his divinity but only his glory (until his resurrection). Bulgakov understands the kenosis as a continuous 'uninterrupted self-emptying'; see Gavrilyuk, "kenotic theology," 260.

> an immeasurable difference certainly exists between creaturely man, who knows the divine principle only as a gift and a task to be accomplished, and the God-Man, who has this divine life as His proper nature and human becoming as the work of salvific love and self-humiliation. That which in man is always as ascent is, in the God-Man, only a divine condescension. The union of the two natures in Christ is therefore not only an abstract dogmatic schema but also a truth of life that we receive on the pathways of our religious experience.[41]

The notion of double kenosis is significant to understand the whole life and ministry of Jesus Christ: the 'hunger and thirst, exhaustion, grief, temptation, and death on the cross' were not docetic dramas but the test of the double kenosis.[42] Since Christ's kenosis was true kenosis, his knowing, as we observe in his earthly ministry, was limited to and could not surpass the knowledge of his human nature. The instances of knowledge of the future were not due to the exercise of his omniscience but his prophetic ministry (through yielding to the Spirit). For Bulgakov, Gethsemane is as significant as Gologotha because it is in the former that the struggle between the two wills reached the climax and a real 'metaphysical' kenosis happened. The kenosis of the Son, according to Bulgakov, involved the whole Trinity (an insight anticipating the work of Jürgen Moltmann *The Crucified God* [1993]; of course, an insight already in Hegel).[43]

As divine-human, Christ fulfilled his prophetic, high priestly and royal works. Bulgakov discusses how Christ, through his infinite sacrifice, restored humanity back to God and he conquered forces of evil.[44] Christ's royal work now continues through the Church's task that prepares the world for the kingdom of God. This task is a task of realising divine-humanity in the world. The unity will continue to be 'realized in the progressive penetration of the world by Wisdom, bringing it gradually into conformity with its prototype in Wisdom'.[45]

What can be concluded from this theological discussion can now be lucidly summarised. First, the world must not be conceived deistically without any interaction with God. It should not be understood as monistic in which case the two are conflated. Rather, the differentiated unity of Christology has furnished us with analogy to conceive ontological commensurability between the divine and the human. Thus, in light of this, an appropriate disposition is neither a-cosmism (a world-denying attitude) nor cosmism (an uncritical world-affirming

41 Bulgakov, *The Lamb of God*, 198.
42 Gavrilyuk, "kenotic theology," 260.
43 Gavrilyuk, "kenotic theology," 263-264.
44 Bulgakov, *The Lamb of God*, 343-378.
45 Bulgakov, *The Wisdom of God*, 143-144.

tendency) but divine-human theo-cosmism (a struggle against the world for the world).[46] The principle of cosmic-mediation has provided the necessary theological ground for the possibility of an appropriate Christian *askesis*. The two interrelated notions – the sophianic and the kenotic – are important notions that help Bulgakov to understand the Christ Event (by resolving the problem of the two natures and wills in Christ) but they have great significance to understand Christian *askesis* in history. History is, according to Bulgakov, 'a further unfolding of the Chalcedonian and ditheletic dogma'.[47] Put differently, 'what was accomplished in Christ was pre-accomplished for the whole of humankind'.[48]

7.3 The Event as Task: A Metanoic Re-turn to the Event

In Bulgakov's view, the realisation of divine-humanity is a common task given to humankind: 'The Kingdom of God has to be won by common work, the creative effort of mankind as well as the creative work of God'.[49] The synergy between the divinity and humanity is a key concept for Bulgakov not only in the conceptualising of the Incarnation but also in history between the 'already here' and the 'not yet' of the Kingdom of God. The Incarnational Event is turned into a task for humanity and human history becomes a demonstration of the further unfolding of the Event. The subject, for Bulgakov, is one engaged in 'transforming action'[50] in order to 'make sense of the world' ('not simply to interpret it') and 'to make new and orderly patterns within it'.[51]

In contrast to theories of knowledge such as that of Hegel and Kant, who abstract the subject 'primarily' as a 'subject of *knowledge*', he argues that the concrete subject is an 'agent involved in labour'.[52] For Bulgakov, knowledge must be conceived as '*labour*' and as 'willed and active engagement in changing the world', thus, the subject is an acting subject who acts and whose actions cannot be understood as outside of relations.[53] For Bulgakov, it is humanity in its

46 Bulgakov, *The Wisdom of God*, 152.

47 Sergius Bulgakov, *The Bride of the Lamb*, trans. Boris Jakim (Edinburgh: T & T Clark, 2002), 332.

48 Bulgakov, *The Bride of the Lamb*, 332.

49 Sergii Bulgakov, "Social Teaching in Modern Russian Orthodox Theology," Williams, *Sergii Bulgakov*, 285.

50 Sergii Bulgakov, "The Unfading Light," Williams, *Sergii Bulgakov: Towards a Russian Political Theology*, 121.

51 Bulgakov, "The Unfading Light," 122.

52 Bulgakov, "The Unfading Light," 121.

53 Bulgakov, "The Unfading Light," 122.

multiplicity that constitutes as the subject of human history.[54] The antinomy of the 'many' hypostases and the 'one' human nature, for Bulgakov, is an important aspect of his sophiology. This antinomy of multiplicity and unity implies the mystic unity of all humans in the first Adam and through the second Adam in the body of Christ. (This point will be further elaborated in the next chapter).

The operation of Christian *askesis* requires the abiding by the principle of relationality whether vertical (toward God) or horizontal (toward the world). A crisis in action or agency entails a crisis in politics or ethics in general. In this regard, Bulgakov rightly recognises the historical link between the failure of Christianity to develop its own humanism and the rise of secular humanistic ideologies (such as Marxism): '[The] acceptance of the world by humanism was a reaction against its non-acceptance [by the Church], which only left it a right to natural existence'.[55] The Church's attitude to the world was a conservative and an ascetic one and in view of this, the Marxist charge that religion is simply a false intermediary or the 'opiate of the people', according to Bulgakov, was a reaction against this 'social nihilism'.[56] The result of such rejection of the world led to the 'secularisation of life' by secular humanistic ideologies (Marxist as well as Liberal). This secularisation implies neither the separation of the Church from the state, which is arguably for the benefit of the former, nor the 'nullification of religion'.[57] Rather, it refers to the 'negation of Christianity' (of its distinctive values and practices).[58]

---

54 Bulgakov, *The Bride of the Lamb*, 316. History, understood from this ground, constitutes a whole and particularly that individuals, though they act independently, contribute to and understand human history in fragments. It is the whole of humanity that is the subject of history.

55 Bulgakov, "The Wisdom of God," 152.

56 Bulgakov, "Social Teaching", 163-164. In his essay on the social teaching of the modern Russian Orthodox Church, Bulgakov opens up his discussion by making allusion to the acquiescence of the Russian Orthodox Church in the face of serfdom in the context of a backward agricultural economy. Despite the debate whether 'serfdom' was a characteristic feature of Ethiopian socio-economic system prior to the socialist revolution of 1974, the parallels with the Ethiopian situation are striking. This is true, especially, with regard to the ascetic and conservative attitude of the Church to social relations. In both cases, the consequence of such ascetic 'worldview' or 'Christian sociology' was the legitimisation of the *status quo*.

57 Bulgakov, "Social Teaching," 165. (He also employs terms such as 'mechanization' and 'paganization' [of life] alternatively in the place of 'secularisation)

58 Bulgakov, "The Wisdom of God," 151. In view of this, Bulgakov develops Christian humanism as the answer to secular humanism, which is the question (as for example,

Bulgakov argues that we need an orthodox and radical Christian *askesis* in relation to the world to overcome the secularisation of life and fulfil the historical task. And such agency is not simply to supplement for a secular political action (e.g. revolutionary praxis) as if the former is 'without a dogma of its own' (if its use is reduced to providing a motivation for secular political action only).[59] Bulgakov recognises this as the danger of 'applying' Christianity: political theology serving as a backup to secular order. He borrows Archbishop Söderblom's phrase 'Nicaea of ethics' to describe such an approach of accommodation, which cannot suffice for a true Christian *askesis*.[60] Bulgakov argues that Christian theology is not expected to write a form of Nicean Creed to secular ethics but rather ethics should be subsumed by the Church: 'Social life is to be organized according to the postulates of Christian love, so also the whole of political life'.[61] If political theology is desired to have a critical edge, then, this mode of understanding is crucial.

Bulgakov understands time as founded in and heading towards eternity. History, for him, is not a 'bad infinity' or a 'negative eternity'.[62] History has a beginning in creation and an ending in eschatology. It is confined within the boundaries of time but it does not refer to the past only. Rather it includes the present as well as the future. For Bulgakov, time is intelligible only from the perspective of eternity because time is 'eternity extended into being' and in this sense eternity is not something subsequent to time. Human individuals 'have their basis in supra-temporal existence' and hence, they 'become tasks for time'. For this reason, '[H]istory is a certain state of becoming being that is included in being in a definite way: an additional creation of the world within itself, as it were'.[63] In other words, history, while it remains open to eschatology, is a potentiality that seeks full realisation/actualisation. Thus, eschatology is conceived by Bulgakov as 'transfigured history' – a conception, which is different from secular notions of linear time (history as progress) that Bulgakov strongly criticises.[64]

---

the Nicene Creed was the answer of the Church to the question called Arianism); Bulgakov, "The Wisdom of God," 165.

59 Bulgakov, "The Wisdom of God," 151-152.

60 Bulgakov, "The Wisdom of God," 151.

61 Bulgakov, "Social Teaching," 165.

62 Bulgakov, *The Bride of the Lamb*, 315.

63 Bulgakov, *The Bride of the Lamb*, 315-316.

64 Cf. Bulgakov, *The Bride of the Lamb*, 347; Sergei Bulgakov, *Philosophy of Economy: The World as Household*, trans. ed. Catherine Evtuhov (New Haven: Yale University, 2000), 8-9.

The Church stands at the intersection between time and eternity, history and eschatology. Since the Church is in the state of becoming who 'acts in history as a creative force', time cannot be understood as an empty passage to eternity.[65] As a creative force, 'the idea of the Church in this sense is applied to the whole world in its real foundation and aim, *entelecheia*'.[66] (Human history, for Bulgakov, is 'the history of the Church, not only the outer and institutional, in the sense of her destiny in the world, but also inner, as the spiritual force that accomplishes Divine-humanity. In this sense, Christian history is, in general, the "last times"'.[67]) The kingdom of God is already here and yet to come and the Church, as an active force, participates in the kingdom of God. Because of their supra-temporal foundation, '[A]ll earthly things must be perceived in the light of the coming end, the eschatological culmination' and it is this 'special music of eternity' that 'gives to earthly works their exclusive significance, placing them in the perspective of eternity'.[68] It is this perspective of eternity that helps the agent to judge or evaluate actions.

This brings us to the question of synergy between divine and human creative activity. Creativity, particularly divine-human creativity, is an important idea for Bulgakov that explains the interaction of God and the world. He conjoins human creativity (*anthrourgy*) and the notion of *theurgy* (divine action).[69] To distinguish it from its pagan counterpart, Bulgakov sometimes uses the term 'sophiurgy'.[70] Theurgy, for Bulgakov, is the work of the Holy Spirit and for this reason; he affirms, 'Pentecost is the absolute foundation of the Christian theurgy'.[71] Theurgy, according to Bulgakov, 'is inseparably connected with the incarnation' and 'it is the incarnation itself extended in time and uninterruptedly in process of

---

65 Bulgakov, *The Bride of the Lamb*, 334.
66 Bulgakov, "Social Teaching," 280.
67 Bulgakov, *The Bride of the Lamb*, 334.
68 Bulgakov, *The Bride of the Lamb*, 347.
69 Bernice Glatzer Rosenthal, "The Nature and Function of Sophia," in *Russian Religious Thought*, eds. Judith Deutsch Kornblatt, Richard F. Gustafson. (Madison, Wisconsin: The University of Wisconsin Press, 1996), 149.
70 Bulgakov, "The Unfading Light," in *Russian Religious Thought*, 166. The role of theurgy in Christian liturgy has been an issue of contention. The dominant attitude is that of rejection of the notion because of its association with pagan rituals. Scholars defined Neoplatonic theurgy as a manipulation of gods through rituals. However, contemporary scholarship has challenged such a misunderstanding; see Gregory Shaw, "Neoplatonic Theurgy and Dionysius the Areopagite," *Journal of Early Christian Studies* 7, 4 (1999): 573- 599.
71 Bulgakov, "The Unfading Light," 320.

accomplishment, the unending action of Christ in humanity'.[72] Thus, 'Christ laid down the absolute and irreversible foundation for theurgy, and passed on to his Church a theurgic power' that is 'realised in the liturgy... above all the Eucharist'.[73]

Bulgakov understands human creativeness – in the form of science, economy, culture, literature, art and performing arts – as sophianic and hence, a 'reflection of God's nature'.[74] Especially, he speaks of 'sophiurgic Art' as 'the Old Testament of Beauty' leading to the 'Comforter'.[75] Bulgakov conceives 'Beauty' as 'transformative' and the 'sophian thirst for beauty' as 'a redeeming force'.[76] However, he draws attention to the latent danger of creativity without/outside of God. Bulgakov warns that human 'creativity in its own name' is a kind of 'luciferian creative intoxication'.[77] If the creative vocation of humanity keeps itself away from the graceful acts of God and does not let human action be absorbed by the divine theurgy, it will obscure the sophianicity of the world and draw back its 'becoming' itself: 'divine grace works only by persuasion, not by external compulsion'[78].

Therefore, Christian *askesis* as a task directs humanity in the direction of divine-humanity (the realisation of Godmanhood) and this requires conversion or *metanoia*. Eschatology as the transfiguration of history is a further unfolding of the Event. In other words, the task is about the re-turn to the Event. Bulgakov makes this explicit when he calls his sophiology a 'dogmatic metanoia'.[79] Sophiology, according to Bulgakov, 'represents a theological or perhaps a dogmatic interpretation of the world (*Weltanschauung*) within Christianity'.[80] Dogmatic

---

72 Bulgakov, "The Unfading Light," 156.

73 Bulgakov, "The Unfading Light," 157. See also Andrew Louth, "Sergii Bulgakov and the Task of Theology," *Irish Theological Quarterly* 74 (2009): 243-259.

74 Louth, "Sergii Bulgakov," 149.

75 Louth, "Sergii Bulgakov," 166.

76 Bulgakov, "The Unfading Light," 157, 166. Here, Bulgakov almost echoes Dostoevskii's famous quotation 'Beauty will save the world'; cf. Bulgakov, "The Unfading Light," 128. See also Louth's association of Bulgakov's theological approach with von Balthassar's theological aesthetics, Bulgakov, "The Unfading Light," 243-244.

77 Bulgakov, *The Bride of the Lamb* (Edinburgh: T & T Clark, 2002), 332.

78 Gavrilyuk, "kenotic theology," 258.

79 Bulgakov, *The Wisdom of God*, 28.

80 Bulgakov, *The Wisdom of God*, 29; Sophiology must be understood not as an opening of new dogmas but rather as a theological hermeneutic or a theologoumenon that makes possible new theological constructions. Paul Valliere offers a good description of sophiology: '[T]he mission of sophiology is [...] to catalyze relationships between dogma and culture, not abolish the distinction [...] guides theologians over the terrain, mostly uncharted, where dogma meets experience, church meets world,

metanoia is not an intellectual exercise excluded from concrete life but implies a 'new apprehension' of Christian dogma, which results in the change of mind that leads to theandric action that co-ordinates Christianity with modern life.[81] In a nutshell, central to the account of Christian *askesis* is what Bulgakov calls Christian humanism.

7.4 Conclusion

To recapitulate what we have discussed thus far, first, I discussed the significance of Bulgakov's differentiated unity of Christology for understanding cosmic-mediation. The positive interrelation between the two natures is conceived based on their ontological similarity (sophianicity) and the unity of the two natures is understood from the point of view of double kenosis. The account of the unity of difference, then, makes it possible for us to think of the operation of Christian *askesis* in relation to the world. From this standpoint, genuine Christian *askesis* is distinguished from world-denying Manicheism whether in the form of 'pseudo-monastic' or ascetic worldview – dominant in Orthodoxy – and emphasis on God's transcendence (common in Protestant pietism), or the secularisation of life leading to the worship of the *status quo*.[82]

Christian *askesis* that takes to genuine political engagement is a metanoic re-turn to the Event or the commitment to the common task. The Incarnational Event is the 'highest theurgic action'[83], which sets the paradigm for human action. The pursuit of human creativity should not be indifferent to the theurgic action of God and the way to the sophianianization of the world is this metanoic re-turn to the Event, which is the highest theurgic action. To re-sophianize the world is to continually remake it culminating in the realisation of the Kingdom of God. It is through metanoia that the theo-political subject can resist ideological *dispositifs* and engage in counter-*dispositif* strategy.

Christianity meets culture, Orthodoxy meets modernity'; see Paul Valliere, *Modern Russian Theology: Bukharev, Soloviev, Bulgakov: Orthodox Theology in a New Key* (Edinburgh: T & T Clark, 2000), 306.

81 Bulgakov, "The Wisdom of God," 151.

82 Bulgakov, "The Wisdom of God," 150-2.

83 Adrian Pabst and Christoph Schneider, eds., *Encounter between Eastern Orthodoxy and Radical Orthodoxy: Transfiguring the World by the Word* (Ashgate, 2009), 87.

8 A Christian Social Ontology

8.1 Introduction

From the perspective of Christian agency or *askesis* (in the previous chapter), I have mentioned that the lethal social ontology of ethno-political ideology should be countered. This brings me to the second theological task: the articulation of ontology. If Christian *askesis* is supposed to be critical, it definitely requires its own ontology – a Christian social ontology. A failure to articulate such ontology will inevitably allow an 'implicit ontology' to fill the vacuum.[1] In view of this, the present chapter will focus on the construction of a Christian ontology whose aim is the 'Christian ordering of society'[2]. And Bulgakov offers adequate resources for this theological project. Before proceeding to the discussion, however, it is important to show how the ontological themes that I will consider correspond to the analysis of the previous part.

As we may recall, the previous part precipitated the main ontological determinants of sociality. We have come across three inseparable and interrelated ontological themes: ethnic-collectivisation, economic activity (labour) and violence. All the narratives of self, which I have examined, expound these themes albeit differently. In that discussion, the aim was to examine and describe these social determinants insofar as they form subjects or shape the self. What was concluded from the analysis is that (a) the 'ethnic' came to be a primary category that aggregates individuals interpellating them as ethno-political subjects leading to the denial of individual personhood; (b) economic process is conceived only in terms of utility: class exploitation or progress expressing a negative construal of work and the subject of labour; (c) ethnic/class difference is perceived as conflictual and that violence is a necessary part of life to assert or negate difference.

In this chapter, I shall first articulate a social ontology grounded on Trinitarian ontology. This will help to reclaim personhood denied by impersonal

1 See Peter Scott, *Theology, Ideology and Liberation: Towards a Liberative Theology* (Cambridge: Cambridge University Press, 1994), 134; and Milbank, *Theology and Social Theory: Beyond Secular Reason*, 429.

2 Williams, *Sergii Bulgakov*, 256.

ethnic categories and show that concrete unity-in-difference is possible only on the basis of an analogical account of being (8.2). Next, I will deal with the second ontological theme: labour. Based on Bulgakov's theology of creation and sophiology, I will contend that labour should not be construed in purely utilitarian and impersonal terms but it must be conceived as divine-human (8.3). Finally, again from a creation perspective, I shall contend that sophianic peace has primacy over violence and that difference can unfold in peace (8.4) before my conclusion (8.5)

8.2 Trinity and Ontology

According to Bulgakov, the 'Holy Trinity is not three, but a triunity; and It is not a series but an enclosed whole, which has the fullness of Its being, Its power, precisely in trinitarity'.[3] This is the starting point for Bulgakov's Trinitarian theology: God is neither a unitaristic 'self-enclosed, singular I' nor a tritheistic '*harmony of three*' I's.[4] Rather, he contends that God is not three and he is not one but 'Trinity-Unity' or 'unifiedness in Trinity'; logically, this may appear a contradiction because 'rational-logical computation knows only things fixed in their separateness' and hence, it can only yield to 'either simply three or simply one; or [...] four, by adding to the three I's, the triune I'.[5] From this arises the question of the relationship between person and nature in the Holy Trinity. Here, Bulgakov does not offer explicit reasons for his preference of the term 'nature' used for the Trinity to the more frequently used ones 'being' and 'substance'. Nevertheless, by using this term he refers to *ousia* – the uncreated, immaterial and eternal essence of the Divinity.[6] Although Bulgakov's Trinitarian theology makes its departure from the patristic tradition, he further develops the doctrine in a unique manner by applying sophiology. At the centre of his theology is the concept of personality

3 This is a restatement of the Athanasian Creed: 'God in Trinity and Trinity in unity'. Sergius Bulgakov, *The Comforter*, trans. Boris Jakim (Grand Rapids, MI: Eerdmans, 2004), 54. Bulgakov considers that the proper point of departure in articulating the Trinitarian relations is 'trinitarity' and this shows the emphasis he gives to personhood (rather than nature) in the Holy Trinity.

4 Bulgakov, *The Comforter*, 53-55.

5 Bulgakov, *The Comforter*, 53-55.

6 Bulgakov, *The Lamb of God*, 94-106. Other Orthodox theologians such as John Zizioulas also use the term 'divine nature' for *ousia*, alongside with the term 'being'; cf. John Zizioulas, *Being As Communion: Studies on Personhood and the Church* (London: Darton, Longman and Todd, 1985), 82.

or personhood.[7] In what follows, I wish to expound his theology and draw out its significance for a Christian social ontology.

Personhood and Differentiated-Unity in the Holy Trinity

Let us begin from Bulgakov's conception of the person/personality. The essence of personality ('I' as subject), according to Bulgakov, needs a relationship with an object (the world or in Fichte's term the *not*-I); put differently, the 'spirit', as 'I', cannot live as self-enclosed but must proceed out of itself to find its *not*-I.[8] In Fichte's analysis of the self, the *not*-I (the non-self) limits the personal *I*, and without it, no personal *I* can find its real nature or necessarily reveal itself. Bulgakov, following Pavel Florensky, employs the Feuerbachian concept of 'Thou' as a substitute for Fichte's *not*-I or non-self and that such relation between 'I' and 'Thou' requires a third, a 'he', which could take the position of either 'I' or 'Thou'.[9] However, Bulgakov notes that the Divine Spirit, the Absolute Subject, is not like the creaturely spirit who needs 'thou' outside itself as its mirror or for its fulfillment, but rather it postulates 'thou', 'he', 'we', and also 'you' within its own confines.[10]

For Bulgakov, God is 'a Trihypostatic Spirit: Father, Word, and Holy Spirit'.[11] A 'singular I' that manifests a uni-hypostatic Absolute (God) is 'not only a contradictio in adiecto, but also an expression of metaphysical egoism'.[12] A uni-hypostatic Absolute is a contradiction in terms precisely because God – as Spirit – cannot be self-enclosed – 'a centre of repulsion and egocentrism' – but rather 'an open continuation' – not to a 'bad infinity' – into a tri-hypostatic mode of being.[13] Spirit, as 'self-moving love', proceeds out, 'beyond its confines to another *I*'

7 His emphasis on the concept of personhood exposes the dangers of impersonalism in philosophies ranging from Marxism to Trinitarian theologies (including the patristic tradition); cf. Valliere, *Modern Russian Theology*, 333.

8 In Bulgakov's Trinitarian theology, the scriptural notion of 'spirit' the concept of persons and nature in the Trinity; see Bulgakov, *The Lamb of God*, 90-91.

9 "Privoda v filosofii," 10 cited in Michael Aksionov Meerson, *The Trinity of Love in Modern Russian Theology: The Love Paradigm and the Retrieval of Western Medieval Love Mysticism in Modern Russian Trinitarian Thought* (Quincy, Illinois: Franciscan Press, 1998), 146-147.

10 Bulgakov, *The Comforter*, 54. The tri-hypostatic Person of God, each 'I' needs the other(s) not as a mirror (as in creaturely spirit; Bulgakov, *The Lamb of God*, 95; "Privoda v filosofii," 10 cited in Meerson, *The Trinity of Love*, 146-147.

11 Bulgakov, *The Comforter*, 61.

12 Bulgakov, *The Comforter*, 54.

13 Bulgakov, *The Comforter*, 54.

because it 'resists the absoluteness of the hypostasis'.[14] God is 'wholly and simultaneously a co-existence of three moments of saying I, each manifest[ing] only through its others'.[15] The 'self-positing of 'I' necessarily implies the co-positing of 'Thou', in which case this 'thou' is another personal 'I-subject' or 'another self'; and, there is perfect unity of personality: that is, despite its tri-hypostatizedness, the Divine Person remains one, but never as mono-hypostatized.[16] Thus, for Bulgakov, the character of consciousness is 'neither impersonal nor unipersonal' but, employing Sergei Trubetskoi's concept, *sobornost'* (roughly translated as conciliarity) - 'multi-unitary' – which is realised in 'we' or 'you'.[17]

This harmony of Trinitarian hypostases does not, however, imply that we have to view the trinity as a community of three Gods. Bulgakov explains,

> But this equi-personal *I* never posits itself in separation from the other equi-personal I's, as unique or even as *one of three I's* (which would transform the trinity into a *community or harmony of three* - a tritheism); rather, it posits itself in the other I's, is composited with them. And there results a unique but also triune divine *I*, for trinitarity is not only trinity but also unity.[18]

Trinitarity is a safeguard against both tritheism and modalism (any form of unitarism). But what connects the persons or hypostases? Bulgakov claims that 'the three hypostases have their nature *not* in common, not in common possession (nor do they have it each one for Himself, which would be tritheism), but as *one* for all, homoousianly, not homoiousianly'.[19] The consubstantiality that exists between the Trinitarian persons, however, should not be understood as static. Bulgakov's concept of personality seeks to show the dynamic relation that exists between the Trinitarian hypostases. This implies that the Divine Spirit, being absolute and free, posits itself as *actus purus*, but not an 'an actualized potential' because there is no opposition between 'perfect act' and 'perfect potential'.[20] In the Divine I, each of the Trinitarian hypostases has his 'nature by a *personal*

---

14 Bulgakov, *The Comforter*, 54. Cf. Bulgakov, *The Lamb of God*, 95.

15 Williams, *Sergii Bulgakov*, 166.

16 See Meerson, *The Trinity of Love*, 143-146; Bulgakov, *The Lamb of God*, 95. However, Bulgakov notes that 'none of the three positings of I – as I, thou, and he - can be defined solely from a single center'; Bulgakov, *The Comforter*, 54-55.

17 "Privoda v filosofii," 10 cited in Meerson, *The Trinity of Love*, 146-147.

18 Bulgakov, *The Comforter*, 55.

19 Bulgakov, *The Lamb of God*, 95. The Divine Spirit, as Bulgakov notes, has a 'personal self-consciousness' (*hypostasis*) and 'nature' (*ousia*) and there is an 'indivisible unity' between the two.

20 "Glary o troichnosti," 33-44 cited in Meerson, *The Trinity of Love*, 146.

self-positing' and each has this nature '*in its own way*, for itself and for the other hypostases in the triune circle'.[21] This requires further clarification.

Within the Holy Trinity, first, there is a relation between the Father and the Son. The Father is 'the principle (*archē*) of the nature of Divinity' and 'has His own nature, and His possession of it is a hypostatic, co-hypostatic, and interhypostatic act'.[22] However, this is not to be understood in terms of 'origination' or 'causality', which Bulgakov strongly critiques because these notions introduce explicitly and implicitly subordination within the Holy Trinity.[23] The Father, as the first principle or the 'primordial hypostasis', 'begets the Only Begotten Son' and in the act of 'begetting', the Father goes out of himself by self-emptying and through this act of self-actualising he finds his 'nature' in the Son.[24] The 'begottenness' of the Son by no means should be understood as introduction from nonbeing, and there is relation but not relativity or becoming within the Trinity, but in such engendering, both the Father and the Son, the begetter and the begotten, enter into an eternal relationship as equi-divine equi-personal *I*s. They become the 'revealing' hypostasis and 'the revealed one' respectively; however, there is no place for equivocation here: the Son is not a sign signifying the Father.[25] The self-emptying is a mutual or reciprocal one. Since 'the Father desires to have Himself outside Himself, in the Son, the Son too does not desire to have Himself for Himself' and this is demonstrated in the Son fulfilling the will of the Father.[26] The relation between the two constitutes a 'sacrifice of love' that consists in the 'self-renunciation' of the 'Father's love' and the 'self-depletion' of the 'Son's love' because the vocation of the latter relates to the redemption of the world, which is sacrifice before the foundation of the world: *eternal kenosis*.[27]

The Holy Trinity, which cannot be exhausted from the point of view of the dyad – Father and Son, requires the completion of its circle by the third hypostasis – the Holy Spirit. As there is no love without sacrifice, there is not also love without the 'joy of sacrificial love, the bliss and actualization of this love', which is the Holy Spirit; the Holy Spirit is a hypostatic love or a hypostasis of love, which overcomes the sacrificial love of the Father and the Son from turning into a

---

21 Bulgakov, *The Lamb of God*, 97-8.
22 Bulgakov, *The Lamb of God*, 98.
23 See Bulgakov, *The Comforter*, 57-61, 68-73.
24 Bulgakov, *The Lamb of God*, 98.
25 Bulgakov, *The Lamb of God*, 98.
26 Bulgakov, *The Lamb of God*, 99.
27 Bulgakov, *The Lamb of God*, 99.

'tragedy'.[28] He is sent by the Father to 'repose' in the Son and become a 'comforter' to both the Father and the Son as well as to himself and since the mutual love of the two hypostatic centres does not complete the Trinitarian circle, the Holy Spirit, 'as a living Hypostatic love of the Two between themselves, locks in triunity the reciprocity of love'.[29] Thus, the interhypostatic act is the relation of 'mutual love'[30] and that the three hypostases are '*distinctly personal as well as trinitarian*' without subjecting them to systems of dyads or originations.[31]

But doesn't the 'economic' Trinity– God as the creator – introduce a change within the Trinity? Bulgakov avoids the bifurcation between the 'immanent' Trinity, God as the Absolute and the 'economic' Trinity. His argument is that regardless of the differences between the two, the 'economic' Trinity does not introduce something (ontologically) new in the Trinity. Even though, it is true that creation introduces 'a certain differentiation, a new distinction', the Trinitarian persons remain inseparable.[32] For example, 'that which the Father accomplishes is accomplished neither by the Son nor the Holy Spirit, and *each* hypostasis has its particular mode of action in the world'; however, the differentiated persons 'characterized by separate actions' are also 'effectively united in we or us ("Let us make man in our image" [Gen. 1:26]).[33] Bulgakov remarks, 'the eternal *taxis* (the order of hypostases) exists supratemporally, and in this sense the *taxis* is the determinate, concrete interrelation between the Father, the Son, and the Holy Spirit. Creation, drawing God's being into temporality, defines the *taxis* in its own way, differentiating the interrelation of the hypostases into a temporal sequence'; however, 'In God, "Alpha and Omega," First and Last, beginning and the end are identical'.[34]

Therefore, in Bulgakov's Trinitarian theology, Trinitarian difference is acknowledged in the Godhead without understanding the *taxis* in terms of subordination.[35] Regardless of the difference the 'economic' Trinity might introduce, the Trinity remains indivisible and consubstantial. The Trinity always remains to be a unity not due to static unity of substance but a dynamic relation of the 'Trinitarian self-moving love'.[36] Such focus on dynamic or produced unity is

28 Bulgakov, *The Lamb of God*, 99.
29 Bulgakov, *The Lamb of God*, 100.
30 Bulgakov, *The Lamb of God*, 100.
31 Bulgakov, *The Comforter*, 141.
32 Bulgakov, *The Lamb of God*, 191-192.
33 Bulgakov, *The Lamb of God*, 192.
34 Bulgakov, *The Lamb of God*, 190-191.
35 Bulgakov, *The Lamb of God*, 190.
36 Bulgakov, *The Lamb of God*, 95.

important to understand humanity created in the image of the Trinitarian God. Of course, this is not to mean that Trinitarian differentiated-unity or relationality should be the model for humans to copy or to imitate.[37]

One of the criticisms against social Trinitarian theology resonates around this issue: how can what is said of the Trinitarian persons become applicable to human persons? Often the answer given by social Trinitarians is that humans are called to imitate or copy Trinitarian relations. But such modelling overlooks the gap between the Trinitarian persons and humans, Kathryn Tanner argues. Tanner suggests a balance between the immanent trinity and the economic trinity and she argues that the latter paves the way for a better understanding of how God entered our world of sin and death to bridge the gap between divine and human relations.[38] Thus, according to this view, we model the trinity insofar as we participate in it.[39] Herein, Bulgakov's view on participation and deification are in tandem with this perspective. '*Methexis*' is the key, here: that is 'the participation of matter in ideal form', 'the desire of earth for heaven'.[40] Humans are called to participate in the divine life.

In the Image of the Holy Trinity

In what follows, I shall discuss how humanity created in the image of the Trinitarian God participates in God, who is a differentiated-unity. But prior to that, I must briefly discuss the 'Image of God in God Himself', which would take us to Bulgakov's theology of two Sophias: the Divine Sophia and the creaturely Sophia (which I briefly discussed in relation to the Incarnation in the previous chapter). Let us begin the discussion by examining Sophia in relation to God's nature. As patristic and post-patristic dogmatic theology have always asserted, the content of the divine esssence (*ousia*) as such remains unknown (i.e., the apophatic element).[41] Bulgakov identifies Sophia with *ousia* but he does not collapse the personal with the impersonal (as his critics hold against him)[42]:

---

37 Cf. Kathryn Tanner, "Trinity," in *The Blackwell Companion to Political Theology* (eds. Peter Scott and William T. Cavanaugh. Malden, Mass.: Blackwell, 2004), 324-331.

38 Tanner, "Trinity," 328.

39 Cf. Tanner, "Trinity," 328-331.

40 Williams, *Sergii Bulgakov*, 137.

41 Bulgakov argues that 'One must, once and for all, overcome the deadening abstractness that is afraid of realism in thought and prefers the abstract nominalism of "properties" of essences'; Bulgakov, *The Bride of the Lamb*, 39.

42 Vladimir Lossky's argues that it is only apophatic theology that can approach the mystery of God. Lossky charges that Bulgakov fails to distinguish between God's

God is Divinity, Ousia-Sophia. It follows that in God there is not only a Person (and Persons) but also Divinity, which is *not* a personality, although it belongs to a Person (and Persons) and is totally hypostatized. Divinity is therefore both personal and impersonal. Such is precisely the Church's dogma of the union of Hypostasis and Ousia in God: Ousia itself is not a personality, although in God it exists only personally. If we consider Ousia only in the aspect of *personal* being, we effectively abolish it. Ousia possesses both personal being (in relation to a Person) and impersonal being (by itself): at no moment of its being does it exist outside of and separately from personality, but also at no moment of its being does it merge with personality, for otherwise the personality too would lose itself, become deprived of nature, be transformed into an empty abstract I, and would not be vital spirit, living in its own nature. The nature must therefore be considered not only as something independent, as Divinity or the Divine world in itself, existent not only in God but also for God. Thus, one can say not only that God *is* Divinity but also that He *has* Divinity, existent by itself, although not for itself (that is, not personally, not as a "fourth hypostasis").[43]

The revealed and knowable 'content of the life' (i.e., the kataphatic element) is love (and glory), which Bulgakov calls Sophia, the Wisdom of God.[44] In this sense, Sophia is the 'love of God for Himself' and his self-revelation.[45] Properly speaking, 'self-emptying love is *what* God is' and 'that "what" [...] is Sophia'.[46] As the 'absolute content of absolute life', it is proper for Sophia to include 'the All as unity and unity as All, *All-unity*' – an 'integral wisdom' or chastity, which is not an aggregation.[47] Thus, with regard to the divinity, Sophia is the fullness of God

essence and God's energies, which St. Gregory Palamas distinguishes. However, Bulgakov appropriates Palamas's distinction between God's nature, ousia, which is 'hidden' and inaccessible and God's *energeia*, which is accessible. The conception of God as Relative Absolute (as one who includes relation but not relativity in Himself) is in a agreement with Palamas's view; see Barbara Newman, "Sergius Bulgakov and the Theology of Divine Wisdom, " *St. Vladimir's Theological Quarterly*, vol. 22 No.1/1978, 42-44.

43 Bulgakov, *The Lamb of God*, 103. Bulgakov carefully uses the Russian term *ipostasnost*, which is not the same as the Greek term 'hypostasis' that refers to 'person' or 'personality'. Sophia is not a person/hypostasis that would turn the Trinity into a quaternity but rather it is 'quasi-personality'. This term has been translated as 'hypostaseity' by Rowan Williams, 'hypostatizedness' by Boris Jakim, and 'hypostacity' by Brandon Gallaher cf. "Protopresbyter Sergii Bulgakov: Hypostasis and Hypostacity: Scholia to *The Unfading Light*," *St Vladimirs Theological Quarterly* 49:1-2 (2005) 14-15.

44 Bulgakov, *The Lamb of God*, 166.

45 Bulgakov, *The Lamb of God*, 105.

46 Williams, *Sergii Bulgakov*, 166.

47 Bulgakov, *The Lamb of God*, 102.

(the *pleroma*) or the 'Image of God in God Himself, the self-Icon of Divinity (according to the doctrine of St. John of Damascus)'.[48]

Sophia is 'the loving of love': 'what God loves is the directness of the world towards the human; God loves the heavenly image of humanity itself'.[49] God's love is never confined within the tri-hypostatic circle but extends to the extra-divine, which is manifested in the creation of the world by God in which his love radiates towards the non-being or 'nothing'.[50] In creation, 'nothing' is included in divine fullness as 'multiplicity'.[51] Sophia is the '*created* plurality of hypostases' that is the foundation or pattern as 'All-unity' of the multiplicity and unity of the created world.[52] It is also 'the plenitude of positive and universal unity'.[53] The multiplicity of creatures differentiated in the Six Days of creation are 'connected and contained in one world soul, the creaturely Sophia'.[54]

The creaturely Sophia is not a different Sophia but it is one with the Divine Sophia that becomes the 'All-unity' of the created world but the two Sophias are differentiated according to their modes of being. The creaturely Sophia is the 'cosmourgic potency' – 'the world's entelechy who is being actualized, or becoming, in the world'.[55] The language of image and likeness properly explains the idea of entelechy: '[T]he Image is the foundation and the given, as the ideal, uncreated image of creation in Sophia. The likeness is the becoming of this image,

---

48 Bulgakov, *The Lamb of God*, 103. Obviously, unlike the creaturely spirit, the Divine Spirit is '*actus purus*, absolute actuality, free of all givenness'; See Bulgakov, *The Bride of the Lamb*, 41. Although, historically, Sophia was associated only with the Logos; however, Bulgakov argues that Sophia cannot be one and the same neither with any or all of the hypostases. Bulgakov avoids attributing Wisdom to the Son of God alone but rather he argues that Wisdom should be attributed to all the three Trinitarian persons. In this manner he transforms the logocentric sophiology of the patristic tradition to a Trinitarian sophiology. In this case he is critical of both the Arian and anti-Arian concept of Sophia; see Newman, "Sergius Bulgakov and the Theology of Divine Wisdom," 45-48.

49 Williams, *Sergii Bulgakov*, 166.

50 Williams, *Sergii Bulgakov*, 134.

51 Bulgakov, *The Bride of the Lamb*, 52.

52 Williams, *Sergii Bulgakov*, 134-135.

53 Williams, *Sergii Bulgakov*, 137.

54 Bulgakov, *The Bride of the Lamb*, 64-65. Her introduction into nonbeing raises the question as to whether Sophia can remain in the extra-hypostatic or impersonal being of the world (after being is taken out of the Trinitarian hypostases). As the world 'soul', she is devoid of spirit (or hypostatizedness) and she is hypostatized by the human person; Bulgakov, *The Bride of the Lamb*, 83-84. Thus, 'the creaturely world is a cosmo-anthropic world' and 'man is a microcosm'; Bulgakov, *The Bride of the Lamb*, 85.

55 Bulgakov, *The Bride of the Lamb*, 80.

through which the image is realized in the creaturely world, ascending from potentiality to actuality'.[56]

Now let us consider the human in the image of the Holy Trinity. As we have noted in the previous chapter, humankind is sophianic because it contains the creaturely Sophia. According to Bulgakov, human-being is created in the image of God as multi-hypostatic multi-unity connected by Sophia, integral wisdom. This multi-unity as a Proto-Image for humankind is substantiated by the indestructible ontological ground, which is commensurate with the divine (this has been discussed in the previous chapter in relation to enhypostatisation of God). The human being is created 'as a co-I of the Holy Trinity, as the creaturely – and in this sense the "fourth" – multi-hypostatic human hypostasis, which is called to have and is capable of having a *personal* relationship with God'.[57]

The sophianicity of humanity, the multi-hypostatic character, which represents humanity as a family, a race or *ethnie* should not be understood as irreconcilable difference. According to Bulgakov, the rational-logic of the sinful and corrupted world fails to comprehend the organic unity of the humanity because it understands 'multiplicity only as extra-position or juxtaposition' or the sense of being as dialectical.[58] The idea of 'fragmentary humanity', which is simply an outcome of 'empirical phenomenon' and 'ontological determination', has a dangerous implication for Christian worldview.[59] If what was not assumed by Christ is not the whole of humanity (past, present, future), 'Integral Adam', but a fragment of humankind, then, the whole edifice of Christian doctrines of Christian anthropology, Christology and soteriology would simply crumble because according to St Gregory the Theologian's maxim 'what is not assumed is not redeemed'.[60]

An account of human multi-hypostatic multi-unity truthful to Christian theology cannot leave aside the concept of consubstantiality of Christ with

---

56 Bulgakov, *The Bride of the Lamb*, 82.

57 Bulgakov, *The Bride of the Lamb*, 89.

58 Bulgakov, *The Bride of the Lamb*, 104.

59 Bulgakov, *The Bride of the Lamb*, 107.

60 See Gregory of Nazianzen, *Letter to Cledonius the Priest Against Apollinarius*, Epistle CI, in *A Select Library of Nicene and Post-Nicene Fathers*, series II, vol. VII, ed. Philip Schaff and Henry Wace (Grand Rapids: Eerdmans, 1978-79), 440; Bulgakov, *The Bride of the Lamb*, 107. The discussion of the 'Original sin' necessarily presupposes the existence of the 'all-man and the all-humanity' because the 'Original sin' cannot be understood in terms of separate events that occurred only in the past; Cf. Bulgakov, *The Bride of the Lamb*, 109.

humanity, which presupposes the existence of integral humanity.[61] Humanity, then, 'is a multi-unity with one nature but multiple hypostases; it is not an indefinite and unfinished series, with ellipsis points indicating continuation but the unity of this series, its integral'.[62] This is a view akin to Gregory of Nyssa's notion of integral body: '[The] plenitude of humankind is included as one body by the providential power proceeding from God'.[63]

Humanity exists not only as 'generic reality' but also as 'ensemble of personalities, as real unity-in-plurality' and Bulgakov, as we noted above, calls this principle: *sobornost'*.[64] This kind of existence or relation is 'not given' but 'proposed'.[65] *Sobornost'* is organic or 'concrete all-unity in divine love' and though this idea undergird Bulgakov's view of eccelsiology, it, as Bulgakov claims, 'can acquire a sociological application, by means of which the lethal doctrine godless sociologism may be overcome'.[66] Ideologically coercive and impersonal 'forced collectivisation' cannot be *sobornost'* but 'the Church possesses the principle of true social order, in which the personal and the collective [...] can be given equal weight and unified harmoniously [through] living *sobornost'*'.[67]

Therefore, Trinitarian ontology offers us a conception of being as analogical. Such a mode of being best accommodates differentiated-unity than the dialectical mode of being that conceives unity only as sameness. In living *sobornost'* we can reclaim back personhood that is often denied by ethno-political ideology in

---

61 Bulgakov, *The Bride of the Lamb*, 109. Here, Bulgakov is reflecting the Council of Chalcedon's Definition of the Faith where we find this statement: 'In agreement, therefore, with the holy fathers, we all unanimously teach that we should confess that our Lord Jesus Christ is one and the same Son, the same perfect in Godhead and the same perfect in manhood, truly God and truly man, the same of a rational soul and body, *consubstantial with the Father in Godhead, and the same consubstantial with us in manhood*, like us in all things except sin;' (italics added); see for example J.N.D Kelly, *Early Christian Doctrines* (London: Continuum, 1977), 339-340. Such a statement reflects the absorption of a key Nicene terminology 'homoousious'; in this case, 'double homoousious' – the consubstantiality of the Son with the Father and with us, which affirms his perfect divinity and perfect humanity. For recent discussions, see Aloys Grillmeier with Theresia Hainthaler, *Christ in Christian Tradition (v.2, pt.4): From the Council of Chalcedon (451) to Gregory the Great (590-604)* (London: Mowbray, 1996), 27-9, 102.

62 Bulgakov, *The Bride of the Lamb*, 108.

63 *De opificio hominis*, c.16, (81-85) n.51 cited in Bulgakov, *The Bride of the Lamb*, 109.

64 Williams, *Sergii Bulgakov*, 260.

65 Bulgakov, *The Lamb of God*, 104.

66 Williams, *Sergii Bulgakov*, 260.

67 Bulgakov, *The Bride of the Lamb*, 262, 264.

favour of abstract categories – ethnic collectives – and challenge those 'impersonal' collectives that place themselves above the organic-collective prescribed to the whole world and practised by the Church.

8.3 The Ontology of Work

The second fundamental ontological determinant of sociality, which shall be considered, here, is labour or work. Bulgakov's treatment of this theme largely relates to the discussion of economy in its broad sense but the notion of labour takes a central place in his thought. For Bulgakov, as we have noted in the previous chapter, the subject, properly defined, is a concrete subject engaged in economic activity – labour/work. Here, we see the close association between economy (economic worldview) and anthropology. Bulgakov observes that every 'economic age has its spirit and is in turn the product of this spirit; each economic age has its particular type of 'economic man' generated by the spirit of economy'.[68] How should the subject, as an economic agent, be conceived in relation to the nature of labour? And how should labour be understood? Seen from the perspective of Christian theology of creation, economic activity should be conceived as a 'joyful' labour 'in Sophia'.[69]

According to Bulgakov, the characteristic feature of 'economic activity is the presence of *effort, labor*' and such activity is never arbitrary but it is always 'directed toward a particular goal'; more precisely, '[*E*]*conomy is the activity of labor*'.[70] Bulgakov defines labour as

> the actuality of human existence, objectivising human being beyond its own limits and making the world 'objective' to us, is a living link between the subject and the object, the bridge by which the ego may go out into the world of [other] realities and which connects that world indivisibly with itself. Thanks to the fact of labour, there is no such thing as a pure subject, as idealism would hold, nor a pure object, as materialism claims: there is a living unity, at once subject and object. Only by examining it from this or that angle by some kind of methodological abstraction can you divide it. But the polarised, 'doubled' state of [our present] being is only transcended in the Absolute, which is at once both subject and object to itself. And the concept of the Absolute also excludes any going-out from subject to object: its character as a subject-object is posited by a unique, self-identical and extra-temporal act. This is the mystery of the life of the Holy Trinity itself.[71]

---

68 Bulgakov, *Philosophy of Economy*, 217. For example, Bulgakov rejects the concept of *homo economicus* arguing that it wrongly construes the human.

69 Bulgakov, *Philosophy of Economy*, 13-14.

70 Bulgakov, *Philosophy of Economy*, 74.

71 *Philosophie de l'économie*, 74 cited in Williams, *Sergii Bulgakov*, 121-122.

Giving epistemological significance to labour, Bulgakov approaches the subject-object problem, which is a concern of idealist as well as materialist philosophy.[72] According to Bulgakov, labour is a subjective-objective act that involves the interaction of the subject and the object. In view of this, Bulgakov rejects two extreme polarities: material determination and absolute freedom. He claims that it is only in the Absolute (the Holy Trinity) that the subject-object division is transcended. Adopting F.W.J. Schelling's philosophy of identity, Bulgakov asserts that the subject-object unity 'finds its explanation in the unity of the world soul [the *natura naturans*]'.[73] (This will be elaborated later)

Bulgakov conceptualises economic activity as a synthesis of freedom and necessity.[74] The subject experiences necessity or 'unfreedom' when the object (nature) sets a limit against it; however, freedom can be realised by the subject insofar as it manages to push back the limit.[75] These two corresponding principles – freedom and necessity – are the principles of life and death respectively. In labour, 'the dependence of human personhood upon nature' is both 'realised and 'overcome'.[76] Through labour, humans struggle against nature to fulfil their material needs and hence, to live (to escape from death).

The principles of freedom and necessity, which always confront the subject, open up to two possibilities: 'polarization' or 'reconciliation'.[77] In the case of polarisation, the object (the non-I) stands opposed to the subject and consequently, as Bulgakov notes, 'the deaf and blind force of necessity, moira, fate – the fate not of divine will but of mechanical necessity, dead and inert matter impossible to blame or complain about' will take control: what one adopts as 'selfness' (the 'empirical I') becomes the 'I' given 'by necessity and received from the surrounding

72 Bulgakov, *Philosophy of Economy*, 18, 114.

73 Bulgakov, *Philosophy of Economy*, 88.

74 According to Bulgakov, freedom should not be understood in relation to 'scientific determinism', lifeless 'mechanism', or 'causal regularity' because freedom is an 'unscientific', 'extrascientific' or 'suprascientific' (but not 'antiscientific') concept. Rightly interpreted, freedom is not only a negative but a positive concept: it 'is not noncausality but self-causality, the capacity to act of oneself (*a se*, hence the unmelodious but convenient expression *aseism*), to commence causality in one's own fashion and thus to disrupt the principle of general mechanism'. For Bulgakov, the source of such freedom as *aseism* is God who is 'Freedom itself' and honoured 'humanity with his image, that is, freedom'. See Bulgakov, *Philosophy of Economy*, 197, 199, 202.

75 Bulgakov, *Philosophy of Economy*, 196.

76 Williams, *Sergii Bulgakov*, 240.

77 Bulgakov, *Philosophy of Economy*, 208, 220.

environment'.[78] The fact that the knowledge of ourselves is only possible through 'life experience' (because 'the non-I becomes the field for the realization of the I's freedom – its object and potential') does not imply that our sense of the self is not 'self-willed self-definition'.[79] Bulgakov argues that determinism 'could be true only if our I were dead'.[80] Even though it is true that freedom and necessity are 'in a state of constant flux', 'motion', and 'struggle', there are instances in which the two are reconciled (if not put in permanent 'equilibrium' for the antinomy continues until the end of times).[81] Bulgakov's conclusion is that human creative activity synthesises freedom and necessity and necessity should permit freedom to prevail.

However, we should note, here, that this struggle against nature for life is not a reality given from the beginning of creation. Rather, it is a phenomenon that indicates to the 'metaphysical Fall', which is, in theological terms, known as the Original Sin.[82] The Fall involved humankind including all creation. It resulted in the loss of the 'original state' ('harmonious interaction' of humankind and nature) and such a state was overtaken by the chaotic state of the empirical world; after the loss of what Bulgakov calls the 'Edenic economy'[83], 'economics becomes [...] labour 'in the sweat of his brow' [Gen. 3.19] for the sake of sustaining life and the incessant struggle against death; it is indeed, in a sense, death itself'[84]. The outcome of such a 'cosmic catastrophe' was not only the chaotic state of the

78 Bulgakov, *Philosophy of Economy*, 210.

79 Bulgakov, *Philosophy of Economy*, 212.

80 Bulgakov, *Philosophy of Economy*, 212. Recently, John Hughes argued that pure utility is contrary to human 'nature' – that it is an impossibility: 'human labour cannot be understood in terms of pure utility, but rather that it has within itself an excessive logic that points beyond itself, a certain 'ideality', a rational, aesthetic, moral nature, not empirically evident, but standing in judgement against the current realities. It is by virtue of this nature that social criticism is possible; there could be no critique at all if labour were nothing but pure utility'; see John Hughes, *The End of Work: Theological Critique of Capitalism* (Oxford: Blackwell, 2007), 224.

81 Bulgakov, *Philosophy of Economy*, 210, 218.

82 Bulgakov, *Philosophy of Economy*, 150.

83 Bulgakov, *Philosophy of Economy*, 150. As an out result of the Fall, humankind 'does not so much govern the world as the world governs him'; Williams, *Sergii Bulgakov*, 152.

84 Williams, *Sergii Bulgakov*, 241. Death, though uncreated by God, became a reality in the empirical world: 'though life reigns in the sophic world, in empirical reality it must, so to speak, obtain death's permission for its mere existence'. 'Life survives only because its seeds, sown by the creator, are indestructible'; Williams, *Sergii Bulgakov*, 152.

empirical world but also a dramatic change in 'the meaning and motivation of economic activity'.[85]

Thus, 'Economic labour is imposed upon us as a penalty for sin, and we are bound to see it as a duty [...] laid upon all mankind'.[86] According to Bulgakov, the historical process (historical humanity), which is the basis for economic conceptualisations, begun only after the catastrophe. It is this empirical reality, which is considered as 'the only real one' by Marxist economic materialism (or better, 'materialist economism').[87] After this catastrophe, economic activity is subjected to death and becomes 'forced and self-interested' ('Marxism has its truth' in this regard).[88]

Nevertheless, materialist economism cannot be the way out of this crisis. Materialist economism makes the mistake of understanding the historical process as linear (the 'theory of progress') and economic activity as mechanical (utilitarian). Bulgakov argues that the consequence of the 'theory of progress', historically, has proved to be 'a theodicy': 'sacrificing the good of present generations for that of the future'.[89] Economic activity, as Bulgakov argues, 'does *not* have an eschatological task' that transcends this age and it does not need 'sacrificial pseudo-eschatology' either, but rather it is a 'malign infinity, which knows 'no fulfilment'.[90] In this regard, the Marxist idea of progress and the belief in the 'new history' is simply futile and in fact, the crisis of this belief/worldview gave rise to the longing of 'a *different* kingdom, not of this world', and Bulgakov argues that it is 'Sophia that determines the teleology of the historical process'.[91]

Bulgakov argues that a 'religious materialism' should perceive economic activity as 'the Christian cycle of Fall and Resurrection' rather than 'revolutionary transformation'.[92] In the economy, humanity restores the lost relation between *natura naturans* and *natura naturata*: the former refers to the principle or the ideal image or the foundation of the world while the latter refers to the created

85 Bulgakov, *Philosophy of Economy*, 150, 154.
86 Williams, *Sergii Bulgakov*, 150.
87 Bulgakov, *Philosophy of Economy*, 10.
88 Williams, *Sergii Bulgakov*, 241.
89 Bulgakov, *Philosophy of Economy*, 8-9.
90 Williams, *Sergii Bulgakov*, 151-153.
91 Williams, *Sergii Bulgakov*, 153.
92 Williams, *Sergii Bulgakov*, 13. This Christian view of history 'anticipates the use of this same resurrective model by existentialist philosophers, and particularly Heidegger, whose notion of the "throweness" of Dasein corresponds to Bulgakov's description of history as the result of the Fall'.

world or universe; in other words, the restoration of such connection is 'the resolution of nature's stiff and lifeless products into the forces that generate them, as the organization of nature'.[93]

This implies that human creativity is the re-creation of that which is already pre-existing, as an 'ideal model', in the 'metaphysical world'; in other words, human creative capacity can never 'create an image' but 'can only reproduce likeness' for human-beings are 'incapable of metaphysical originality'.[94] Since nature is already *nata* (created), the creative activity of humanity relates to the re-creation of nature (*natura*) by culture, thus eliminating the opposition between nature and culture.[95] The human is 'as a microcosm in the sense that he is the *logos* and the soul of the world' and makes nature its 'peripheral body' (humanise it through directing and governing it).[96] Nature, according to Bulgakov, 'always perceives her reflection in man, just as man [...] perceives his own reflection in Sophia', and as a sophianic being and the proper *metaxu* who mediates between God and the cosmos, human-being 'reflects the wise rays of the divine Logos'.[97] Humanity aspires to restore the gap created in the created order by

> transforming its mechanistic character once more into an organism and its lifeless products into the living forces that generated them, changing nature – which has become an object – once more into a subject-object, reestablishing the lost and forgotten unity of *natura naturans* and *natura naturata*.[98]

Such economic activity, Bulgakov describes is like the 'work of art, in which each product radiates 'with its own idea, and the world as a whole turns into a cosmos – a chaos that has been conquered, tamed, and illuminated from within'.[99] Thus, in Sophia, we find the ideal model of economy while in living *sobornost'*, we find a participatory vision of the individual and society.[100]

---

93 Bulgakov, *Philosophy of Economy*, 142.
94 Bulgakov, *Philosophy of Economy*, 145-146.
95 Bulgakov, *Philosophy of Economy*, 147.
96 Bulgakov, *Philosophy of Economy*, 145; Williams, *Sergii Bulgakov*, 241.
97 Bulgakov, *Philosophy of Economy*, 145.
98 Bulgakov, *Philosophy of Economy*, 135.
99 Bulgakov, *Philosophy of Economy*, 135.
100 Daniel P. Payne and Christopher Marsh, "Sergei Bulgakov's 'Sophic' Economy: An Eastern Orthodox Perspective on Christian Economics," *Faith & Economics* 53 (Spring 2009): 46. *Sobornost'* guarantees the rights of the individual but unlike Liberal capitalism, which dehumanises the person, it properly links the individual to society.

8.4 States of Peace and Privation

Thus far, we have seen that difference/multiplicity – whether group or class – can be reconciled in integral wisdom, All-unity (as ideal model), and that this unity-in-plurality can be experienced in living *sobornost'* (concretely). Then how can we give a Christian account of evil and violence? Sophia as the mediating principle bringing multiplicity (All) into unity is a peaceful principle – 'gentle and bloodless'.[101] Bulgakov often distinguishes between class-conflict and class-consciousness showing that how we can have the latter without the former: 'the class struggle in our society of class divisions must not be defined by hatred; it can be defined in terms of class-*conscience* and the awareness of mutual duties'.[102] He strongly argues that a 'model of the world as essentially conflictual will not do'.[103] In the discussion that follows, leaning on Bulgakov's theology of creation, I shall argue that creation *ex nihilo* implies that evil does not have an ontological existence and that evil/violence is a privation (failure to do the 'good' or rejection of peace, which is God's gift).

Evil and the Concept of Limitation

Does evil ontologically exist? Bulgakov answers this question in the negative. He denies evil any ontological existence. He denies evil a positive being. 'In the positive sense', Bulgakov claims, 'only Good, only God and His power in creation, exists', and evil, for Bulgakov, means 'an absence of good, *sterĕsis*, *privatio*, an accident, a parasite of being'; it is failure to do the good.[104] Thus, evil should not be understood as an independent ontological being (e.g., an evil god) or a principle that competes with the Good God (as in Oriental dualism). Having no positive being or substance, evil is simply a *state* of a living being.

If evil is not a positive being but a state of being, then how could this state become possible? To address this question, we need recourse to Bulgakov's concept of limitation, which is central to his doctrine of creation. Commenting on God's creation of the world *ex nihilo*, Bulgakov remarks, 'nothing' does not exist but simply implies an 'empty metaphysical hole, a bottomless abyss, in which there is no content'.[105] Nothing, which is not a hypostatic being with concrete nature, can be intelligible only in relation to something. Being content-less, nothing does

101 Rosenthal, "The Nature and Function of Sophia," 163.
102 Williams, *Sergii Bulgakov*, 265.
103 Williams, *Sergii Bulgakov*, 123.
104 Williams, *Sergii Bulgakov*, 147.
105 Bulgakov, *The Bride of the Lamb*, 54.

not exist *in*, *by* or *for* itself. 'Absolute nothing' can only exist in the human mind – conceiving absolute nothing as 'supracreaturely' being or an 'equidivine freedom' that juxtaposes alongside God rescinds the 'absoluteness of God's being' and introduces a dualism.[106] Thus, there is no absolute nothing (*ouk on*) but 'relative nothing' (*me on*), which exists and *me on* becomes intelligible only in a relation.[107] It is the relative nothing, which Bulgakov, following Dionysius, asserts that God, when he created the world, also generated nothing and included it in the very being of creation.

By its inclusion into the being of creation, nothing becomes the 'container' or 'potency' of the relative being (Plato's *ekmagein*).[108] Because of the endowment of creaturely freedom and creativity, relative being is in process of becoming. Creaturely freedom and creaturely creativity make it possible for creaturely/relative beings to realise or actualise the divine fullness of the Divine Sophia by creating out of 'the given and on a given theme'.[109] Since it has nothing as its constituting reality, the creativity of the relative being, however 'free' it might be, can never attain absolute perfection (if/when seen in relation to divine perfection). Thus, the becoming of the relative being signifies that, 'even though it enters *potentially* into the whole, every individual part or stage of being is necessarily *limited*, for it actually separated from the whole'.[110]

In view of the perfect being, the limitation of creaturely being can be considered as imperfection. In addition to this, creaturely creativity is fragmentary in nature because the response of creatures to God's call opens up to different prospects. In light of these two aspects – imperfection and diverse possibilities – one can conclude that creaturely limitation shows the disproportion (between the perfect being and the relative being), which implies that the latter is 'not infallible'.[111] However, imperfection or the presence of multiple possibilities should not be regarded as evil but only as the 'precondition' for evil, and what limitation implies is the state of non-infallibility or the possibility of fall from which the

---

106 Bulgakov, *The Bride of the Lamb*, 54.

107 Bulgakov, *The Bride of the Lamb*, 44, 55.

108 Bulgakov, *The Bride of the Lamb*, 54.

109 Bulgakov, *The Bride of the Lamb*, 148. The relation of the Divine Sophia and creaturely Sophia is not actually according to the mode of repetition. There is a differentiation.

110 Bulgakov, *The Bride of the Lamb*, 148.

111 Bulgakov, *The Bride of the Lamb*, 148-151. In Paul Ricoeur's expression, humans have the 'capacity to fail'; see Paul Ricoeur, *Fallible Man* (New York: Fordham University Press, 1965 [1986]), 138, 141.

idea of freedom cannot be detached. And actually, God freely and graciously bestowed the gift of self-determination 'even at the price of limitedness'.[112]

Freedom or Self-determination

Here, we need a brief account of the relation between creaturely freedom and evil. For Bulgakov, evil is an outcome of creaturely freedom, not a creation of God. With the manifestation of creaturely freedom arose two ways of life or possibilities.[113] The first possibility was a resolute obedience to the will of God. Such a path reveals a way of life beyond or prior to any opposition between good and evil. The second possibility was non-conformity to the will of God and this path clearly shows the introduction of the opposition between good and evil. This latter path is not part of the original creation and it is with this possibility that evil is associated. But both possibilities – whether the capacity for good, which is 'conformity with objective law', or evil, which is 'arbitrariness or caprice' – only affirm creaturely freedom.[114]

As a parasite of being, evil gets 'its strength from being' and 'arises in being as its sickness' but only as an outcome of self-determination and creativity.[115] Evil can be a reality as an actualised nothing only in the exercise of free self-determination. For Bulgakov, the 'very character of creatureliness' is 'the union of free self-determination and the natural given', which must be received as God's 'gift'; however, Bulgakov notes that 'it can be stolen by self-deifying creation' (as in the case of Lucifer) and he warns that creaturely beings should overcome the Luciferian temptation of 'pretend genius and self-deification'.[116] The exercise of self-determination or freedom by humans can have a devastating effect:

> Hidden in the metaphysical nature of the creature, which rests upon nothingness may be activated by human freedom, so that the abyss opens up. Nothingness is simply the texture of things – what lies between the threads in the weave of reality, the limitation of being as becoming. To the extent that becoming remains incomplete and the likeness has not been attained full identity with the image, this limitation may be the source of an illegitimate self-assertion, a creaturely egoism (already expressed in our

112 Bulgakov, *The Bride of the Lamb*, 148-149.

113 Bulgakov, *The Bride of the Lamb*, 151.

114 Self-determination or 'freedom' is 'without cause' or 'that which it determines itself on the basis of itself'; Bulgakov, *The Bride of the Lamb*, 153-154.

115 Bulgakov, *The Bride of the Lamb*, 153. Evil exists in its 'pure form' as a result of 'direct' rebellion to God in the world of fleshless angels but in the human domain evil, as an outcome of self-determination, is based on deception.

116 Bulgakov, *The Bride of the Lamb*, 155.

reciprocal impenetrability in space); it can represent the force of disintegration that belongs to the chaos 'waiting' and 'stirring' within it. Finally (but primarily, in ontological terms), the created spirit carries in itself the satanic temptation of putting its own selfhood in the place of the Primary Image.[117]

Participation in Sophia as All-unity or multi-unity is a peaceful unfolding of difference but not a violent self-assertion.[118] Sophia builds but does not destroy: 'Wisdom hath built herself a house' (Proverbs 9: 1).[119] Living *sobornost'*, which is participation in divine love, cannot allow the exercise of freedom/self-determination for the destruction of other selves. In *sobornost'*, collective existence cannot be simply reduced into a war of all against all. Rather, the connectedness of life and mutuality in divine love prevails. Sophia is about this peaceful re-ordering of society.

8.5 The Church as Counter-polity

Prior to extending the discussion to ecclesiology and the enactment of ontology, let me briefly clarify the connection of the foregoing theological discussion with social ontology. I started by elaborating Trinitarian ontology with two interrelated goals: (a) the ontology of individual personhood, and (b) a relational ontology of differentiated-unity. The concern with individual personhood has to do with the rights of the individual often conflated by the communitarian emphasis of ethno-nationalism. In the ethno-federal arrangement of Ethiopia, it is the ethnic-collective that has primacy over the individual. A Christian social ontology resists the denial of individual personhood by collectivist ethno-political ideology. The second relates to the ontology of coexistence. The concept of *sobornost'* expresses this social ontology of common life. Such ontology sanctions a differentiated-unity within the social order. On the one hand, it is opposed to the nationalistic practice of unity-as-homogeneity, which effaces difference and enforces a single centre, and on the other, it rejects the kind of difference practiced by violent ethno-nationalist struggles and the reification of abstract categories of the nation and the ethnic.

---

117 Williams, *Sergii Bulgakov*, 216.

118 Here, I am not intending to say that unjust ordering of society should be left untouched for the sake of maintaining peace. Social ordering that does not express sophianicity (the beauty of unity-in-plurality) is itself violent/evil. However, sophianic reordering cannot resort to violence as a means of reordering society.

119 Rosenthal, "The Nature and Function of Sophia," 162.

The theme of human labour further develops the ontology of personhood affirming that the person is irreducible to instrumentalisation. It resists both the mechanical conception of ethno-political ideologies and also the meritocratic view of the subject of labour (cf. the notion of *idil* discussed in Part II). Here, I wish to accentuate the need for a greater participation of the subject of labour in economic activities in modular voluntary associations free from state collectivisation and control. This has relations with what I say about corporatism in the next chapter. Finally, the primacy of the ontology of peace is discussed as a critique of the ontology of violence or 'the myth of ethnic conflict' presupposed by ethno-nationalist discourses to ground ethno-federal system in Ethiopia.

However, such discussion will not be complete without an account of the Church (*as* a counter-polity[120]) that enacts the Christian social ontology (counter-ontology) expounded thus far. This discussion, which will focus on the essence and operation of the Church, will have an anthropological significance (social or political) and serves as a theoretical bridge to the more constructive chapter. First of all, what is the Church? And what constitutes its essence? In his theological work, Bulgakov approaches the doctrine of the Church from the perspective of the theology of two Sophias according to which he claims that the essence of the Church is Sophia in both of its aspects: Divine and creaturely.[121]

The Church has a supra-temporal foundation as well as a temporal existence (appearing 'in time or in history' to share with 'creation the destinies of becoming').[122] The New Testament Church, which is inaugurated by the Incarnation and Pentecost (and whose head is Christ), is characterised by the synergy between the divine and the human: 'divine-humanity *in actu*'.[123] In light of this synergy, two implications can be drawn, here: the affirmation of the Church as a corporeality that presupposes the unity of the divine and human dimensions; and ecclesial existence presupposes discerning and enacting noumenal ontology. Noumenal ontology, or noumenal ontologism, is all about the

120 Here, I recognise the Church as a body that resists its marginalisation to the private sphere and that the manifestation of its life or inner dynamics stands as a critique of the 'immanentist self-ordering of the world'; see for example, Graham Ward, *Cities of God* (London: Routeledge, 2000), 94. See also John Milbank, *Being Reconciled: Ontology and Pardon* (London: Routledge, 2003), 105.

121 Bulgakov, *The Bride of the Lamb*, 253.

122 Bulgakov, *The Bride of the Lamb*, 253-254.

123 Bulgakov, *The Bride of the Lamb*, 261.

understanding of the life of the Church in its Divine-humanity, in its noumenal depth, in its supra-temporality, beyond the historical or empirical aspect.[124]

Holy Corporeality: The *Sobornost'* of the Church

As divine-humanity *in actu*, the Church is 'in-hypostatized' in Christ as 'the Bride of the Lamb'[125], and is also affirmed as the body of Christ (who is divine-human). As Bulgakov remarks, two dimensions are included in this affirmation: 'first, that it is proper to God, as well as to man, and therefore to the God-man, to have a body; and second, that the body of the God-man, the body of Christ, is the Church as deified humanity, as divine-human life'.[126] This statement stresses the theological importance of the notion of bodiliness and corporeality in relation to Christ and the Church. Bulgakov is against a negative metaphysical construal of the body, which argues that a 'bodiless' Christ needed flesh only insofar as he could accomplish our salvation.[127] He argues that such a construal is 'ontologically contradictory' because a bodiless being cannot put on corporeality; in this regard, what we discussed in Chapter 7 about the positive correlation of the two natures in Christ is relevant here because this union presupposes the existence of two – divine and human – corporealities.[128] The important point, here, is that it is quite proper for divinity to have a body, corporeality and that:

> In its essence, bodiliness is absolutely not the opposite of spirit, because there exists a spiritual bodiliness, the 'spiritual body' St Paul speaks of in 1 Cor. 15.44: '[I]f there is

124 Bulgakov, *The Bride of the Lamb*, 270.

125 Bulgakov, *The Bride of the Lamb*, 265.

126 Bulgakov, *The Bride of the Lamb*, 258. Scripture clearly attests the significance of bodily life in relation to Christ, the Church and human-beings. Of course, without this notion of bodiliness Christian doctrines such as the Incarnation, resurrection, the Church and salvation cannot not be properly understood; Williams, *Sergii Bulgakov*, 141.

127 A negative metaphysical construal of the body is the conception of the body as the opposite of 'spirituality', as the 'non-spiritual'; but rather, 'Christianity is the apotheosis of the body and holds out the promise of its redemption' because Christianity is not merely about the 'salvation of the soul' but also of the 'body'; Williams, *Sergii Bulgakov*, 141-2. St. Irenaeus of Lyon, St. Gregory of Nyssa, and St. Gregory of Palamas affirm that the name 'man' applies to both soul and body and that both are created in the image of God; Vladimir Lossky, *Orthodox Theology: An Introduction*, trans. Ian and Ihita Kesarcodi-Watson (NY: St. Vladimir Seminary Press, 1989), 120.

128 Bulgakov, *The Bride of the Lamb*, 259.

a physical body there is also a spiritual (*pneumatikon*) body' and indeed this kind of bodiliness contains in itself the ontological norm of bodily life'.[129]

Thus, when we say that the Church is a *body*, a 'mystical'[130] body, we mean that it is not 'a figure, a simile: *like* a body or *similar* to a body'.[131] To be sure, the Church as a mystic body is the revelation of both the Word (Logos) and the Holy Spirit: that is, as body of Christ ('panchristism') and as the temple of the Holy Spirit ('panpneumatism').[132] These aspects that properly describe the life of the Church as 'Holy corporeality' have great anthropological significance.[133] The anthropological significance has to do with the antinomy of the one and the many. In panchristism and panpneumatism, this antinomy, which cannot be resolved in any logical or static synthesis, is surmounted dynamically: 'the unity of *multiple* members' and 'their differentiation in *one* body'.[134] According to Bulgakov, the main difficulty in ecclesiology is this unity-in-difference. In the Holy corporeality: 'each member of the body is thereby the body, belonging to the *whole*; and in this sense each member is this whole [...] at the same time each member is also different from the whole'.[135]

In light of the above discussion, I wish to make a point in relation to the ethno-political context examined in Part II. As we have noted above, the antinomy between the one and the many is dynamically surmounted in the holy corporeality. This implies that incorporation into the body of Christ transforms and redefines social relations. This incorporation entails a different mode of

---

129 Williams, *Sergii Bulgakov*, 142.

130 This notion of the Church being a 'mystical body' refers not to the invisibility of the Church but it implies Bulgakov's ecclesial realism. In the same vein, Henri De Lubac employs this notion to explain that the Church 'originates beyond the natural order' (which is neither invisible nor virtual) – a body 'signified and realized by the Eucharist'; cf. David Grumett, *De Lubac: A Guide for the Perplexed* (London: T & T Clark, 2007), 57. The correlation between the ecclesial body and the sacramental body will be discussed later.

131 The term 'church' is used in two ways in the Scripture: when it is used in the plural, it refers to communities of Christians, and in the singular, it signifies the life that unites the churches – 'one mystical essence' and this essence/life is expressed as the body of Christ; Bulgakov, *The Bride of the Lamb*, 255.

132 Bulgakov, *The Bride of the Lamb*, 259-261.

133 Williams, *Sergii Bulgakov*, 142.

134 Bulgakov, *The Bride of the Lamb*, 255-258.

135 Bulgakov, *The Bride of the Lamb*, 259. It is only in the Church that persons realise their true nature; cf. Vladimir Lossky, *In the Image and Likeness of God* (ed. John H. Erickson and Thomas E. Bird. NY: St. Vladimir Seminary Press, 1974), 108.

existence: a spiritual existence irreducible to mere biological existence. Through the operation of the Spirit (in this holy corporeality) a new ordering of persons emerges. With such incorporation, not only a new form of unity but also a new form of difference (based on the distribution of spiritual gifts and hence, places/statuses) arises.

While acknowledging the fact that individuals can be products of their culture, individuals incorporated in the body of Christ can transcend the ideological conditioning of their respective ethnic communities. Panchristism (panpneumatism) is a Christic-politics that stands against the logic of ethno-political ideology, which is solidarity of the *ethnos* (achieved through ethnic-interpellation). Therefore, from this perspective, the Church is a living organism of collective harmony and peace, as we have already noted in the previous chapter: a living *sobornost'*. Enacting *sobornost'* is manifesting a new ordering of persons in a harmonious and peaceful order. We will discuss this enactment below.

Noumenal Ontologism: Enacting *Sobornost'*

The idea of *sobornost'*, as Bulgakov argues, is understood not only ontologically but also pragmatically, and this pragmatism or realism demonstrates the synergism of the Church.[136] As Divine-human, the Church is the synergy of the divine and the creaturely principles, which are united *without separation* and *without confusion* in the manner of the union of the two natures in Christ. In practical terms, this synergy implies 'a giving and a receiving of divine gifts'.[137] The understanding of the body of Christ in terms of operations of gifts implies an organic and creative life. This aspect of the Church is 'free ecclesiality' to which Bulgakov attributes ontological precedence over the Church in its aspect of institutional hierarchism.[138] In view of this, the organised institutional Church must not suppress the ontological (sophiological) aspect of the Church (that is, free ecclesiality).[139]

---

136 Bulgakov, *The Bride of the Lamb*, 262.

137 Bulgakov, *The Bride of the Lamb*, 262. With the receiving and the operation of gifts within the body of Christ arises a notion of difference that emanates from the diversity of the nature of the gifts themselves and the various levels of responses (the economy of responses might vary according to the measures of faith/giftedness of each members of the body). In the operation of gifts, the members of the body are equi-corporeal or equivalent but equivalence, here, does not imply equality. This indicates the necessity of a healthy form of hierarchism, which does not transform itself into a pathological/parasitical mode of existence in relation to the body.

138 Bulgakov, *The Bride of the Lamb*, 262.

139 Bulgakov, *The Bride of the Lamb*, 262-263.

Bulgakov's argument does not go in the direction of regarding church history (the development of the Church as institution with hierarchical charismata) as completely an accident foreign to God's providence. Rather, he argues that the Divine-human foundation of the Church implies that the Church is 'essentially historical' and in fact, the Church, in its creaturely aspect, properly belongs to '*history*': Bulgakov claims that the institutional, or the 'phenomenal', Church is indivisible from the *sobornost'* of the Church, that is, 'noumenal ontologism'.[140]

The evolvement of sacramental powers (priestly ministry) in church history is associated with the central sacrament of the Church, the Eucharist, which attests and manifests the Incarnation.[141] What is at stake, here, is that there is a deep correlation between ecclesial realism and Eucharistic realism, which Bulgakov strongly asserts because it is the principal way by which the Church reveals and realises its divine-humanity in the world. This is central to the continuation and realisation of the Incarnation and Pentecost.[142] Hierarchy, according to Bulgakov, 'originally appeared in connection with the performance of the sacraments [...] the Eucharist'.[143] As directly administered by Christ, and afterwards in the 'primitive' Church, this sacrament, simply known as the 'breaking of bread', was without a definite hierarchic-liturgical form.[144]

Bulgakov comments that this is but a '*postulate* of hierarchy as an organ of the sacraments'[145] (i.e., in service of *sobornost'*) and not an unhealthy kind of hierarchy that suppresses noumenal ontologism. (Here, Bulgakov does not clearly

140 Bulgakov, *The Bride of the Lamb*, 270.

141 Bulgakov mentions the differences that exist between Western (Protestantism) and Eastern Orthodox theology. The former reduces the Eucharist into communion while the latter conceives it as both a sacrifice and a communion (in its one complex act). It is the 'divine "It is finished" (John 19:30), as sacrificial and abiding Incarnation' – the 'abiding of Christ in the world, *despite* the ascension'; Bulgakov, *The Bride of the Lamb*, 286.

142 Similarly, De Lubac claims 'Although the Church produces the Eucharist, the Eucharist realizes the Church' and he argues that the Eucharist is not an empty sign (or a mediatorial sign – because that which is signified by a sign disjoined from the sign itself but rather it 'unites them by making present that which it evokes'; see Henri De Lubac, *The Splendor of the Church*, trans. Michael Mason (San Francisco: Ignatius, 1986), 202 cited in Grumett, *De Lubac*, 56-57.

143 Bulgakov, *The Bride of the Lamb*, 287.

144 Bulgakov, *The Bride of the Lamb*, 284.

145 Bulgakov, *The Bride of the Lamb*, 287. In the initial stage of institutionalism, hierarchism developed without suppressing 'charismatism'/the prophetic dynamism of the early Church; see Bulgakov, *The Orthodox Church*, 45.

spell out who knows when noumenal ontologism is suppressed and who is responsible to speak about and implement the necessary reforms). The historical context for this healthy hierarchism is the necessity of authentication raised due to inauthentic performances of the Eucharist such as 'false, emotional ecstasy' and 'anticommunal, non-koinonic ("monatanistic") exaltation'.[146] Such ecclesial guarantee for the Eucharist, however, as Bulgakov remarks, must not be at the cost of placing the hierarchy over the ecclesial *sobornost'*.

In Bulgakov's thought, the noumenal and the phenomenal aspects of the Church are non-contradictory and are not opposed to each other. However, he also observes the development of an unhealthy form of hierarchism – 'clericalization' – that is different from the healthy hierarchism. This concerns the recognition of bishops as 'vicars of Christ', which led to the equation of hierarchy with the Church – an identification of the Church with the hierarchy as '*pars pro toto* or, at least, as the head' 'replaces the whole body'.[147] In consequence, earthly hierarchy is elevated (the aim of which is) uniting it with the heavenly hierarchy; however, 'this diminishes the true significance of the Head of the Body, Christ, who, we repeat, is not the head of the body (with which a hierarchy is most comparable) but the Head from, by, and in which the body exists – the Body of Christ'.[148] Clerical absolutism, in all its diverse forms (papal infallibility as well as corporate episcopate infallibility in Catholic and Orthodox churches respectively), 'subverts the very principle of ecclesial hierarchism' and introduces a division in functional/operative ecclesiology: a cleft/cleavage between 'the rulers and the ruled, the teachers and the taught, those who command and those who obey'.[149]

Therefore, according to Bulgakov, the principle should be that of 'First the Church, then the hierarchy, not vice versa' and that the 'universal priesthood is the *prius* (the first condition) of the episcopate, not vice versa'.[150] The crux of Bulgakov's argument is that as far as the history of the Eucharist is concerned, it is the 'koinonic character', rather than the hierarchical, which has the

146 Bulgakov, *The Bride of the Lamb*, 287. While acknowledging that both the 'charism' and the 'hieratic principle' are equally important, Bulgakov indicates that the exaltation of the former at the expense of the latter can lead to 'pseudo-prophetic excitement', which can undermine the real significance of ecclesial as well as Eucharistic realism; cf. Bulgakov, *The Orthodox Church*, 50.

147 Bulgakov, *The Bride of the Lamb*, 276. Here, Bulgakov indicates the dangers of the notion of apostolic succession in Catholic as well as Orthodox churches.

148 Bulgakov, *The Bride of the Lamb*, 276.

149 Bulgakov, *The Bride of the Lamb*, 279.

150 Bulgakov, *The Bride of the Lamb*, 281.

precedence. Even though this koinonic character was 'replaced [...] by hierarchism', it (unhealthy hierarchism) 'did not completely eliminate it, but was capable of obscuring it'.[151]

While acknowledging the positive benefits of healthy hierarchism, Bulgakov draws attention to the prophetic and royal Church, but not the hierarchical Church that is not governed by canonical or hierarchic regulation. Herein, Bulgakov distinguishes between the hierarchism of the institutional Church and the gifts of the prophetic Church: prophecy is conceived as dynamics and movement while the hierarchism is understood as its support.

In conclusion, I want to say the following in relation to ecclesiology and a counter-*dispositif* strategy. As we have noted in Part II, the challenge facing the Church has been the nationalistic absorption of Christian identity. To counter the instrumentalisation of religion by the state and its ideology (a counter-*dispositif*), (operative) ecclesiology takes a central place. Now, what has been said so far has a great relevance for this strategy: that is, letting free ecclesiality (the sophiological or the ontological aspect of the Church).

In the Ethiopian case, historically, there have been varied forms of active or passive resistance against state ideology: monastic movements, evangelical movements, etc. (of course, there have always been contradictory tendencies within Christianity). What has been made clear in the discussion above is that the institutional Church is the place where we discern and enact noumenal ontologism. This does not mean, however, that the enactment should be confined in the Church. The Church is not understood as a static, self-sufficient and enclosed polity. We have made clear this in Chapter 7 in the account of cosmic-mediation. Through its prophetic dynamism and sacramental realism, the Church enacts its noumenal ontology that counters secular ordering of society.[152] Therefore, in light of the discussion of this chapter on the ontological themes, concluded in an account of the Church as counter-polity, offers a resource for a counter-*dispositif* theological strategy. This will be the task of the next chapter, which will be more constructive.

---

151 Bulgakov, *The Bride of the Lamb*, 287.

152 For example, Alexander Schmemann, who is one of Orthodox theologians influenced by Bulgakov, argues that secularism is a form of a '*negation of worship*', which in theological terms is 'a heresy about man (homo adorans) and that in sacramental act (Eucharist), 'It is not "grace" that comes down, it is the Church that enters into "grace," and grace means the new being, the Kingdom, the world to come'; Alexander Schmemann, *For the World: Sacraments and Orthodoxy* (NY: St. Vladimir's Seminary Press, 1995), 118-121, 31.

8.6 Conclusion

Before proceeding to the next chapter that deals with the politics of metanoia, a summary of the argument of this chapter might be helpful. First, I discussed the significance of Bulgakov's Trinitarian ontology for sociality. The exposition of this theology precipitated the importance of the concept of personality. For Bulgakov, each Trinitarian hypostasis has its nature by a *personal* self-positing. And the unity of the Holy Trinity is not of mere possession of a common static nature but rather through a dynamic relation or produced unity. Bulgakov's use of the concept of 'spirit' and his identification of God's essence *ousia* with 'Sophia' is directly related with finding theological tools to reverberate the idea of personhood for countering impersonalism in all its forms.

The implications of these for social ontology are clear. It offers a way of articulating the relation of personhood to collective existence without compromising the significance of individual personality. It also offers us an account of unity-in-plurality (differentiated-unity) – the reconciliation of multiplicity in Sophia, integral wisdom or All-unity. Generally, the significance of Trinitarian ontology for social ontology can be summarised by one word/concept: *sobornost'*. This notion of organic collective existence leads neither to liberal individualism nor to impersonal collectivisation.

We also discussed the sophic nature of economic activity. Despite theories of economy that consider labour as a single factor (among others) in economic calculations and contrary to conceptions of the 'economic man' that narrowly define labour in terms of utility, we argued that economic activity is the synthesis of freedom and necessity. Although the relation between the human-being and nature is affected by the metaphysical Fall, there is the hope of joyful labour in Sophia as labour gradually restores the division between the two Sophias. In *sobornost'*, the individual person practices freedom (from impersonal mechanisation of life) to participate in economic activity that restores her personhood.

Next, we noted that evil does not have an ontological existence but rather it is a privation (not doing the good). It only exists as a parasitic being. This becomes possible because the created being is a limited relative being and this provides the condition for evil (but limitation is not by itself evil). What needs attention is the fact that we are given the gift of self-determination, which is the freedom to act (without causality), and that we can use this capacity for good or vice. Therefore, in this chapter, I have, then, outlined the social ontology, which Christian *askesis* requires.

Finally, we concluded with an account of the Church. We noted that to know the Church only in its temporal existence, creaturely essence and phenomenal reality, is to deprive it of its divine essence, eternal/supra-temporal ground, and noumenal ontologism. Understanding the Church as a synergy of the heavenly and earthly realities is significant to counter the contemporary appellation of the Church as a form of society or association (e.g. as civil society), which practically depoliticises the Church by either marginalising it to the sphere of the private or limiting its public/political visibility. The Church, as divine-humanity *in actu*, is the 'ultimate purpose of creation'[153]. And the idea of *sobornost'*, which is central to Bulgakov's ecclesiology, cannot be extricated from social and political life. Through its prophetic dynamism and sacramental realism, the Church enacts its noumenal ontology that counters the secular ordering of society.

153 Graves, *The Holy Spirit*, 68.

9 The Politics of Metanoia

9.1 Introduction

In the preceding chapters, and particularly in the previous one, I have articulated a Christian ontology and ecclesiology, which further elaborated the account of Christian *askesis* I articulated in Chapter 7. My concern in those chapters has been largely a critique of both Church and society (articulating counter-anthropology, counter-ontology, counter-polity). We are now in a position to integrate the arguments in a constructive manner.[1] I wish to organise the arguments of this chapter in response to the following question: what are the consequences of the theological discourse, developed thus far, to the ethno-political context (analysed in Part II)? This reconstructive chapter develops the outlook articulated in the previous chapters by giving expression to a political perspective consistent with the Christian theology outlined there: the politics of metanoia.

As I will argue, the politics of metanoia is the way out of the dead-end produced by ethno-political ideology, which identifies politics with the identity/self of the community (the *ethnos*). This will pave the way for us to risk thinking politics in an altogether different way beyond ethno-national logic. The discussion will proceed in three stages: first, I shall start by accentuating the need for a metanoic community constituted by a distinctively Christian culture of the self that enhances the transformation of persons and communities that go beyond the ideological conditioning of their own communities (9.2). Second, I shall further elaborate the politics of metanoia by placing it within its utopic horizon, the ideal of the Kingdom of God (9.3). Third, I shall briefly explain that the theological implication of the Kingdom of God is not only serving as an active principle but also presupposes another kind of authority (9.4) before I conclude the discussion (9.5).

1 Even though the emphasis has been on self-criticism and critique, there has been a constructive side to the arguments deployed in the preceding chapters. Self-criticism, critique and construction that constitute the three-fold theological task of cultural hermeneutics are often overlapping.

9.2 The Metanoic Community

The analysis of the political technologies that have shaped the self is meant to draw attention to the need to counter those historically inbuilt *dispositifs* that 'make only particular kinds of action possible'[2]. As noted above, the identification of politics with the identity/self of the community (whether ethnic or national) has led Ethiopian politics to a dead-end. Now, going beyond this impasse demands going beyond the 'limits' of *what we are* (to use Foucault's terms) through what Foucault calls the *practices of freedom* (See Chapter 2). Freeing the self from the practices and thinking that historically limit its experience involves a (re)turn to aesthetics of existence.

In what follows, I wish to make two points: first, I shall explain that a theological counter-*dispositif* strategy that aims to dissociate identity/self of the community from politics needs a metanoic return to transcendent aesthetic values, which makes possible a new culture of the self. In so doing, I shall show the ontological possibility of a new political subject that transcends ethno-political ideology. This leads to my second point: solidarity beyond the *ethnos* that characterises the metanoic community (the new political subjects).

A Metanoic Return: Towards a Christian Culture of the Self

Back in Chapter 7, I quoted Bulgakov's remark that suggests that the sophianic thirst for beauty (art) is a redeeming force, which I think, has a direct implication to the conception of ethical self-formation. Seen from this perspective, ethical self-formation looks like a work of art.[3] Ethical self-formation as the work of art assumes the work of freedom or moral creativity. Granted, Foucault's practices of freedom are important to understand how we transform our relation to the self, but I reject the idea that freedom *per se* suffices to be the ontological precondition and the *telos* of ethics (and politics).[4] Here, I consider it important to

---

2 See John Rajchman, *Michel Foucault: The Freedom of Philosophy* (New York: Columbia University Press, 1985), 110–111.

3 The following remark by William Desmond (in connection to our 'aesthetic potency') alludes to this fact: 'we live in our response to beauty'; *Ethics and the Between* (Albany, NY: State University of New York Press, 2001), 11.

4 As we may recall, Foucault's stance is post-metaphysical in so far as it asserts that limits are not universal but contingent and hence, his idea is that the 'historical ontology of ourselves' should avert from those projects (metaphysical and ahistorical) that claim to be 'global or radical'; however, I want to make a brief remark, here, using William Desmond's work: 'In claiming to be beyond metaphysics, we become

surpass Foucault's account of *askesis* because I contend that the aesthetic values and stylistic criteria (needed for ethical self-formation) should not be sought within the bounds of the self. Rather, they have to be sought in and beyond the self (I will further clarify this point later).

Although I am not suggesting probing into the complex notion of 'freedom', which Bulgakov calls a 'logical Chameleon', but it is quite important, here, to clarify at least how this notion is being used in connection to moral creativity. One way of approaching this issue is by recalling what I have already said in Chapter 7 in connection to creation from the perspective of the theology of two Sophias. From that discussion, we can draw the fact that creation and its moral creativity cannot be divorced from its supra-temporal foundation – its *entelecheia*.

This implies that creation cannot be understood 'in and from itself'.[5] Of course, 'the true domain of freedom in its multifarious manifestations belongs precisely to creaturely Sophia' and 'its source must be sought in the Divine Sophia'.[6] The point is that freedom is not an 'ontological substance' but a 'modality': it does not exist 'in and for itself'.[7] Thus, moral creativity has to be understood within a relational matrix (having a vertical [towards the transcendent] and horizontal [towards the other] axis).

For now, let us take into account the vertical axis. What we said of the potency of sophiurgy (in Chapter 7) is relevant, here. Double-agency – divine-human synergy – is the key to understand aesthetic life. This does not undermine the place of freedom or self-determination in ethics and politics. 'Ethical self-determination', Bulgakov claims, 'cannot be free, and conversely, only free self-determination can have an ethical goal'.[8] Put another way, ethical self-formation or aesthetic life requires synergy; otherwise, we slip into a 'formless creativity of the self'[9]. Even though there is an anarchic element (un-conformity) in the constitution of the self/subjectivity, the Christian's ethical goal is that of conformity (to Christ, to the sophianic). What is proper is not moral creativity 'in its own name', which is

---

unknowing metaphysicians – an inarticulate sense of the meaning of being informs our post-metaphysical, or non-metaphysical thinking. There seems no escape from metaphysics', *God and the Between* (Oxford: Blackwell Publishing, 2008), 9.

5 See Bulgakov, *The Bride of the Lamb*, 126.

6 Bulgakov, *The Bride of the Lamb*, 126.

7 Bulgakov, *The Bride of the Lamb*, 125-126.

8 Williams, *Sergii Bulgakov*, 41. Without freedom or self-positing a person does not exist but since the creaturely 'I' (self) is not absolute 'its very freedom is unfree'; see Bulgakov, *The Bride of the Lamb*, 126-127.

9 Williams, *Sergii Bulgakov*, 66. Unlike Berdiev, Bulgakov makes no appeal to anarchism.

'asophianic' or 'anti-sophianic'; therefore, moral creativity requires freedom that 'does not abolish this sophianic regularity but only concretely applies it'.[10]

A paradigm expressive of this form of aesthetics that involves divine-human synergy is the Christ Event, which is, in fact, a task for humanity (See Chapter 7). The Event defines the ontological horizon of Christian *askesis* and the condition for transformation. For Christians, a re-turn to aesthetics of existence entails a re-turn to the event. Ethical self-formation, as the work of art, involves a certain theandrism and dithelitism, and metanoia names this re-turn to the event.[11] Metanoia, for Bulgakov, is not understood in terms of a pietistic individualistic repentance but rather as a return to first principles that transforms Christians and the world. It is for this reason that he calls his sophiology a 'dogmatic metanoia', a 'new apprehension' of Christian dogma, which results in the change of mind and action towards the world. Metanoia is, in the words of Rowan Williams, 'a comprehensive self-questioning'.[12] Without such self-questioning, Christians cannot generate critique of society and have a meaningful socio-political engagement. Thus, comprehensive self-questioning, or metanoia, is proper to Christian *askesis* whose aim is meaningful action in relation to self and the world.

As an aspect of Christian *askesis*, metanoia is inseparable from *paideia*. The transformation of our relation to the self can be made possible only in thinking differently, which is acquired through proper *paideia*. Through metanoia, a shift in worldview, theo-political subjects can challenge the worldview unleashed by ethno-political ideology. Within the Ethiopian context, in which ethno-national self-writing proliferate, and in which the educational apparatus is subservient to ethno-political ideology, Christians should give due attention to the necessity of thinking the relation about theology and pedagogy (ethics and *askesis*) seriously. What is overlooked in this process of politicising abstract categories is the concrete notion of the 'personal'; here, personal in the sense of the virtuous.[13]

---

10 What is argued for, here, has nothing related to predeterminism or determinism for 'creative activity' according to Bulgakov, is 'free of the fetters of determinism'; see Bulgakov, *The Bride of the Lamb*, 342.

11 The use of the notion of 'Event', here, is not to evoke associations with Alain Badiou's notion of the Event because Badiou's notion of the Event awaits for singularising (revolutionary) moments and figures and mobilises coercion, which are elements or aspects I am critical of; cf. Creston Davis and Patrick Aaron Riches, "Metanoia: The Theological Praxis of Revolution," in *Theology and the Political: The New Debate*, eds. Creston Davis, Slavoj Žižek and John Milbank (Durham, N.C.: Duke University Press, 2005), 22-46, 255-256.

12 Rowan Williams, "Introduction," in *Theology and the Political*, 3.

13 Williams, *Sergii Bulgakov*, 65.

Such a focus on the personal makes 'the *education* of the will' quite significant.[14] It is the task of Christian pedagogy to elaborate what we are transformed from and transformed to because such pedagogy is pedagogy of difference/transformation (for there is a disjunction between the Christian account of personhood and that of ethno-political modes of self-writing). The *paideia* that informs and informed by Christian *askesis* cannot ignore our identity (who we are in Christ). This Christian understanding of personhood or selfhood cannot be divorced from the Christology (already articulated in Chapter 7). The in-hypostatisation or the incorporation in Christ and our participation in divine life entails a new formation of and relation to the self, a new culture of the self. Incorporation into the body of Christ implies a transformation of the bond of togetherness. Christian pedagogy, which is pedagogy of difference, makes a new culture of the self that smoothes the progress of solidarity beyond the *ethnos*.

Solidarity beyond the *Ethnos*

If we revisit the theological argument on personhood based on Trinitarian ontology in the context of ecclesial *sobornost'* (in the previous chapter), and join it with the above discussion on a new culture of (relation to) the self, we are now in a position to see where the whole discussion is leading to (vis-à-vis ethno-political ideology or the ethno-federal polity): that is, solidarity beyond the *ethnos*. In what follows, I wish to briefly explain fostering solidarity beyond the *ethnos* entails going beyond self-assertion, autonomy, or self-determination, and towards the enactment of *sobornost'*.

From our discussion in the foregoing chapter, we recall that there is a correlation between freedom and necessity, which helps to clarify the notion of autonomy. In that discussion, the notion of freedom (corresponding to necessity) was raised in relation to material determinism. But here, we have to see it in connection to the relation of the self (self-assertion; self-determination) to the other (what we mentioned above as the horizontal axis). It might be helpful to start by quoting Bulgakov on the notion of freedom:

> Creaturely freedom is necessarily a play of light and shadow: The rays of freedom must be reflected from a wall which is its boundary just as the I in Fichte's system requires a not-I in order to posit itself. Autonomous being collides here with what is given, and the self-positing of freedom reflexively appears only in connection with or as dependent

14 Williams, *Sergii Bulgakov*, 65. 'Will' mediates between desire and action; see Desmond, *Ethics and the Between*, 126.

upon unfreedom. Creaturely freedom is always relative or, what is the same thing, modal. This freedom is correlative with necessity.[15]

What such a remark makes clear, in the first instance, is the fact that freedom is a modality, and that conceiving it as absolute is a '*contradictio in adjecto*'[16] because freedom, as applied to human creatures, is a relative concept. From this we can draw the conclusion that the non-absolutism of freedom makes it impossible for the meaning of creaturely freedom to be coextensive with autonomy.[17] Then, since autonomy or self-determination cannot be an end in itself, there arises the need to go beyond self-determination. Going beyond self-determination is a release of the self towards the other beyond autonomous will and calculating self-interest of self-determination.[18]

In Part II, we noted how the self of self-determination has been constructed as a self-asserting ethno-political entity. We recall that the foundational myth of the ethnic-federal polity is ethnic-egotism (and as a remedy and safeguard to inter-ethnic domination or exploitation, they need to assert their own autonomous will and use it in rational calculation of self-interest). Here, I would suggest resorting to the interrelated theological motifs of kenosis and sophianicity, which we mentioned in Chapter 7 albeit in relation to the commensurability between the divine and the human. Indeed, it is theologically more appropriate to speak of such surpassing of the self (by the self of self-determination or the ethno-political entity) using the language of kenosis. Such desire for the other (which we may call the 'neighbour' in biblical terms) beyond the calculation of self-interest emanates from the kenotic self that aspires to surpass (transcend) itself. Through accepting otherness as otherness and relating to the other through kenotic self-giving, the self becomes truly itself. This implies that the relation of the self to the other should not be simply because the self (the 'I') needs the *not*-I (the other) for its fulfilment but rather because the self should respond to the call, which the other (*not* I) poses on the self. This directly implies that without the kenotic, the *pleroma* (fullness/wholeness) of sophianic All-unity cannot manifest (it is kenosis that makes *koinonos* or *sobornost'* possible).[19]

---

15 Bulgakov, *The Bride of the Lamb*, 127.

16 Williams, *Sergii Bulgakov*, 126.

17 See William Desmond, *Ethics and the Between*, 8.

18 Bulgakov, *The Bride of the Lamb*, 126-7. See also Desmond, *Ethics and the Between*, 8.

19 For Bulgakov, the self releases itself to the other (beyond 'egoism') through kenosis, which makes the self relate to the other in a loving relation. In the same vein, William Desmond argues that however wholeness is important to the self, the motivating factor should be doing this move for the sake of the other; see *Ethics and the Between*,

Although dialectical sense of being can make us acknowledge the importance of drawing attention to issues of sameness and difference, the conception of life as a struggle (war of all against all) by ethno-political ideology cannot offer the ground for peacefully resolving the struggle between the self and the other. In contrast to the 'self-mediating wholeness' of the 'dialectical', it is only being-as-analogical (see Chapter 8) or the 'metaxological' that offers the possibility of resolving the tension in an 'open wholeness' related to what William Desmond calls the 'ovedetermined milieu'.[20] The question raised by autonomy or self-determination takes us from kenosis to sophianicity: Integral Wisdom or multi-hypostatic unity. But does not this recourse to Integral Wisdom seem monistic or univocal? To make myself clear, I have to make the following two points.

First, the sophianic All-unity is a differentiated-unity that is well attuned to our equivocal condition (cf. the previous two chapters). The supra-ethnic order of the sophianic All-unity does not simply erase differences (ethnic or other differences) but resolves the antinomy of difference in organic unity, in the togetherness of *sobornost'* (see Chapter 8). This is different from the attempt to effect a supra-ethnic order through the transcendence of ethnic loyalties through civic-nationalism – imagined community – which is a metaphysical void. Rather, it is an organic unity of *sobornost'* – one with a metaphysical depth and dense in meaning (as we have seen in the previous chapter). As we recall, *sobornost'* involves a transformation of the bond of togetherness. The panchristic theo-logic replaces the ethnic-logic without (the former) demanding the abolition of difference. Differentiated-unity remains to be a characteristic feature of solidarity beyond the *ethnos*.[21] Therefore, unlike the univocal, which upholds sameness,

---

354-355. The necessity of going towards the other is not self-return, though; there is a return to the self. Here, the issue of generosity (gift) cannot be neglected (a notion inherent in panpneumatism). The generosity of the kenotic self does not demand or require for a return. Of course, the return might be repeated in a different form or it might not come at all. Even if the latter becomes the case, the self-transcendence of the kenotic self is not a failure. See Desmond, *Ethics and the Between*, 8, 355; Graham Ward makes the link between sociality and the economy of the gift highlighting that 'sociality, which moves beyond ourselves and into a permanent journeying towards the other is only possible within an economy of the gift in which I am constituted in the transit of plenitudinous grace' and for example, 'Abraham does not give to the strangers because he will get something in return. Though he later receives'; *Christ and Culture*, 79-80.

20 Desmond, *Ethics and the Between*, 2.

21 However, the notion of differentiated-unity requires a qualification. It should not be reduced to ethnic difference and its affirmation. It should be broadly understood as a promise of discord.

my account gives proper attention to the equivocal condition of sociality. In fact, it stands as a critique of the federal polity in its institutionalisation of territorial identities with political ones, which, through achieving ethnic homogeneity, exclude the 'ethnic'-others (a mechanism of in/exclusion). But, how should difference or differentiated-unity unfold? This leads to my second point.

Second, the sophianic-All does not enforce a single centre. This is true to our sophianic condition. Such condition can be captured by an important Platonic term cherished by Bulgakov: *metaxu* (the 'meta' is both a 'beyond' and an 'in the midst').[22] In the metanoic community, the ethos (of freedom; the good) derives out of the *metaxu* or the 'metaxological' milieu that implies that the ethos is always already 'overdetermined'.[23] The overdetermined good that emerges out of this metaxological milieu (constituted by multi-hypostatic multi-unity) transforms the bond of togetherness: that is, *sobornost'* that knows no 'peripheries'.[24] From this standpoint, there can only be plurality of centres resulting in the distribution of freedom, which perturbs what William Desmond calls 'erotic sovereignty'.[25]

In a sense, federalism is not exclusively incompatible with the notion of *sobornost'*.[26] Federalism presupposes a collaborative ethics and conceives politics

---

22 Bulgakov, *The Bride of the Lamb*, 123; also cf. Desmond, *Ethics and the Between*, 7.

23 See Desmond, *Ethics and the Between*, 8-9, 466-467.

24 Cf. Desmond, *Ethics and the Between*, 126.

25 Desmond, *Ethics and the Between*, 8; Desmond comments that the 'metaxological view demands a plurality of mediating centres of power to prevent the social intermediation of erotic sovereignty from the project of seeking to become the one absolute center that seeks to ingest all others, subjecting them to itself as mirrors of itself. This middle way respects the pluralism of centers of power, keeping alive in the *metaxu* the promise of power beyond sovereignty, the power of agapeic service that frees from bewitchment'; Desmond, *Ethics and the Between*, 481.

26 Historically, the federal idea has its roots and legitimation in religion. Its philosophical basis was the idea of covenant (the Latin *foedus* and its Hebrew equivalent *berith* meaning peace and 'covenantal wholeness'). In the West, such covenantal (federal) theologico-political concept was secularised as '*pactum*' (contractual bond), which is often associated with the work of Johannes Althusius's *Politica Methodice Digesta* in the late 16th century; see Daniel J. Elazar, *Exploring Federalism* (Tuscaloosa, AL: Alabama University Press, 1987), 115-153; Glenn A. Moots, "The Covenant Tradition of Federalism: The Pioneering Studies of Daniel J. Elaza," in *The Ashgate Research Companion to Federalism* (eds. Ann Ward and Lee Ward. Surrey, England: Ashgate, 2009), 391-399. In Russian philosophical-theological tradition, federalist thought has sometimes been associated with the concept of sobornost understood as 'coming together' of people in loving mutual relationship (co-operation); for example, cf.

as 'the art of associating' that furthers mutuality and 'harmonious exercise of social life'.[27] However, as I have already argued, federalism tends to devalue its own values of federalism because of its ethnic nature and its bias or resonance towards the centre (a slide to tyranny). I contend that the apotheosis of the bond of togetherness endangered by federalism (federalism that is not federal enough) lies in the ideal of *sobornost'*. *Sobornost'* operates by the postulate of love that fosters the coming togetherness of people and is opposed to coercive holding-togetherness of people.

Therefore, going beyond our cultural (ideological) conditioning, beyond the confines of solidarity of the *ethnos*, and beyond self-determination, the metanoic community opens the door for the possibility of larger solidarities. Here, I am suggesting the need for corporatism between the individual and the State, which the latter should not seek to control. However, I am not suggesting another politics of subjectivity nor do I propose a politics of identity of a religious sort.[28] The politics of metanoia, which I am proposing, is the politics of the Kingdom of God.

9.3 Metanoia and the Kingdom

In the above discussion, it has been hinted that political metanoia leads to the questioning of earthly forms of authority. This leads us to the discussion of the ideal of the Kingdom of God, which is the context for metanoia: 'Repent – *metanoeite* (change your mind, examine yourselves), for the Kingdom of God is at hand'.[29] The Kingdom of God is *in* but not *of* this world. It is *entoshēmōn* ('within us', 'among us'), and it also 'comes' 'so that one presupposes the other'.[30] The Kingdom of God is the utopic horizon for metanoia insofar as it is a 'prophecy of the future', which is yet invisible and unrealised in a definite form in any

---

Elena Chebankova, "Russia's Noncovenantal Federalism: Past and Present," *Journal of Church and State* 51, 2 (November 10, 2009): 317.

27 Johannes Althusius, "Politics as the Art of Associating," in *Theories of Federalism: A Reader* (eds. Dimitrios Karmis and Wayne Norman. New York, N.Y.: Palgrave Macmillan, 2005), 27-33.

28 For example, see Kenneth Surin, "Rewriting the Ontological Script of Liberation: On the Question of Finding a New Kind of Political Subject," in *Theology and the Political*, 254-255. On liberal utopia, see also Robert Nozick, *Anarchy, State, and Utopia* (Oxford: Blackwell, 1974), 316.

29 Williams, *Sergii Bulgakov*, 251.

30 Williams, *Sergii Bulgakov* 252; see also Bulgakov, *The Bride of the Lamb*, 341.

definite place.[31] However, because utopia (*ut-topos*) implies a no-where, utopianism should not be regarded as 'the direct opposite of realism'; but rather 'it can and must be united with it'.[32] I am not intending to open another discussion on the congruence between utopia and realism (see Chapter 3). The point, which I wish to make, is that the politics of metanoia can be understood as recognition of the utopic horizon of Christianity.

What is the effect of this recognition? As we have already noted in Part I, it is utopian imagination (of another social order) that provides us with the critical distance to resist ideology. The ideal of the Kingdom of God, which inspires Christian utopianism, informs Christian *askesis*. This ideal is not a prophecy of the future, which Christians simply expect or anticipate in a passive disposition. Rather, it implies a projection of the present to the future as well as a directedness of the future to the present. For this reason, Bulgakov remarks, 'Is this *metanoia* not a summons to new kinds of action, and, above all, to the testing and rethinking of what we imagine to be self-evident, the foundations on which we rest?'[33] Christian utopianism is not about static hope but about practices of hope (faith).[34] Political metanoia requires active faith (i.e., 'the assurance of things hoped for, the conviction of things not seen'; Heb. 11.1) and faithful action in the present.[35]

The politics of metanoia has the propensity for revolutionary change (the challenging of what is regarded as self-evident) because its utopian element furnishes the *idée-force* necessary to infuse social change.[36] As there is a strong aspiration for the future in revolutionary praxis, so is it with political metanoia. Political metanoia is love of and faith in the future: '*amor futuri*'[37], which contains the dynamicity of irrupting in the present. However, it should be noted that there is a gap between revolutionary praxis, inspired by secular utopias, and Christian practices of hope, informed by the ideal of the Kingdom of God.[38] Since the former is wedded to the idea of progress (history as a dialectical movement), it

---

31 Bulgakov, *The Bride of the Lamb*, 248-249.

32 Bulgakov, *The Bride of the Lamb*, 248.

33 Bulgakov, *The Bride of the Lamb*, 251.

34 See Ward, *The Politics of Discipleship*, 179. Stefan Skrimshire, *Politics of Fear, Practices of Hope* (London: Continuum, 2008), 87-110.

35 Williams, *Sergii Bulgakov*, 248.

36 Revolution is both a 'fact' and a 'principle'; as a 'fact' it has an uprooting effect while as a 'principle' it is generated by the ideal of transformation. It is derived not only by hatred but by passion or faith in a changed future; Williams, *Sergii Bulgakov*, 246-247.

37 Williams, *Sergii Bulgakov*, 248.

38 Williams, *Sergii Bulgakov*, 253.

tends to be a 'nihilistic revolt'- destructiveness of the spiritual ideal (against faith and historical tradition).[39]

> But a faith that has lost its spiritual balance turns into superstition or fanatical fantasy, which is inspired no longer by the vision of the city to come but by deceptive mirages. As soon as the utopianism that forms the soul of revolution has lost its religious roots, it ceases to have any spiritual balance. Its social idealism finds itself at odds with the tired positivism with which it has been yoked in the name of an imaginary 'scientific' perspective. Marx's utopianism – like that of other positivists – is wholly irrational, full of contradictions and religiously vacuous. Its conception of history goes no further than 'prehistory' – the epoch of class struggle [...].[40]

Such negative remark on secular revolution (inspired by secular utopianism) by Bulgakov reminds us of the radicalisation of the Ethiopian Student Movement and the legacy of Ethiopian messianism (cf. Chapter 4).[41] Nonetheless, the point I am trying to make, here, has to be confined to the relation between the ideal of revolution and Christianity. What has been noted in the rise of Ethiopian messianism is said to be the lack of utopian mentality (see Chapter 4). Bulgakov's remark, which I quoted in Chapter 7, which suggests that the rejection of the world by Christianity led to the rise of secular (atheistic) humanism, agrees with this. In fact, the lack of utopian mentality does not imply an altogether lack of spiritual sensibility of the tension between the supra-mundane and the mundane orders, which is ineradicable from Christianity (and also Islam) (especially, within the monastic tradition). Indeed, from the stylising of the self (image of the self) by the revolutionaries using quasi-religious motifs such as sacrifice and martyrdom strongly suggest that the religious worldviews of the revolutionaries had become favourable for the germination of Marxist revolutionary ideas (see Part II).

So seen, the appropriate question is not whether Christianity has or lacks utopian vision that infuses the propensity for revolutionary praxis but rather whether this predilection is suppressed or not. Pursuing transformation (as mentioned above), ought we not place emphasis on the need for utopian imagination

---

39 Williams, *Sergii Bulgakov*, 249.

40 Williams, *Sergii Bulgakov*, 249.

41 Since then, of course, the idea of revolution (Amharic; *abiot*) has become a reference that defines the self-understanding of Ethiopians. And for that matter, the incumbent government calls its ideological programme 'Revolutionary Democracy' enacting 'brave new world' of ethnic-federalism. The response to the discourse of revolution is varied. Some like it while others dislike it. Given the trauma associated with the experience of secular revolution and chaotic regime changes, there seems to be a justifiable aversion towards the discourse of revolutionary praxis in Ethiopia. See also Chapter 5.

in the contemporary socio-political milieu? Political metanoia is informed by utopian mentality and opens the possibility for resurrecting the suppressed: that is, noumenal ontologism.

It is for this reason that we need to clarify the Christian philosophy of history (Christian historiosophy). Historiosophy is related to an understanding of history and metaphysics. While philosophy of history concerns itself with questions of experiential knowledge such as historical evidence and objectivity, historiosophy espouses an understanding of history originating from 'ontological speculation', 'revelation' or 'religious faith'.[42] Since there is a history for Christians, Christian historiosophy makes history pre-history. From this standpoint, the authentic form of revolutionary dynamics and the genuine kind of progress belong to the teleology of the Kingdom of God.[43] In this regard, secular revolutionary utopia and Christian utopianism differ: the Christian idea of progress grounds itself in the ideal of the kingdom: '[…] to a divine act of violence that interrupts the contentless bad infinity of human history. On the contrary, a positive goal is set for history: its inner ripening to a good end'.[44]

Although the ideal of the Kingdom of God has a transformative power for reordering society, there is a 'polarisation' or struggle between 'love' for the Kingdom of God and 'enmity towards it'. For this reason, Christianity does not have the vision of 'earthly paradise' (like socialism) or messianic paradise (like the Jewish apocalypse).[45] As this might suggest there is obviously a struggle between these opposing forces throughout history. Nonetheless, since history is dependent upon eschatology, as we noted in Chapter 7, there is definitely an end or 'end times' and the struggle cannot simply continue for 'evil infinity'.[46] But here, we need to be cognizant that the New Testament Apocalypse is a revelation about history not only about the end times'.[47]

> As experienced in religious terms, history is the apocalypse coming to fruition – apocalypse understood *not* as eschatology but as historiosophy, which is something linked with the sense of an orientation towards the future, with the consciousness of obligatory tasks to be performed and of continuing historical labour. Time is measured not in years but in *acts*, […].[48]

---

42 Bulgakov, *The Bride of the Lamb*, 316.
43 Williams, *Sergii Bulgakov*, 253.
44 Bulgakov, *The Bride of the Lamb*, 341.
45 Williams, *Sergii Bulgakov*, 252
46 Williams, *Sergii Bulgakov*, 252-253.
47 Williams, *Sergii Bulgakov*, 252.
48 Williams, *Sergii Bulgakov*, 253.

Therefore, the apocalyptic is an important aspect that draws the present to the future through the unfolding of events or acts. But it should be noted that the Heracletian notion of reversals does not suffice for the apocalyptic gesture of the Kingdom of God.[49] This striving to realise the Kingdom of God is what Bulgakov (following Soloviev) regards as the 'common task', which requires 'courage, work and inspiration': 'Christian historiosophy reveals the apocalyptic breadth and scale that lies within the struggle to move from the city that now is to the one that is to come, for 'the form of this world is passing away' [I Cor. 7:.31]'.[50] Although the Church is not conterminous with the Kingdom of God, it participates in the kingdom of God as an active creative force. As such the Church is applied to the whole world in its real foundation and aim, *entelecheia* (see Chapter 7).

9.4 *Sobornost'*, Free Theocracy?

In the above discussion, we have seen that the politics of metanoia belongs to the Kingdom of God, which has significant implications for the socio-political reordering of society. The ideal of the Kingdom of God, as we have noted, has the propensity for change (*idée-force*) insofar as it is conceived as an active principle. Now, there is another important aspect of this: that is, conceiving the Kingdom of God as such entails acknowledging another form of authority: that the Kingdom of God, as an active principle, must not remain only above but must also be in us as the *ruling force* to free humanity. Basically, this is recognition of *another* authority, which is already above (beyond) us that actually must have a legitimate

---

49 Messay argues that 'Sensitivity to reversals and occurrences prevents the Ethiopians from thinking in terms of continuity and progression, from conceiving of the future as the product of the past. [...] Event and time are inseparable, both being equally discontinuous. In a word, time is destiny itself, fate at work, doing and undoing the world' and he continues, 'Heracletus's thinking has certain affinities with the Ethiopian conception. The vulnerability of things and reversal of events have been strongly expressed by the Heracletian notion of cycle based on the unity and struggle of opposites'; See *Survival and Modernization*, 216. The Heracletian chaos might only bring the reversal of positions (regime change): 'war is the father of all and king of all ... some he makes slaves, others free'; Heracletus, *The Presocratic Philosophers* (Cambridge: Cambridge University Press, 1991), 193 cited in Messay Kebede, *Survival and Modernization*, 186. What we need to consider is the danger of 'the sacralisation of conflict' in the Heraclitian view; cf. John Milbank, "Multiculturalism in Britain and the Political Identity of Europe," *International Journal for the Study of the Christian Church* 9, 4 (November 2009): 279.

50 Williams, *Sergii Bulgakov*, 253.

place in us (in the midst of us). In a nutshell, this is a vision of theocracy, or more precisely, 'free theocracy'.[51] And the politics of metanoia is recognition of this form of authority.

Since a great deal of misapprehension surrounds the notion of theocracy, I must begin by briefly distinguishing the notion of free theocracy from other forms of theocracy (pseudo-theocracies). As the history of political philosophy shows, the concept of theocracy has been associated with forms of government that evoke immediate divine guidance, which might take different, and sometimes confused, forms: pure theocracy and ecclesiocracy.[52] In the first, secular leaders claim to have a direct connection with God while in the second, religious leaders assume political positions to carry out political duties without necessarily claiming any divine guidance.[53] It might be helpful, here, to draw brief attention to historical examples of such forms of government.

Historically, there is an association between Christianity and theocracy, Church and State. Such a relation, within Orthodox traditions, is often defined in terms of symphony: the State should not interfere in Church affairs or otherwise the Church felt persecuted and the Church had to be faithful to the State that must provide protection. The Russian Orthodox theologian, John Meyendorff, remarking on the social and political thought of Byzantium, argues that prominent Church fathers of the time such as St. John Chrysostom, St. Maximus the

---

51 The idea of 'free theocracy' was first developed by Vladimir Soloviev and later Dostoevsk. Bulgakov absorbed this idea but he often employs a variant term 'sobornost'. It is known that Bulgakov developed '*metaphysical* [and political] issues raised by Soloviev' and the vision of the Kingdom of God and its rule (theocracy) receive their expression in Bulgakov's work; cf. Williams, *Sergii Bulgakov*, 120. To Soloviev, free theocracy is based on the conception of the three-fold ministry of Christ correspond ing to the royal (political), priestly and prophetic forces of society. Some argue that Soloviev had abandoned this view in his later years but Brandon Gallaher contends that there is continuity between Soloviev's earlier and later writings; see Gallaher, "Vladimir Solovi'ev's Sophiology," 637: "Free theocracy is that society in which all three spheres—the Church, the State, and the local authority—each maintaining its relative independence, are not externally or mechanically separated, but mutually penetrate each other as integral parts of a single organic being, indispensable to each other and united in a common goal and a common life."; Konstantin Mochulsky, "Social Philosophy in Russia," *St. Vladimir's Seminary Quarterly* 12 (1968): 163.

52 Emil Brunner, *Dogmatics II: The Doctrine of Creation and Redemption* (Cambridge, UK: James Clarke & Co., 1952), 320.

53 Ran Hirschl, *Constitutional Theocracy* (Cambridge, MA: Harvard University Press, 2010), 2.

Confessor, St. John of Damascus, and St. Theodore the Studite did not denounce the formula of harmony (symphony) defined by Justinian. Nor did they encourage apocalyptic withdrawal from the world giving the secular autonomy. Rather, they hold onto the principle of divine-humanity and from this emanated their conviction of the symphony between the Church and the State. Nevertheless, Meyendorff makes two important points: first, 'Byzantine Christianity never accepted the belief that the emperor had absolute authority in matters of faith or ethics'; and second, 'it is not opposing to the emperors another competing authority (i.e. that of the priesthood) that Byzantine society avoided caesaropapism, but by referring all authority directly to God'; and Meyendorff adds that the monastic tradition was a reminder that total harmony between the Kingdom of God and human society before the *parousia* cannot happen (the polarity between the already here and the not yet aspect of the Kingdom).[54] Therefore, the contention is not basically against the theocratic ideal as such but the forgetfulness of the eschatological and the consequent worship of the *status quo*.

In such pseudo-theocratic forms, according to Bulgakov, the character of authority as well as the distinction between God and Caesar is obscured.[55] Authority, whether in its 'purely' secular version or pseudo-theocratic form, exhibits its 'feral' quality or 'animal' principle ('of unregenerate human power').[56] This form of authority, according to Bulgakov, is 'a *negative revelation* of true authority': '*another* kind of authority' (belonging to '*another* kingdom').[57] In point of fact, the recognition of theocracy, which I am highlighting here, dovetails with 'the *transfiguration* of authority' ('power and its expression in the *kenosis*, self-emptying').[58] From this standpoint, then, what must fall under critique is autocracy, not theocracy.

In light of this, the distinction between the Church and the State (as we noted earlier) is desirable (favourable). Now, the Church should remain a free theocracy. What does this imply? It implies that it should be free from State interference (and also the

---

54 John Meyendorff, *Living Tradition: Orthodox Witness in the Contemporary World* (Crestwood, NY: St. Vladimir's Seminary Press, 1978), 192-194.

55 Williams, *Sergii Bulgakov*, 159.

56 Williams, *Sergii Bulgakov*, 159. Power whose aim is not only disciplining subjects but also subjugating the whole of life.

57 Williams, *Sergii Bulgakov*, 160.

58 Williams, *Sergii Bulgakov*, 160. Although he has no intention to offer a theological legitimation of the monarchy, Bulgakov describes the monarchy in terms of 'authority as a cruciform', which suggests 'bearing ... authority like the cross of Christ'; Williams, *Sergii Bulgakov*, 60, n.25.

Church should not involve itself in party politics). In this sense, it is both political and apolitical. It is political in the sense that it is the 'democracy of souls' because the people are potentially the ecclesia; but, at the same time, it is apolitical in terms of its role as the 'conscience of society', which cannot be reduced to any ideology or party politics.[59] Thus, as free theocracy, the Church must be free to teach its doctrine (including its social doctrines).[60] In brief, the Church, as the divine-humanity *in actu*, embodies and enacts the Kingdom of God (though it cannot have monopoly of it).

Therefore, free theocracy does not look forward to establish an earthly (messianic) paradise (as is the case of utopianisms and pseudo-theocracies) – it does not seek to merge earthly and divinely sovereignties.[61] In fact, what is proper for free theocracy that belongs to the Kingdom of God, then, is what we referred to as 'permanent revolution' (that never surrenders to any *status quo*).[62] Although the exact/full details of how, when or where of the free theocratic cannot be worked out, there should be an aspiration or a quest (expressed in faithful acts/practices of hope) that will always remain meaningful. The historical quest itself is the place of metanoia and maturing: 'empirically speaking, there has been, on the face of things, a dissolution of the religious principle of authority; secularisation has triumphed', however, 'in the mystical depths a new revelation of the nature of authority has been prepared and matured, a revelation of theocracy, announcing its ultimate victory on the threshold of this new age'.[63]

9.5 Conclusion

To recapitulate what we have discussed so far, we began by looking at the possibility of cultivating a new culture of the self. The emphasis has been on the

---

59 Williams, *Sergii Bulgakov*, 256.

60 This can imply a direct politics meaning a 'direct intervention in political events' ('e.g. Solov'ev's defence of the Jews, opposition to capital punishment, commitment to women's rights, etc.'); cf. Gallaher, "Vladimir Solovi'ev's Sophiology," 637.

61 Rowan Williams makes the following three important presuppositions of theocracy, which Christians should be wary of: the assumption that 'dialogue and discovery' can 'end' (which can lead to the outlawing of unbelief); assuming an 'end to history' (seeking to 'foreclose the eschaton' denies us of the gift of repentance/conversion in the time between the resurrection and the *parousia*); and 'the fusion of divine and earthly sovereignty' is 'foreign to the language and practice of Jesus'; *On Christian Theology* (Oxford: Blackwell, 2000), 36.

62 Rowan proposes this 'long revolution' that goes with 'conversion' (in a broader sense), which is 'creative renewal of persons and communities'; Williams, *On Christian* Theology, 36-37.

63 Williams, *Sergii Bulgakov*, 161.

need to return to the aesthetic of life – the Christ Event (as task). Through re-aligning themselves to the Event, subjects redirect their allegiance to the Subject (God); put in Althusserian terms, subjects are 'interpellated' by Christ (Christic-interpellation). It is possible to go beyond Althusser (and Balibar) who can only tell us about how religion (the Church), as ideological State apparatus, can produce subjects who are loyal to the State but does not yield as a possible site of resistance. In their account, the individual, through apparatuses and their practices, is instituted as *homo nationalis* and simultaneously, she is instituted as *homo religious* (*economicus*, *politicus*, etc.).[64] I contend that such interrelation (between *homo nationalis* and *homo religious*) can be challenged as theo-political subjects, who are interpellated by grace, begin to question where technologies or ideological *dispositifs* stand in relation to the Sovereign (God) whose Kingdom demands their allegiance. The Church can and must go beyond ethno-phyletism (see Theological Introduction).

Theo-political subjects who surpass their cultural (ideological) conditioning constitute the metanoic community. An important feature of this community is its capacity for forging solidarity beyond the *ethnos*. Such propensity disassociates the identification of ethnic identity from politics and takes politics out of the present dead-end. The politics of metanoia belongs to the kingdom of God, which is an active principle for transformation (in the present). The ideal of the kingdom is not only an *idée-force* but also a *ruling-force* in and over us. The idea of anti-secularisation permeates the spirit of *sobornost'*, which fits together with political metanoia.[65] The metanoic community with its metaxological nature – as a community of intermediation – transforms the bond of togetherness beyond ethno-political federal polity, beyond erotic sovereignty.

Reflections on Part III

Employing the three-fold theological task of cultural hermeneutics, I began this part (Chapter 7) by a theological self-criticism of the Church. The focus of this chapter has been articulating an account of Christian agency since to act is central to being political. This account of Christian *askesis* (Christian humanism) was developed based on Bulgakov's two-Sophias Christology (divine-humanity). As we have noted, the relation and distinction between the divine and the human

64 See Balibar, "The Nation-form," 93.

65 Pauliina Arola and Risto Saarinen, "In Search of Sobornost and 'New Symphony': The Social Doctrine of the Russian Orthodox Church," *The Ecumenical Review* 54, 1 (2002): 136.

provides the basis for an analogical imagination for Christian act in the world and serves as a protocol against Christian tendencies – cosmism and acosmism that cannot yield as possible sites of ideological *dispositifs*.

The theological task of the subsequent chapter (Chapter 8) has been that of critique. There I presented a distinct Christian ontology that counters the lethal ontology engendered by ethno-political ideology. The Trinitarian ontology countered the impersonal category of the 'ethnic' that aggregates subjects. It laid the foundation for a differentiated-unity (*sobornost'*) against the views represented in the politics of integration, which conceives unity as sameness, and the politics of identity, which holds a view of radical difference. Based on the conception that economic activity should be a joyful act in Sophia (between necessity and freedom), I argued that the subject, in living *sobornost'*, can overcome the impersonal modes (whether state controlled economy [state developmentalism] or free market economy) that operate under utilitarian spirit. In living *sobornost'*, the individual participates in personal systems (voluntary collectives). By denying evil ontological existence, the chapter also offered an account of a peaceful sophianic order and that the sophianic-All implies a peaceful unfolding of difference. Generally, the chapter articulated a harmonious peaceful social order of significant relevance for social reordering of society fragmented by ethnic hostility. This has been grounded in ecclesiology (the *sobornost'* of the Church).

The final chapter (Chapter 9) constituted the constructive theological task of cultural hermeneutics. This chapter elaborates the politics of metanoia that advocates for a comprehensive questioning and transformation of society. Such politics summons for a Christian culture of the self that enables transcending the solidarity of the *ethnos*. Placing the politics of metanoia within its context – utopic horizon – I argued that the ideal of the Kingdom of God can be an *idée-force* for social change. I also recognised that the ideal of the Kingdom of God is not only an active principle (*idée-force*) but also a ruling force, which entails another form of authority. The politics of metanoia was understood as a recognition of a theocratic form of authority (free theocracy), which is opposed to autocratic or 'false' theocracy.

Conclusion

In this study, I claimed that those secular modes of thought and the political discourses they sanction have led Ethiopian politics to a dead-end. I argued that such modes of thought are not only flawed on their accounts of collective existence but also in their conceptions of the religious (the theological). A theological turn, as I argued, not only appropriately re-positions the theological vis-à-vis the secular discourses but also connects the political and the theological discourses insofar as it generates theological resources to transcend the pathos of ethno-nationalism. Contra such modes of thought that conceive original violence, the whole gist of the study aimed at constructing a political theology that advocates a harmonious peaceful order. The study has made an original contribution by generating theological resources to transcend the current political impasse.

It was by means of a meaningful juxtaposition between 'Ethno-political Imagination' (Part II) and 'Theo-political Imagination' (Part III) that I hope to have provided a theological out-narration of secular discourses on Ethiopia. In fact, first, I needed a conceptual framework – 'Imaginative Practices' – in which ideology and utopia figure as two polarised imaginative practices (Part I). In that part, I analysed the most salient aspects of social imagination and introduced a number of methodological and conceptual landmarks on subject formation mechanisms. It was in light of such a conceptual framework that I examined the Ethiopian case in Part II.

I started the discussion in Chapter 4 of the second part by outlining the grand narrative of Greater Ethiopia and in the subsequent discussion (critique) I demonstrated that the constitution of the people of Ethiopia as Ethiopians involved the production of fictive Amhara ethnicity (Amharic speaking linguistic community). Instead of defining the singularity (unity) of Ethiopians in objective (sociological) terms, I argued that such singularity should be understood as an outworking of imaginative practices (national ideology); thereby, demonstrating how the Ethiopian citizen-subject (*homo Æthiopicus*) emerged as a consequence of ideological institutions developed in the modern state of Ethiopia over the past century. This chapter has also pinpointed the nationalistic absorption of Christian identity, which is an important discussion that has implications to understand not only the interplay between political ideology and religion in imperial Ethiopia but also to look at what this legacy might mean in the present.

Subsequently, I began Chapter 5 by drawing attention to the peculiar ways in which the ideal of national self-determination became the ideological frame for political movements (liberation fronts) in Ethiopia (formed based on the solidarity of the *ethnos*). The conclusion of this discussion asserted that it was not because of the theoretical clarity but due to *practices of war* and inter-ethnic hostility that this notion came to be an ideal for such movements. Then, I examined the modes of self-writing against this background. We noted that such narratives of the self are held in the tension between victimhood and voluntarism, which legitimise violence. In contradiction to the narrative of Greater Ethiopia, such modes of self-writing (particularly the narrative of domination) legitimise an Ethiopian ethnic-federal polity where national self-determination is respected. Nevertheless, despite the claim that a brave-new-world was inaugurated – following the regime change in 1991 in Ethiopia – we witness new forms of ex/inclusion and the impeding of *practices of freedom*.

Due to the selective function of such narratives not only is the manipulations of memory at stake but the polarisation of subjectivities is also sanctioned. Producing a new culture of the self (*ascesis*) that institute and consolidate collective identities (fostering solidarities of the *ethnos*), such modes of self-writing have become the *dispositifs* of the day that capture Ethiopian subjects. Such alternative imaginative practices have made possible collective action through ethnic-interpellation. The federal polity has not completely transformed the old centre-periphery dialectic into centre-centre dialectic but rather regions, on which are bestowed a number of rights by the Constitution, are highly controlled from the centre (according to the principle of democratic centralism of the governing party) rendering national self-determination a simple rhetoric and the Constitution a hypocritical dogma. In recent years, there is an evident move towards authoritarianism and the depletion of a genuine expression of interest for an overdetermined societal good.

In Chapter 5, it was argued that the way out of the political impasse produced by ethno-political imagination cannot be sought in the emerging perspective that gives much emphasis to Ethiopia's native condition. The conclusion reached in Part II shows that the identification of politics with identity by ethno-political ideology has led Ethiopian politics to a dead-end. Difference is understood in terms of ethnicity but not as the *topos* of an argument (or political rhetoric) and hence, politics has been reduced to the enactment of identity (not equality as such, which exemplifies a crisis of emancipatory politics/impossible identification). This led to the conclusion that the way out of this dead-end requires rethinking politics and the notion of the subject in a different way.

The originality of this work is evident in the methodology (Part I) and the way it offers analytical tools for Part II, which in turn prepares the ground for Part III. Nevertheless, the originality of this work lies largely on the last theological part (Part III): Theo-political Imagination. This part claimed that a theological turn opens the ontological possibility of a new political subject (the theo-political subject) and a reinvention of politics that transcends the contemporary political dead-end (see Theological Introduction).

Employing a three-fold theological task of cultural hermeneutics, I organised my arguments in three stages. First, I started the theological discussion by giving an account of Christian *askesis* (Christian humanism) as a theological self-criticism of the Church. Based on an articulation of cosmic-mediation employing two-Sophias Christology as developed by Bulgakov, I developed a protocol against tendencies that do not serve as possible 'sites' of resistance to ethno-political ideology. Second, since defining what it means to act is inseparable from being political, I articulated a distinct Christian social ontology based on Trinitarian ontology (that was complemented by perspective from creation) and grounded in ecclesiology. The ontological themes explored have direct relevance to counter the rival/lethal ontology engendered by ethno-political ideology: a social ontology (differentiated-unity), the ontology of work/labour, and the state of peace.

In the final stage, I developed the more constructive chapter: the politics of metanoia. In this part, I have demonstrated how we can transcend the current impasse through the transformation of our relation to the self by cultivating a Christian culture of the self. Such a transformation, as we have argued, is a counter-*dispositif* strategy that enables going beyond ethnic-interpellation and solidarity of the *ethnos*. The ideal of the Kingdom of God, as has been argued, is the utopic horizon that informs the politics of metanoia. We concluded the part with the realisation that the politics of metanoia was understood as a recognition of a theocratic form of authority (free theocracy), which, of course, should not be confused with other forms of autocratic or 'false' theocracies.

Such a theological standpoint, which seeks to transform the context within which it is situated, exemplifies a political-theological gesture that refuses the worship of the *status quo* in contemporary Ethiopian socio-political context offering an alternative account of society. Demonstrating the possibility of a new political subject and the rethinking of the interplay between the political and the theological, this study has made an original contribution seriously lacking in studies of Ethiopia.

Bibliograpy*

Abdul Mejid Hussein. "Ethiopia and Ethiopianism." *Struggle* 3, 1 (1968): 9-11.

Abebe Zegeye and Siegfried Pausewang, eds. *Ethiopia in Change: Peasantry, Nationalism and Democracy*. London: British Academy Press, 1994.

Addis Hiwot. *Ethiopia: From Autocracy to Revolution*, Occasional Publication No.1. London: Review of African Political Economy, 1975.

Adem Abebe. "Rule by Law in Ethiopia: Rendering Constitutional Limits on Government Power Nonsensical." Working Paper 1. Cambridge: University of Cambridge Centre of Governance and Human Rights, 2012.

Adhana Haile Adhana. "Tigray-The Birth of a Nation within the Ethiopian Polity." Pages 42-49 in *Ethnicity and the State in Eastern Africa*. Edited by M.A. Mohamed Salih and and John Markakis. Uppsala: Nordiska Afrikainstitutet, 1998.

Agamben, Giorgio. "Poiesis and Praxis." Pages 63-93 in *The Man Without Content*. Stanford: University of Stanford Press, 1999.

—. *What is an Apparatus? And Other Essays*. Edited by Hamacher, Werner. Stanford, CA: Stanford University Press, 2009.

Ahmad, Aijaz. "Orientalism and After." Page 169 in *Colonial Discourse and Post-colonial Theory: A Reader*. Edited by Patrick Williams and Laura Chrisman. New York: Columbia University Press, 1994.

Althusius, Johannes. "Politics as the Art of Associating." Pages 27-33 in *Theories of Federalism: A Reader*. Edited by Dimitrios Karmis and Wayne Norman, New York, N.Y.: Palgrave Macmillan, 2005.

Althusser, Louis. *For Marx*. London: Allen Lane, 1969.

—. "Ideology and Ideological State Apparatuses (Notes Towards an Investigation)." In *Lenin and Philosophy and Other Essays*. New York: Monthly Review Press, 1971.

* Note: In line with Ethiopian convention, Ethiopian authors are listed by their first name, rather than their family name.

—. *Essays in Self-Criticism*. London: NLB, 1976.

—. *On Ideology*. London: Verso, 2008.

Althusser, Louis and Étienne Balibar. *Reading Capital*. London: Verso, 1979.

Ambrosio, John. "Writing the Self: Ethical Self-formation and the Undefined Work of Freedom." *Educational Theory* vol. 58 Number 3, (2008): 251-267.

Andargachew Tiruneh. *The Ethiopian Revolution, 1974-1987: A Transformation from an Aristocratic to a Totalitarian Autocracy*. Cambridge: Cambridge University Press, 1993.

Anderson, Benedict. *Imagined Communities: Reflections on the Origin and the Spread of Nationalism*. London: Verso, 1991.

Armstrong, John. *Nations before Nationalism*. Chapel Hill: University of North Carolina Press, 1982.

Arola, Pauliina and Risto Saarinen. " In Search of Sobornost and 'New Symphony': The Social Doctrine of the Russian Orthodox Church." *The Ecumenical Review* 54, 1 (2002): 130-141.

Asafa Jalata. *Oromia and Ethiopia: State Formation and Ethnonational Conflict, 1868-1992*. London: L. Rienner, 1993.

—. *Oromo Nationalism and the Ethiopian Discourse: The Search for Freedom and Democracy*. Lawrenceville, NJ: Red Sea Press, c1998.

—. "Celebrating Oromo Heroism and Commemorating the Oromo Martyrs' Day (Guyya Gootota Oromiyaa)." The University of Tennessee, Knoxville. Accessed 24 April 2010, http://trace.tennessee.edu/utk_socopubs/12.

Atkins, Kim. *Self and Subjectivity*. Oxford: Blackwell, 2005.

Aymro Wondmagegnehu and Joachim, Motovu. *The Ethiopian Orthodox Church*. Addis Ababa: The Ethiopian Orthodox Mission, 1970.

Backhouse, Stephen. "Nationalism and Patriotism." Pages 41-58 in *The Oxford Handbook of Theology and Modern European Thought*. Edited by Nicholas Adams, George Pattison and Graham Ward. Oxford: Oxford University Press, 2013.

Bahru Zewde. *A History of Modern Ethiopia*. London: James Currey, 1991.

—. "Hayla-Sellase: From Progressive to Reactionary." In *Ethiopia In Change: Peasantry, Nationalism and Democracy*. Edited by Abebe Zegeye and Siegfried Pausewang. London: British Academy Press, 1994.

—. *Pioneers of Change in Ethiopia: The Reformist Intellectuals of the Early Twentieth Century*. Oxford: James Curry, 2002.

—. *Society, State and History.* Addis Ababa: Addis Ababa University Press, 2008.

—. *Documenting the Ethiopian Student Movement: An Exercise in Oral History.* Addis Ababa: Forum for Social Science, 2010.

Balibar, Étienne. "The Nation Form: History and Ideology." Pages 86-106 in *Race, Nation, Class: Ambiguous Identities.* Edited by Étienne Balibar and Immanuel Wallerstein. London: Verso, 1991.

—. "Culture and Identity (Working Notes)." Pages 180-189 in *The identity in Question.* Edited by John Rajchman, New York: Routledge, 1995.

Balsvik, Randi Rønning. *Haile Sellassie's Students: The Intellectual and Social Background to Revolution, 1952-1977.* East Lansing: Michigan State University, African Studies Centre, 1985.

—. *The Quest for Expression: State and the University in Ethiopia under Three Regimes, 1952-2005.* Addis Ababa: Addis Ababa University Press, 2007.

Bandrés, José L. and Ugo Zanetti. "Christology." Pages 729-732 in *Encyclopaedia Aethiopica.* Edited by Siegbert Uhlig. Wiesbaden: Harrassowitz Verlag: 2003.

Baur, John. *2000 Years of Christianity in Africa: An African Church History.* Nairobi: Paulines Publications Africa, 1998.

Baxter, P.T.W., Jan Hultin & Alessandro Triulzi, eds. *Being and Becoming Oromo: Historical and Anthropological Enquiries.* Uppsala: Nordiska Afrikainstitutet, 1996.

Baye Yimam, "Academic Freedom at Addis Ababa University: An Overview of Its Past and Current Experiences." Pages 19-57 in *Academic Freedom in Ethiopia: Perspectives of Teaching Personnel.* Edited By Taye Assefa. Addis Ababa: Forum for Social Studies, 2008.

Bediako, Kwame. *Theology and Identity: The Impact of Culture upon Christian Thought in the Second Century and in Modern Africa.* Oxford: Regnum Books, 1999.

Benhabib, Seyla. *Another Cosmopolitanism.* Oxford: Oxford University Press, 2008.

Berghe, Pierre van der. *Race and Ethnicity: Essays in Comparative Sociology.* London: Basic Books, 1970.

Berhanu Gutema Balcha. "Ethnicity and restructuring of the state in Ethiopia." Working Paper no.6. Denmark: Aalborg University DIIPER & Department ofHistory, International and Social Studies, 2008.

Biesta, Gert. "Toward a New 'Logic' of Emancipation: Foucault and Rancière." *Philosophy of Education*, 2008: 169-177.

Brake, Donald. "Historical Investigation of Monophysitism in the Ethiopian Orthdoox Chruch." PhD diss., Dallas Theological Seminary, 1977.

Brubaker, Rogers. "Rethinking Nationhood: Nation as Institutionalized Form, Practical Category, Contingent Event." *Contention* (Fall 1994): 3-14.

Brunner, Emil. *Dogmatics II: The Doctrine of Creation and Redemption.* Cambridge: James Clarke & Co., 1952.

Bujo, Bénézet. *African Theology in Its Social Context.* Translated by John O'Donohou. Maryknoll, NY: Orbis Books, 1992.

—. *The Ethical Dimension of Community: The African Model and the Dialogue between North and South.* Nairobi: Paulines Publications Africa, 1997.

Bulgakov, Sergius. *The Orthodox Church.* London: The Centenary Press, 1935.

—. *The Wisdom of God: A Brief Summary of Sophiology.* London: Williams and Norgate, 1937.

—. *Philosophy of Economy: The World as Household.* Translated and edited by Catherine Evtuhov. New Haven: Yale University, 2000.

—. *The Bride of the Lamb.* Edinburgh: T & T Clark, 2002.

—. *The Comforter.* Grand Rapids, MI: Eerdmans, 2004.

—. *The Lamb of God.* Grand Rapids, MI: Wm. B. Eerdmans, 2008.

Bureau of Democracy, Human Rights, and Labor. *Country Reports on Human Rights Practices.* Accessed 10 March 2010 http://www.state.gov/j/drl/rls/hrrpt/2001/af/8372.htm

Butler, Judith. *The Psychic Life of Power: Theories in Subjection.* Stanford: Stanford University Press, 1997.

Carver, Terrell and Chambers, Samuel. *Judith Butler's Precarious Politics: Critical Encounters.* London: Routledge, 2008.

Caulk, Richard. "Dependency, Gebre Heywet Baykedagn and the Birth of Ethiopian Reformism." *Proceedings of the Fifth International Conference on Ethiopian Studies* (1978): 569-581.

Chebankova, Elena. "Russia's Noncovenantal Federalism: Past and Present." *Journal of Church and State*, vol. 51 no. 2 (2009): 312-340.

Clapham, Christopher. "Centralization and Local Response in Southern Ethiopia." *African Affairs* vol. 74, Issue 294, (1975): 72-81.

—. *Transformation and Continuity in Revolutionary Ethiopia*. Cambridge: Cambridge University Press, 1988.

—. "Ethnicity and the National Question in Ethiopia." Pages 27-40 in *Conflict and Peace in the Horn of Africa: Federalism and Its Alternatives*, by Peter Woodward and and Murray Forsyth (eds.). Aldershot, UK: Dartmouth Publishing, 1994.

—. "Degrees of Statehood." *Review of International Studies*. (1998): 143-157.

—. "Controlling Space in Ethiopia." Pages 9-30 in *Remapping Ethiopia: Socialism and After*, by Wendy James, Eisei Kurimoto, Donald Donham, and Alessandro Triulzi. Oxford: James Currey, 2002.

—. "War and State Formation in Ethiopia and Eritrea." *Proceedings, XIVth International Conference of Ethiopian Studies*, vol. 3. Addis Ababa University Press, (c2002): 1420-1435.

Cohen, Anthony. *The Symbolic Construction of Community*. London: Tavistock Publications, 1985.

Cohen, Gideon. "Identity and Opportunity: the Introduction of Local Languages for the Purpose of Primary Education in the SNNPR, Ethiopia." PhD diss., University of London, 2000.

—. "The Development of Regional and Local Languages in Ethiopia's Federal System." Pages 170-172 in *Ethnic Federalism: The Ethiopian Experience in Comparative Perspective*. Edited by David Truton. Ohio: Ohio University Press, 2006.

Crisp, Oliver D. " Problem with Perichoresis." *Tyndale Bulletin*, 56.1 (2005): 119-140.

Crummey, Donald. "Imperial Legitimacy and the Creation of Neo-Solomonic Ideology in 19th-Century Ethiopia." *Cahiers d'Études africaines*, 109, XXVIII-I (1988): 7-18.

—. "Personality and Political Culture in Ethiopian History: The Case of Emperor Tewodros." Pages 78-89 in *Personality and Political Culture in Modern Africa*. Boston: Boston University Press, 1998.

—. "Ethiopian Historiography in the Latter Half of the Twentieth Century: A North American Perspective." *Journal of Ethiopian Studies* Xxxiv (2001): 13-43.

Davis, Creston and Riches, Patrick Aaron. "Metanoia: The Theological Praxis of Revolution." Pages 22-51 in *Theology and the Political: The New Debate*. Edited by Creston Davis, Slavoj Žižek and John Milbank. Durham, N.C.: Duke University Press, 2005.

Deleuze, Gilles. *Foucault*. Translated & edited by Seán Hand. Minneapolis, MN: The University of Minnesota, 1988.

Dereje Feyissa. "The Experience of Gambella Regional State." Pages 215-228 in *Ethnic Federalism: The Ethiopian Experience in Comparative Perspective*. Edited by David Truton. Ohio: Ohio University Press, 2006.

Desmond, William. *Ethics and the Between*. Albany, NY: State University of New York Press, 2001.

—. *God and the Between*. Oxford: Blackwell Publishing, 2008.

Donham, Donald L. "Old Abyssinia and the new Ethiopian empire: themes in social history." Pages 3-48 in *The Southern Marches of Imperial Ethiopia*. Edited by Wendy James et al. Cambridge: Cambridge University Press, 1986a.

—. *Marxist Modern: An Ethnographic History of the Ethiopian Revolution*. Berkeley; Oxford: University of California Press, 1999.

Dreyfus, Hubert L. and Rabinow, Paul. *Michel Foucault: Beyond Structuralism and Hermeneutics*. London: Harvester Wheatsheaf, 1982.

Eagleton, Terry. *Ideology: An Introduction*. London: Verso, 2007.

Editorial. "The National Democratic Revolution in Ethiopia." *Challenge* 12, No. 1 (1972): 8.

Ehrlich, Charles. "Ethnicity and Constitutional Reform: the Case of Ethiopia." *Journal of International and Comparative Law* 6 (1999): 51-71.

Eide, Øyvind. *Revolution and Religion in Ethiopia: A Study of Church and Politics with Special Reference to the Ethiopian Evangelical Church Mekane Yesus 1974-1985*. Stavanger, Uppsala: Misjonshøgskolens forlag; Uppsala Universitet, 1996.

Elazar, Daniel J. *Exploring Federalism*. Tuscaloosa, AL: Alabama University Press, 1987.

Ann Ward and Lee Ward, eds. *The Ashgate Research Companion to Federalism*. Surrey, UK: Ashgate, 2009.

Erlich, Haggai. *Ethiopia and the Challenge of Independence*. Colorado: Lynne Reinner Publishers, 1986.

Ethiopian Observer, Addis Ababa: December 1956.

Federal Democratic Republic of Ethiopia Central Statistical Agency. "Population Projection of Ethiopia for All Regions at Wereda Level from 2014-2017." n.p. Accessed 20 January 2014, http://www.csa.gov.et/

Eyasu Lulseged. “Why Do The Orthodox Christians In Ethiopia Identify Their Faith with Their Nation?” *Proceedings of the First National Conference of Ethiopian Studies.* Addis Ababa: Addis Ababa University Press, (1990): 7.

Fargher, Brian L. *The Origins of the New Churches Movement in Southern Ethiopia, 1927-1944.* Leiden: Brill, 1996.

Fasil Nahum. *Constitution for a Nation of Nations: the Ethiopian Prospect.* Lawrenceville, NJ: Red Sea Press, 1997.

Fernyhough, Timothy. “Interpreting Ethiopian Banditry: A Revisionist View.” Pages 57-81 in *Ethiopia in Broader Perspectives, vol. 1.* Edited by Katsuyoshi Fukui et al. Kyoto: Shokado Book Sellers, 1997.

Feuerbach, Ludwig. *The Essence of Christianity.* Translated by George Eliot. New York: Harper & Brothers, 1957.

Fikre Tolossa, “A Historical Explanation as to Why Members & Supporters of the TPLF are Ethnocentric.” Jan.-Feb. 1997. Ethiopian Review. Accessed 20 March 2012, http://www.ethiopic.com/Fikre1er.htm

Foucault, Michel. *Power/Knowledge: Selected Interviews and Other Writings, 1972 -1977.* Edited by Colin Gordon. Brighton: Harvester, 1980.

—. “Preface to The History of Sexuality, Vol. 2.” In *The Foucault Reader.* Edited by Paul Rabinow. New York, 1984.

—. “About the Beginning of the Hermeneutics of the Self.” In *Michel Foucault, The Essential Works of Foucault 1954-1984 volume 1.* Edited by Paul Rabinow. London: Penguin Books, 1994.

—. “On the Genealogy of Ethics: An Overview of Work in Progress.” In *The Essential Works of Foucault 1954-1984, volume 1.* Edited by Paul Rabinow. London: Penguin Books, 1994.

—. “On the Government of the Living.” In *The Essential Works of Foucault 1954-1984 volume 1.* Edited by Paul Rabinow. London: Penguin Books, 1994.

—. “Security, Territory, and Population.” In *The Essential Works of Foucault 1954 -1984 volume 1.* Edited by Paul Rabinow. London: Penguin Books, 1994.

—. “Self Writing.” In *The Essential Works of Foucault 1954-1984 volume 1.* Edited by Paul Rabinow. London: Penguin Books, 1994.

—. “Society Must Be Defended.” In *The Essential Works of Foucault 1954-1984 volume 1,* by Paul Rabinow (ed.). London: Penguin Books, 1994.

—. “What is Enlightenment?” In *The Essential Works of Foucault 1954-1984 volume 1.* Edited by Paul Rabinow. London: Penguin Books, 1994.

—. “What is Critique?” In *What is Enlightenment? Eighteenth-Century Answers and Twentieth-Century Questions*. Edited by James Schmidt. Berkeley: University of California Press, 1996.

Fukui, Katsuyoshi and John Markakis, eds. *Ethnicity and Conflict in the Horn of Africa*. Athens: Ohio University Press, 1994.

Gallaher, Brandon. “Protopresbyter Sergii Bulgakov: Hypostasis and Hypostacity: Scholia to The Unfading Light.” *St Vladimirs Theological Quarterly*, 49:1-2 (2005): 14-15.

—. “The Christological Focus of Vladimir Solovi'ev's Sophiology.” *Modern Theology*, 25 (4 October 2009): 617-643.

Gavrilyuk, Paul L. “The kenotic theology of Sergius Bulgakov.” *Scottish Journal of Theology* 58, 3 (2005): 251-269.

Gebru Tareke. *Ethiopia: Power and Protest*. Cambridge: Cambridge University Press, 1991.

Geertz, Clifford. *The Interpretation of Cultures*. London: Hutchinson, 1975.

—. *Old Societies and New States: The Quest for Modernity in Asia and Africa*. New York; London: Free Press; Collier-Macmillan, 1963.

Gellner, Ernest. *Nations and Nationalism: New Perspectives on the Past*. Ithaca New York: Cornell University Press, 1982.

Getachew Haile. *The Faith of the Unctionists in the Ethiopian Church (Haymanot Masihawit)*. Louvain, 1990.

—. *THE GƎʿƎZ ACTS OF ABBA ƎSṬIFANOS OF GᵂƎNDAGᵂƎNDE*. Louvain: Corpus Scriptorum Christianorum Orientalium, 2006.

Graves, Charles Lee. *The Holy Spirit in the Theology of Sergius Bulgakov*. Geneva: World Council of Churches, 1972.

Greenfield, Richard. *Ethiopia*. New York: Frederick A. Praeger Publishers, 1968.

Gregory of Nazianzen, “Letter to Cledonius the Priest Against Apollinarius, Epistle CI.” Page 440 in *A Select Library of Nicene and Post-Nicene Fathers*, series II, vol. VII. Grand Rapids: Eerdmans, 1978-79.

Grumett, David. *De Lubac: A Guide for the Perplexed*. London: T & T Clark, 2007. (Abba) Hailemariam Melese Ayanew. “Influence of Cyrillian Christology in the Ethiopian Orthodox Anaphora.” Doctoral diss. University of South Africa, 2009.

Hainthaler, Aloys Grillmeier with Theresia. *Christ in Christian Tradition (v.2, pt.4): From the Council of Chalcedon (451) to Gregory the Great (590-604).* London: Mowbray, 1996.

Hammond, Jenny. *Fire From the Ashes: A Chronicle of the Revolution in Tigray, 1975-1991.* Lawrenceville N.J. & Asmara: Red Sea Press, 1999.

Hastings, Adrian. *The Construction of Nationhood: Ethnicity, Religion, and Nationalism.* Cambridge: Cambridge University Press, 1997.

Heran Sereke-Berhan. "Ethiopia: A Historical Consideration of Amhara Ethnicity." *New Trends in Ethiopian Studies: Papers of the 12th International Conference of Ethiopian Studies.* East Lansing, Michigan: Michigan State University Press, (1994): 742-774.

Heur, Bas van. "The Spatial Imagination of Oromia: The Ethiopian State and Oromo Transnational Politics." Masters thesis, Utrecht University, 2004.

Hirschl, Ran. *Constitutional Theocracy.* Cambridge, MA: Harvard University Press, 2010.

Hobsbawm, Eric. *Nations and Nationalism Since 1790: Programme, Myth, Reality.* Cambridge: Cambridge University Press, 1990.

Hofmeyr, A. B. "The meta-physics of Foucault's ethics: Succeeding where Levinas fails." *South African Journal of Philosophy* 25, 2 (2006): 113-125.

Holcomb, Bonnie K. and Sisa Ibssa. *The Invention of Ethiopia.* Trenton, NJ: Red Sea Press, c1990.

Hughes, John. *The End of Work: Theological Critique of Capitalism.* Oxford: Blackwell, 2007.

Human Rights Watch. *Suppressing Dissent: Human Rights Abuses and Political Repression in Ethiopia's Oromia Region.* May 2005 Vol. 17 (A).

—. *Collective Punishment War Crimes and Crimes against Humanity in the Ogaden area of Ethiopia's Somali Regional State.* June 2008.

Isichei, Elizabeth. *A History of Christianity in Africa: From Antiquity to the Present.* London: SPCK, 1995.

Johnson, Doglas H. "On the Nilotic frontier: imperial Ethiopia in the southern Sudan, 1898-1936." Pages 219-244 in *The Southern Marches of Imperial Ethiopia: Essays in History and Social Anthropology.* Edited by Wendy James et al. Cambridge: Cambridge University Press, 1986a.

Jones, A.H.M. and Elizabeth Monroe. *A History of Ethiopia.* New York: Negro University Press, 1961.

Kaplan, Steven. *The Monastic Holy Man and the Christianization of Early Solomonic Ethiopia.* Stuttgart: Franz Steiner Verlag Wiesbaden GMBH, 1984.

Keller, Edmond J. *Revolutionary Ethiopia: From Empire to People's Republic.* Indianapolis: Indiana University Press, 1988.

Kelly, J.N.D. *Early Christian Doctrines.* London: Continuum, 1977.

Kiflu Tadesse. *The Generation: The history of the Ethiopian People's Revolutionary Party (Part 1).* Trenton, NJ: The Red Sea Press, 1993.

Kinfe Abraham. *Ethiopia from Empire to Federation.* London: Ethiopian International Institute for Peace and Development, 2001.

Kymilcka, Will. "Emerging Western Models of Multination Federalism: Are They Relevant for Africa." Pages 32-64 in *Ethnic Federalism: The Ethiopian Experience in Comparative Perspective.* Edited by David Turton. Ohio: Ohio University Press, 2006.

Lee, Ralph. "Symbolic Interpretation in Ethiopic and Ephremic Literature." PhD diss., University of London, 2011.

—. "The Conversion of King Caleb and the Religious and Political Dynamics of Sixth-Century Ethiopia." Pages 77-87 in *An Age of Saints? Power, Conflict and Dissent in Early Medieval Christianity.* Edited by Peter Sarris *et al.* Leiden, The Netherlands: Brill, 2011.

Levine, Donald. *Gold and Wax: Tradition and Innovation in Ethiopian Culture.* Chicago: Chicago University Press, 1965.

—. *Greater Ethiopia: The Evolution of a Multiethnic Society.* Chicago; London: University of Chicago Press, 1974.

Leslau, Wolf. *English-Amharic Context Dictionary.* Wiesbaden: Otto Harrassowitz, 1973.

Lossky, Vladimir. *Orthodox Theology: An Introduction.* NY: St. Vladimir Seminary Press, 1989.

—. *The Mystical Theology of the Eastern Church.* Cambridge: James Clarke, 1991.

Loukeris, Kostas. "Contending Political Ideologies in Ethiopia: After 1991: The Role of Intellectuals." *Polis, Revue Camerounaise De Science Politique, Vol. 12, Numero Special 2004-2005* (2005): 1-11.

Louth, Andrew. " Sergii Bulgakov and the Task of Theology." *Irish Theological Quarterly,* 74 (2009): 243-259.

Lubac, Henri De. *The Splendor of the Church.* San Francisco: Ignatius, 1986.

Luther H. Martin; Huck Gutman; and Patrick H. Hutton, eds. *Technologies of the Self: A Seminar with Michel Foucault.* London: Tavistock, 1988.

MacIntyre, Alasdair. *After Virtue.* Notre Dame: Notre Dame University Press, 1981.

Mannheim, Karl. *Ideology and Utopia: An Introduction to the Sociology of Knowledge.* London: Routledge and Kegan Paul, 1936, 1968.

Markakis, John. *National and Class Conflict in the Horn of Africa.* Cambridge: Cambridge University Press, 1987.

—. *Ethiopia: The Last Two Frontiers.* Oxford: James Currey, 2011.

Markakis, John and Nega Ayele. *Class and Revolution in Ethiopia.* Nottingham: Spokesman Books for the 'Review of African political economy', 1978.

Marx, Karl. *Critique of Hegel's Philosophy of Right.* Cambridge: Cambridge University Press, 1970.

—. "The German Ideology." in *Early Writings*, trans. Rodney Livingstone and Gregor Benton, Gregor. Penguin Books in association with New Left Review, 1975.

Mbembe, Achille and Nuttall, Sarah. "Writing the World from an African Metropolis." *Public Culture* 16, 3 (2004): 347-372.

Mbembe, Achille. "African Modes of Self-Writing." *Public Culture* 14, 1 (Winter 2002): 239-273.

—. "Necropolitics." *Public Culture* (2003): 11-40.

McGuckin, John A. "Scholia on the Incarnation of the Only Begotten." Pages 294-335 in *St. Cyril of Alexandria: The Christological Controversy: Its History, Theology and Texts.* Leiden: Brill, 1994.

Mebratu Kiros Gebru. *Miaphysite Christology: An Ethiopian Perspective.* Gorgias Press, 2010.

Meerson, Michael Aksionov. *The Trinity of Love in Modern Russian Theology: The Love Paradigm and the Retrieval of Western Medieval Love Mysticism in Modern Russian Trinitarian Thought.* Quincy, Illinois: Franciscan Press, 1998.

Mekuria Bulcha. *The Making of the Oromo Diaspora: A Historical Sociology of Forced Migration.* Minneapolis: Kirk House Publishers, 2002.

Merera Gudina. *Ethiopia: Competing Ethnic Nationalisms and the Quest for Democracy, 1960-2000.* Maastricht: Shaker Publishing, 2002.

—. "Contradictory Interpretations of Ethiopian History." Pages 119-130 in *Ethnic Federalism: The Ethiopian Experience in Comparative perspective.* Edited by David Turton. Ohio: Ohio University Press, 2006.

Mesfin Wolde-Mariam. *An Introductory Geography of Ethiopia.* Addis Ababa: Berhanena Selam H.S.I. Printing Press, 1972.

Messay Kebede. *Survival and Modernization: Ethiopia's Enigmatic Present: A Philosophical Discourse.* Lawrenceville, NJ: The Red Sea Press, 1999.

–.'The Rehabilitation of Violence and the Violence of Rehabilitation: Fanon and Colonialism'. *Journal of Black Studies* 31, 5 (May 2001): 539-562.

—. *Radicalism and Cultural Dislocation in Ethiopia, 1960-1974.* Rochester, NY: University of Rochester Press, 2008.

—. "Return to the Source: Aleqa Asres Yenesew and the West." 2008. Accessed 15 June 2010, http://abbaymedia.com/2008/03/14/return-to-the-source-aleqa-.. asres-yenesew-and-the-west/

Meyendorff, John. *Imperial Unity and Christian Divisions: The Church 450-680 A.D.* Crestwood, NY: St Vladimir's Seminary Press, 1989.

—. *Byzantine Theology: Historical Trends and Doctrinal Themes.* New York: Fordham University Press, 1974.

—. *Living Tradition: Orthodox Witness in the Contemporary World.* Crestwood, NY: St. Vladimir's Seminary Press, 1978.

Milbank, John. *Being Reconciled: Ontology and Pardon.* London: Routledge, 2003.

—. *The Suspended Middle: Henri de Lubac and the Debate Concerning the Supernatural.* Grand Rapids, MI: Wm. Eerdmans, 2005.

—. *Theology and Social Theory: Beyond Secular Reason.* Oxford: Blackwell, 2006.

—. *The Future of Love: Eassays in Political Theology.* London: SCM Press, 2009.

—. "Multiculturalism in Britain and the Political Identity of Europe." *International Journal for the Study of the Christian Church*, Vol. 9 No. 4 (November 2009): 268-281.

—. *Sophiology and Theurgy: the New Theological Horizon.* Accessed April 19, 2012, <http://www.theologyphilosophycentre.co.uk/papers/Milbank_SophiologyTheurgy.pdf.

Mochulsky, Konstantin. "The Idea of Social Philosophy in Russia." *St. Vladimir's Seminary Quarterly*, 12 (1968): 163.

Moseley, Carys. *Nations and Nationalism in the Theology of Karl Barth.* Oxford: Oxford University Press, 2013.

Nairn, Tom. *Faces of Nationalism: Janus Revisited.* London: Verso, 1997.

Negaso Gidada and Donald Crummey. "The Introduction and Expansion of Orthodox Christianity in Qelem Awraja, Western Wallaga, from about 1886 to 1941." *Journal of Ethiopian Studies* vol. X. No. 1, (1972): 103-112.

Newman, Barbara. "Sergius Bulgakov and the Theology of Divine Wisdom." *St. Vladimir's Theological Quarterly*, vol. 22 No.1 (1978): 41-73.

Nozick, Robert. *Anarchy, State, and Utopia.* Oxford: Blackwell, 1974.

Ottaway, Marina and David Ottaway. *Ethiopia: Empire in Revolution.* New York: Africana, 1978.

Pabst, Adrian and Christoph Schneider, eds. *Encounter between Eastern Orthodoxy and Radical Orthodoxy: Transfiguring the World by the Word.* Ashgate, 2009.

Pain, James and Nicolas Zernov. *A Bulgakov Anthology.* Philadelphia: The Westminster Press, 1976.

Pankhurst, Richard. "'Fear God, Honor the King': The Use of Biblical Allusion in Ethiopian Historical Literature, Part I." *Northeast African Studies* 9, 1 (1987): 11-30.

Papanikolaou, Aristotle. "Orthodoxy, Post-Modernism, and Ecumenism: The Difference that Divine-Human Communion Makes." *Journal of Ecumenical Studies* 42:4 (Fall 2007): 527-546.

Parsons', Talcott. *Societies: Evolutionary and Comparative Perspectives.* London: Prentice Hall, 1967.

Paulos Milkias. "Authoritarianism and the Ethiopian Body Politic Dissonance between Democratization and Elite Political subculture." *Proceedings of the 16th International Conference of Ethiopian Studies*, 2009: 673-696.

Pausewang, Siegfried. "The Oromo and the CUD." *Oromo Studies Association XX Annual Conference Proceedings* (2006): 71-73.

—. "Political Conflicts in Ethiopia – in View of the Two-Faced Amhara Identity." *Proceedings of the 16th International Conference of Ethiopian Studies* (2009): 550-551.

Payne, Daniel P. and Christopher Marsh. "Sergei Bulgakov's 'Sophic' Economy: An Eastern Orthodox Perspective on Christian Economics." *Faith & Economics*, Number 53 (Spring 2009): 35-51.

Plowden, Walther C. *Travels in Abyssinia.* Westmead: Gregg InternationalPublishers Limited, 1972.

Prestige, G.L. *God in Patristic Thought.* London: SPCK, 1952.

Rajchman, John. *Michel Foucault: The Freedom of Philosophy.* New York: Columbia University Press, 1985.

Rancière, Jacques. "Politics, Identification, and Subjectivization." Pages 58-64 in *The identity in Question*. Edited by John Rajchman. New York: Routledge, 1995.

—. *The Politics of Literature.* Cambridge: Polity, 2011b.

Ricoeur, Paul. *Fallible Man.* New York: Fordham University Press, 1965; 1986.

—. *Lectures on Ideology and Utopia.* Edited by George H. Taylor. New York: Columbia University Press, 1986.

—. *Time and Narrative,* vol.3. Chicago: The University of Chicago Press, 1988.

—. *Oneself as Another.* Chicago: Chicago University Press, 1992.

—. *The Just.* Chicago; London: University of Chicago Press, 2000.

—. *From Text to Action: Essays in Hermeneutics, II.* London: Continuum, 2008.

—. *Memory, History, Forgetting.* Chicago: Chicago University Press, 2004.

Rosenthal, Bernice Glatzer. "The Nature and Function of Sophia." Pages 149-163 in *Russian Religious Thought.* Edited by Judith Deutsch Kornblatt and Richard F. Gustafson. Madison, Wisconsin: The University of Wisconsin Press, 1996.

Samuel Wolde-Yohannes. "The Vision of Man and Humanity in Ethiopian: A Politico-Philosophical Perspective." Pages 93-99 in *Faith and Culture in Ethiopia: Towards A Pastoral Approach to Culture.* Addis Ababa: Ethiopian Review of Cultures, 1997.

Sbacchi, Alberto. *Ethiopia under Mussolini: Fascism and the Colonial Experience.* London: Zed, 1985.

Schmemann, Alexander. *For the World: Sacraments and Orthodoxy.* NY: St. Vladimir's Seminary Press, 1995.

Schlee, Günther and Abdulahi A. Shongolo. "Local War and Its Impact on Ethnic and Religious Identification in Southern Ethiopia." *GeoJournal,* 36, 1 (1995): 7-17.

Scott, Peter. *Theology, Ideology and Liberation: Towards a Liberative Theology.* Cambridge: Cambridge University Press, 1994.

Seliger, Martin. *The Marxist Conception of Ideology: A Critical Essay.* New York: Cambridge University Press, 1977.

Semir Yusuf. "Contending Nationalisms in a Transnational Era: The Case of Ethiopianist and Oromo Nationalisms." *Journal of Asian and African Studies* 44 (June 2009): 299-318.

Sergew Hable Sellassie. *Ancient and Medieval Ethiopian History to 1270.* Addis Ababa: United Printers, 1972.

Serra-Horguelin, Arnoult. "The Federal Experiment in Ethiopia: A Socio-political Analysis." n.p. Institut d'etudes politiques de Bordeaux, Université Montesquieu-Bordeaux IV, 1999. Accessed 27 January 2009. Centre D'etude D 'Afrique Noire.

Seyoum Hameso. "'Myths and Realities of the Ethiopian State.'" Pages 97-111 in *Arrested Devlopment in Ethiopia: Essays on Underdevelopment, Democracy and Self-determination.* Edited by Seyoum Hameso and Mohammed Hassen. Trenton, NJ: The Red Sea Press, 2006.

Shaw, Gregory. "Neoplatonic Theurgy and Dionysius the Areopagite," *Journal of Early Christian Studies* 7, 4 (1999): 573- 599.

(Pope) Shenouda III, H. H.. *The Nature of Christ.* St Mark Coptic Orthodox Church, 1999.

Shils, Edward. *Political Developments in the New States.* Netherlands: Mouton, 1962.

Simons, Jon. *Foucault & the Political.* London: Routledge, 1995.

Skrimshire, Stefan. *Politics of Fear, Practices of Hope.* London: Continuum, 2008.

Smith, Anthony. *The Ethnic Origins of Nations.* Oxford: Balckwell, 1986.

—. *Theories of Nationalism.* London: Duckworth, 1971.

—. *Myths and Memories of the Nation.* Oxford; New York: Oxford University Press, 1999.

—. *Ethno-symbolism and Nationalism: A Cultural Approach.* London: Routledge, 2009.

Sodipo, J. O. "Some Philosophical Aspects of the African Historical Experience." Pages 346-354 in *African Philosophy*. Edited by Claude Sumner. Addis Ababa: Addis Ababa University Press, 1998.

Sorenson, John. *Imagining Ethiopia: Struggles for History and Identity in the Horn of Africa.* New Jersey: Rutgers University Press, 1993.

Strauss, Steve. "Creeds, Confessions, and Global Theologizing: A Case Study in Comparative Christologies." Chapter 6 in *Globalizing theology: belief and practice in an era of world Christianity.* Edited by Craig Ott and and Harold A. Netland. Grand Rapids, MI: Baker Academic, 2006.

Sumner, Claude. *Ethiopian Philosophy.* Addis Ababa: University of Addis Ababa, 1974.

Sundkler, Bengt and Christopher Steed. *A History of the Church in Africa*. Cambridge: Cambridge University Press, 2000.

Surin, Kenneth. "Rewriting the Ontological Script of Liberation: On the Question of Finding a New Kind of Political Subject." Pages 240-266 in *Theology and the Political: The New Debate*. Edited by Creston Davis, Slavoj Žižek and John Milbank. Durham, N.C.: Duke University Press, 2005.

Szakolczai, Aprád. *Identity Formation Mechanisms: A Conceptual and Genealogical Analysis*. San Dominico, Italy: European University Institute, 1998.

Taddesse Tamrat. *Church and State in Ethiopia, 1270-1527*. Oxford: Clarendon Press, 1972.

Tanner, Kathryn. *The Politics of God: Christian Theologies and Social Justice*. Minneapolis: Fortress Press, 1992.

—. "Trinity." Pages 324-331 in *The Blackwell Companion to Political*

Theology. Edited by Peter Scott and William T. Cavanaugh. Malden, Mass.: Blackwell, 2004.

Taylor, Charles. *Modern Social Imaginaries*. Duke University Press, 2005.

Teodros Kiros. "Zera Yacob and Ethiopian Traditional Philosophy." Pages 183-190 in *A Companion to African Philosophy*, by Kwasi Wiredu. Oxford: Oxford: Blackwell Publishing, 2004.

Tesfazghi Uqbit. *Current Christological Positions of Ethiopian Orthodox Theologians*. Roma: Ponitificium Insitutum Studiorum Orientalium, 1973.

Teshale Tibebu. *The Making of Modern Ethiopia 1896-1974*. Lawrenceville, NJ: The Red Sea Press, 1995.

—. "Modernity, Eurocentricity, and Radical Politics in Ethiopia, 1961-1991." *African Identities* 6, 4 (November 2008): 345-371.

Tibebe Eshete. *The Evangelical Movement in Ethiopia: Resistance and Resilience*. Waco, Texas: Baylor University Press, 2009.

"The Interim Secretariat Oriental Orthodox Conference." *The Oriental Orthodox Churches Addis Ababa Conference*. Addis Ababa, January 1965.

Tolo, Arno. *Sidama and Ethiopian: The Emergence of the Mekane Yesus Church in Sidama*.Uppsala: Uppsala Universitet, 1998.

TPLF/EPRDF. "TPLF/EPRDF's Strategies for Establishing its Hegemony & Perpetuating its Rule." *Ethiopian Register* 3 (1996): 20-29.

Trimingham, J. *Islam in Ethiopia*. London: Frank Cass, 1952.

Triulzi, Alessandro. "Competing Views of National Identity in Ethiopia." Page 119 in *Nationalism and Self-determination in the Horn of Africa*. Edited by I. M. Lewis. London: Itheca Press, 1983.

—. "Nekemte and Addis Abeba: dilemmas of provincial rule." Page 68 in *The Southern Marches of Imperial Ethiopia*. Edited by Wendy James et al. Cambridge: Cambridge University Press, 1986a.

Tronvoll, Kjetil. *War & the Politics of Identity in Ethiopia: Making Enemies & Allies in the Horn of Africa*. Cumbria, UK: James Curry, 2009.

Ullendorff, Edward. *The Ethiopians*. Oxford: Oxford University Press, 1960.

Valliere, Paul. *Modern Russian Theology: Bukharev, Soloviev, Bulgakov: Orthodox Theology in a New Key*. Edinburgh: T & T Clark, 2000.

Vaughan, Sarah. "The Addis Ababa Transitional Conference of July 1991: Its Origins, History, and Significance." *Occasional Papers* 51. Edinburgh: University of Edinburgh: Centre of African Studies, 1994.

—. "Ethnicity and Power in Ethiopia" PhD diss., University of Edinburgh, 2003.

Vestal, Theodore. *Ethiopia: A Post-Cold War African State*. Westport, Conn.: Praeger, 1999.

Vladimir Lossky, John H. Erickson and Thomas E. B, eds. *In the Image and Likeness of God*. NY: St. Vladimir Seminary Press, 1974.

Walden, Treadwell. *The Great Meaning of Metánoia: An Undeveloped Chapter in the Life and Teaching of Christ*. New York: Thomas Whittaker, 1896.

Walleligne Mekonen. "On the Question of Nationalities in Ethiopia." *Struggle* (1969): 4-7.

Ward, Graham. *Cities of God*. London: Routeledge, 2000.

—. *Christ and Culture*. Oxford: Blackwell, 2005.

—. *Cultural Transformation and Religious Practice*. Cambridge: Cambridge University Press, 2005.

—. *The Politics of Discipleship: Becoming Postmaterial Citizens*. Grand Rapids, MI: Baker Academic, 2009.

Williams, Rowan. *Sergii Bulgakov: Towards a Russian Political Theology*. Edinburgh: T & T Clark, 1999.

—. *On Christian Theology*. Oxford: Blackwell, 2000.

—. "Eastern Orthodox Theology." Pages 572-578 in *The Modern Theologians An Introduction to Christian Theology Since 1918*. Edited by David F. Ford, Oxford: Blackwell Publishing, 2005.

Wiredu, Kwasi. "Introduction: African Philosophy in Our Time." Pages 1-27 in *A Companion to African Philosophy*. Edited by Kwasi Wiredu. Oxford: Blackwell Publishing, 2004.

Young, John. *Peasant Revolution in Ethiopia: The Tigray People's Liberation Front, 1975-1991*. Cambridge: Cambridge University Press, 1998.

Zizioulas, John. *Being As Communion: Studies on Personhood and the Church*. London: Darton, Longman and Todd, 1985.

www.ingramcontent.com/pod-product-compliance
Ingram Content Group UK Ltd.
Pitfield, Milton Keynes, MK11 3LW, UK
UKHW021842100926
8556IPUK00019B/1010

9 783631 658505